After the Bomb

After the Bomb

Civil Defence and Nuclear War in Britain, 1945–68

Matthew Grant

palgrave
macmillan

First published 2010 by
PALGRAVE MACMILLAN

Palgrave Macmillan in the UK is an imprint of Macmillan Publishers Limited, registered in England, company number 785998, of Houndmills, Basingstoke, Hampshire RG21 6XS.

Palgrave Macmillan in the US is a division of St Martin's Press LLC,
175 Fifth Avenue, New York, NY 10010.

Palgrave Macmillan is the global academic imprint of the above companies and has companies and representatives throughout the world.

Palgrave® and Macmillan® are registered trademarks in the United States, the United Kingdom, Europe and other countries.

ISBN-13: 978-0-230-20542-0 hardback

This book is printed on paper suitable for recycling and made from fully managed and sustained forest sources. Logging, pulping and manufacturing processes are expected to conform to the environmental regulations of the country of origin.

A catalogue record for this book is available from the British Library.

A catalogue record for this book is available from the Library of Congress.

10 9 8 7 6 5 4 3 2 1
19 18 17 16 15 14 13 12 11 10

Printed and bound in Great Britain by
CPI Antony Rowe, Chippenham and Eastbourne

For Tracey

Contents

List of Figures

Preface

This is a book based overwhelmingly on primary sources, a considerable amount of which were initially withheld from public scrutiny for more than the traditional 30 years. These were sensitive documents, dealing with how the government would deal with a nuclear attack on Britain, whether it be building a secret chain of government post-attack headquarters, or the various ways the state would help – or in many cases not help – ordinary Britons survive enemy attack. Before 2000 a considerable number of documents cited here would have been unavailable, and many were only opened after the 2006 implementation of the Freedom of Information Act. More may be expected to surface in the coming years. In many ways then, the writing of this book has involved keeping up with the latest archival revelations, and although some areas require greater archival openness, the archive on British nuclear war planning in the 1940s, 1950s and 1950s can be said to be largely complete. These newly opened documents serve two purposes. First is the obviously beneficial one of telling us what actually happened in the secret cold war world of Whitehall. But the second is probably even more important, for we can now place civil defence and nuclear war planning in its correct context as one of many British responses to the cold war, and one which, like the others, was subject to the same constraints of the diplomatic, strategic, economic and political contexts of the time. For too long the study of this subject has fallen into a pattern of 'now I can reveal' rhetoric, an understandable reaction to the intense secrecy which traditionally surrounded it. The main thing this book reveals is the subject's hitherto unknown normalcy; it was a standard subject for successive governments, a problem which at times seemed intractable but which demanded time and money. It was, in short, an integral and inescapable part of Britain's cold war role.

Thanks must go to the staff of two institutions. The first is Queen Mary, University of London, and profuse thanks must be given to Professor Peter Hennessy, doctoral supervisor and source of sound advice, and Professor John Ramsden, doctoral mentor and robust encourager. Other former Mile End colleagues who must be thanked include Dr Catherine Haddon, Dr Dan Todman, Dr Alban Webb, Dr James Ellison and Pete Davies. The second institution is the University of Sheffield. Although many of my conclusions about the subject had been formed before my arrival in Yorkshire, I must thank my colleagues en masse for helping to create an atmosphere of intellectual rigour which has radically influenced my attitude to history. I would also like to thank Professors Len Scott and Jane Lewis for their respective help at vital stages of the endeavours.

Special acknowledgements must go to Dr Peter Catterall for allowing me to look at the transcript of the unpublished portions of the Harold Macmillan diary; Alan Glennie and others at the Cabinet Office for their sympathetic attitude and can-do approach to the thorny question of Freedom of Information, which has allowed rich material to be released quickly enough to be included here; to the staff at the various libraries and archives at which I spent much fruitful time researching this work; to the organisers and participants of various research seminars and conferences at which some of this research was first aired; to the Trustees of the Mass-Observation Archive, University of Sussex, for allowing extracts to be quoted here; to the Arts and Humanities Research Board (as was), for funding the doctoral research this book is based on; and to the Department of History, University of Sheffield for providing the research funds which ensured that the images discussed within the text could be reproduced.

It is a book which was written over a 22-two month period in 2007–09 that encompassed five houses in three cities, Manchester, Sheffield and Cardiff. In addition, the bulk of the research was undertaken during my doctoral studies in London between 2002 and 2006. Life as a pair of peripatetic academics has meant near constant upheaval for myself and my partner; and it is for her understanding and all-round inspirational role as sounding-board, critic, historical adventurer and proof-reader that I dedicate this book to Tracey Loughran.

Matthew Grant
Cardiff, March 2009

List of Abbreviations

AFS	Auxiliary Fire Service
ARP	Air Raid Precautions
BMEWS	Ballistic Missile Early Warning System
CDJPS	Civil Defence Joint Planning Staff
CDM	Ministerial Committee on Civil Defence
CDO	Official Committee on Civil Defence
CDPC	Civil defence Planning Committee
CND	Campaign for Nuclear Disarmament
CWPS	Central War Plans Secretariat
DTC	Defence (Transition) Committee
FCDA	Federal Civil defense Administration
HDC	Home Defence Committee
HDM	Ministerial Committee on Home Defence
HDR	Home Defence Review Committee
JIC	Joint Intelligence Committee
JIGSAW	Joint Inter-Services' Group for the Study of All-out War
JTWC	The Joint Technical Warfare Committee
MDC	Mobile Defence Corps
MoD	Ministry of Defence
NATO	North Atlantic Treaty Organisation
PR	Policy Review Committee
RAF	Royal Air Force
ROC	Royal Observer Corps
RSG	Regional Seat(s) of Government
SRC	Sub-Regional Control
UKAEA	United Kingdom Atomic Energy Authority
WRVS	Women's Royal Voluntary Service
WVS	Women's Voluntary Service

Introduction

Confronting nuclear war

In the spring of early 1953 a group of civil servants led by the respected Treasury official Robert Hall sat down to think about what Britain would look like after an atomic war.[1] They were not the first committee of officials to do this, and they certainly would not be the last. Before Hall's little group reported, a similar group had completed much the same task in February 1947,[2] and others also attempted to confront the reality of post-attack Britain in 1955 and in 1960.[3] These four reviews were each deemed essential not because of the perceived intractability of the problem of defending the UK home base against Soviet attack, but because developments in weapons technology demanded it. In 1947, the effects of a limited atomic bombardment (allied to a massive conventional one) were analysed. In 1955, the effects of thermonuclear weapons and radioactive fallout were investigated; the reviews of 1953 and 1960, however, were instigated when it became clear that the Soviet stockpiles of atomic and thermonuclear weapons respectively, had become so large as to make the initial assessments of the effects of attack with these weapons redundant. This is why the Hall group is such an illuminating starting point. In the conventional history of nuclear warfare, the 'thermonuclear moment' of 1954–55 is the point when the story of complete nuclear destruction truly begins. Before the development of these enormous weapons, or rather before their true nature was understood in 1954, war fought with *atomic* weapons of the sort used on Japan in 1945, though actually rather more powerful by the 1950s, would have been brutal, bloody, but still prosecuted along recognisable lines. Armies would clash in Northern Europe, industrial production would continue – the theory was called 'broken-backed warfare'. Although immensely destructive, atomic bombs could not destroy everything, especially when possessed in limited numbers. When the *thermonuclear*, or hydrogen bomb, was invented, the factor of devastation was vastly increased – to the point where a single bomb could destroy an entire city and its inhabitants.

But when Hall received the intelligence assessment on the likely nature of a Soviet attack on Britain, it seemed to make a mockery of 'broken-backed warfare': it was estimated by the Joint Intelligence Committee that there would have been 132 atomic bombs delivered on industrial and 'population' targets and 40 on airbases, leaving a cool 28 bombs in reserve. Even if extensive evacuation had been successfully carried out, the casualties would have been horrendous: 1,378,000 people dead and 785,000 seriously injured.[4] The picture of civilian and industrial dislocation Hall presented made it clear that 'broken-backed warfare' was no longer a viable posture, and 'emphasised even more than before the importance of the allies building up a powerful deterrent'.[5] It also signalled the start of what became the key civil defence policy of the 1950s and 1960s: the strengthening of the machinery of government to attempt to maintain some semblance of state control in wartime. Hall made it clear that civil defence as it was popularly understood – dedicated to saving lives in wartime – was dead, that the key issues now were nuclear deterrence and the machinery of government: other plans were either futile, too costly, or a combination of both. The lasting impact of the Hall report was actually slight, as the revelations about the destructive power of thermonuclear weapons and the lasting effects of their subsequent radiation meant a new committee had to be formed to reconsider the whole issue, but it does show that even in the *atomic* era, civil defence could not achieve its traditional role as it had been understood in the last war.

But the point remains that Hall and his colleagues, as others did before and after, confronted the grim possibility of Britain being attacked with the most destructive forces ever unleashed. These groups peered into the abyss, seeking to understand what life could possibly be like after a nuclear attack, and even to ask, after the hydrogen bomb, whether Britain would still exist as an organised community. What did they see? At whatever point during the cold war insiders confronted nuclear war they would have seen enormous human suffering and destruction. It was understood that a single atomic bomb on a British city would probably kill around 50,000 people.[6] It was estimated in 1960 that an all-out attack with hydrogen bombs would kill 8 million people instantly with between 13 and 27 million others dying slowly and painfully from radiation sickness, with virtually no chance of medical relief.[7] Although planners could estimate casualties, when it came to mapping patterns of life after the bomb, they understood that the results of thermonuclear war were 'beyond the imagination'.[8] Some of the most difficult, unanswerable questions were rarely if ever asked, such as how those who survived would cope psychologically with the trauma of nuclear war. For the planners involved, aware that what was left of Britain would need to strain every sinew in order to allow a semblance of organised life to continue after an attack, psychological well-being would be an issue to confront only after law and order were re-established – almost certainly by a military government in the first instance – and the basic amenities of existence put on an adequate footing. They feared a society collapsing in on itself, a shattering of the rule of law, and survivors slowly starving.[9] For all those involved with civil defence, envisaging nuclear war meant facing up to the prospect of the country being ripped apart and British power being destroyed in what might well be one simultaneous attack. For later planners, it also meant facing up to the fact that a war might kill nearly three quarters of the population and destroy organised society in Britain.[10]

Civil defence always had a role to play, one that shifted as the feared scale of attack grew to proportions unimaginable even to those who, in 1945, had just witnessed a true military revolution. Defence against nuclear war was an obvious and natural consequence of taking part in the cold war; certainly as obvious as building Britain's own nuclear strike capability. Successive British governments firmly believed that the Soviet Union was a major threat both to world peace and to British national interests around the globe. An enormous amount of effort was dedicated to countering this threat, both in military terms in case of war, and in diplomatic terms to lessen international tension.[11] Britain manned and equipped a large army in Germany (the British Army of the Rhine, or BAOR), was committed to an independent nuclear strike force, and of course carried out civil defence preparations. The cold war must be seen as a dominant backdrop to British history after 1945, as dominant as the story of economic decline which traditionally haunts any discussion of contemporary British history.[12] Of course, one major reason for Britain's economic plight was the huge defence burden placed on it by the nation's cold war activities.[13] British diplomacy, technological innovations and 'colonial' wars all took place within the cold war paradigm. If Britain avoided the worst excesses of McCarthyesque anti-communism, many people were held in suspicion because of their views and the careers of many with no concern with the 'secret' areas of the cold war were hampered.[14] The cold war is central to modern British history, and civil defence was a vital – if misunderstood – part of Britain's cold war story.

Civil defence in cold war Britain

Civil defence is vital to our understanding of cold war Britain in a number of ways. First, and most obviously, is that it allows us to penetrate Whitehall thinking about nuclear war, what a post-attack Britain would look like, and what measures could be implemented to alleviate the effects of such an attack. Hence we can understand the contingency plans that were prepared to meet the gravest emergency Britain could ever face. But civil defence is important not just for the plans to meet an attack that never came, vital though that is, it is also central to what actually happened in the cold war. Civil defence was a real, living and breathing cold war policy that had ramifications for the government's wider defence policy and which itself can only be understood as part of a set of interlocking factors shaping Britain's early cold war response. Without civil defence, it was inconceivable that Britain could have pursued an active cold war policy in the manner it did: only by showing people that their survival was taken seriously could the government convince them to support its actions. For successive governments, preparations to save lives had to proceed alongside active defence. Although evacuation plans cannot be said to come close to rivalling building the atomic bomb in importance, it was as inconceivable to the Attlee Government that an evacuation plan would *not* be produced as it was that Britain would not command the latest weaponry. It may not have been the highest priority, but it was a priority all the same.

The importance of civil defence can be even more amply seen beyond the environs of Whitehall. Every year from 1950 to 1963, bar the election year of 1959, ordinary Britons were confronted with a vast array of advertising encouraging them to volunteer for training to fight a nuclear war in one of the civil defence services, with the Civil Defence Corps taking the lead. Newspaper advertisements, ministerial broadcasts and public speeches, cinema shorts, television and radio items, and local measures such as door-to-door approaches, leafleting, and the staging of pageants and demonstrations at fetes and county fairs all showed the public what civil defence was, what it could do, and how important it was. Over 300,000 people during this time responded to the call and signed up to the Civil Defence Corps alone by 1953.[15] Millions of others decided not to and, later, thousands became openly hostile to it. Either way, civil defence was an integral part of the British way of life in the cold war period. Its importance explains why it was attacked by nuclear disarmers who argued – correctly – that the volunteers of the Corps were being used to create the impression that people would survive an attack in order to convince people to support the nuclear deterrent. Civil defence, then, was at the forefront of contemporary debates about nuclear war.

This, however, is the first academic monograph on the subject. Before 2000 even a rough study of the subject could not have been written due to a regime of archival secrecy which was slow to release cold war files, especially those relating to civil defence decision-making. John Baylis' *Ambiguity and Deterrence*, an excellent study of strategic decision-making in early cold war Britain, was published in 1995 and understandably failed to discuss civil defence issues.[16] Since the turn of the century, and especially since 2002, there has been a steady flow of records reaching the reading rooms at the National Archives in Kew, and this flow turned into a stream after the Freedom of Information Act of 2000 came into force in 2005. These records have allowed the various policies to be pieced together. But more than that, they have allowed civil defence to be placed back into its correct context as part of a cold war response to the nuclear threat which rested as much on the international, economic and political context as it did on technical evaluations of the destructive power of nuclear weapons.

Phases of civil defence

The chronology of civil defence in this period can be divided into three broad phases: the 'atomic age' lasting from 1945 to 1954, the 'thermonuclear age' lasting from 1954 until about 1960,[17] and finally what we can call the 'deterrent age' lasting from 1960 until civil defence was wound-down in 1968.[18] In the first phase, civil defence planners operated on lines familiar from the Second World War, and concentrated on both saving lives *and* ensuring that Britain's economy could operate after an attack. It is not surprising that both the public and officials had a set view of civil defence. During the war against Hitler, civil defence had been rather a success story.[19] Overcoming initial fears and problems, the programme of life-saving measures could be deemed to have succeeded. The evacuation of 'priority' groups may have been problematic, but undoubtedly saved the lives of thousands of children who might have perished in the blitzed cities. Civil defence workers from ARP (Air Raid Precaution) wardens to fire fighters and ambulance drivers, certainly rescued countless people at great personal risk. Perhaps above all, the provision of shelters, both communal and – on a massive scale – domestic, saved lives *and* provided those living in target areas with valuable peace of mind throughout the long war. Another aspect of policy, central to the Second World War, was the dispersal of industry and the 'due functioning' of essential services and utilities: of vital importance if industrial production were to be maintained under attack. So when people in Britain, both within Whitehall and outside, thought of civil defence in the early cold war, it would only be natural for them to conceptualise it along the lines of their experience of the Second World War, and specifically on the trio of key live-saving policies that were evacuation, shelter and ARP.

After the initial work on understanding atomic war, therefore, policies such as evacuation, the founding of the Civil Defence Corps, shelter provision, stockpiling (of food, medical supplies and industrial materials), increasing port capacity and industrial dispersal were pursued.[20] A great deal of effort was spent in the late 1940s drafting these policies, but planners struggled to secure the required sums. The history of industrial dispersal – decisively rejected – demonstrated that plans were often produced which, though desirable in a strategic sense, were far too expensive for any government to implement.[21] Even when the Korean War (1950–53) triggered enormous increases in the civil defence budget, the most expensive measures such as shelter policy were not funded. Clement Attlee, in 1951, concluded that civil defence spending must be limited in favour of funding the active measures that would deter aggression.[22] This period saw substantial work completed on various areas such as the ports system, the publishing of an evacuation scheme, and most importantly the Civil Defence Corps putting the issue into the public sphere. By the end of the period, however, it was becoming clear that advances in nuclear technology and the size of atomic stockpiles were endangering the validity of these measures.[23]

The second, thermonuclear phase from 1954–60, saw the priorities of the atomic age overturned. Planners realised that Britain would be totally crippled and unable to continue to support a continuing war effort. Instead, the fundamental review of civil defence, the Strath Report (1955), divided policy into three strands: life-saving, national survival and national recovery. To save lives, huge sums would be needed to fund shelters and equipment for the Civil Defence Corps. To survive as a nation, an entire alternative system of government – from Regional Seats of Government to an alternative central government headquarters – would be required to take the place of the smashed traditional centres.

To recover, enormous stocks of food and medical supplies would be needed, as would physical preparations to protect vital services.[24] Despite a sustained attempt to secure funds by Home Office Ministers and officials, Strath's recommendations were ultimately deemed too expensive.[25] This left the door open for civil defence priorities to be revised in 1956 when the government was seeking expenditure cuts.[26] Abandoning the 'recovery' strand saved millions, and planners had to fight to retain 'life-saving measures' as well. Such cuts, coming at a time when the destructive power of the new weapons suggested that more not less money should be devoted to the issue, undermined the government's claim that civil defence was a worthwhile policy which could save lives. From 1956 governments essentially turned away from the traditional role of civil defence and were increasingly preoccupied by defending their stance that the money was better spent on offensive measures. One manifestation of this was an increasingly trend to talk of 'home defence' rather than 'civil defence'. The two terms had distinctive meanings in the Second World War,[27] and it has been suggested that this continued after 1945.[28] In fact, the two terms were interchangeable for both the government and the public throughout the cold war and no real distinction between can be made.[29]

As the 1950s drew to a close, then, it was becoming obvious that the life-saving measures the government funded, never thorough, would have a limited impact on casualties. Only the fear of political repercussions kept Macmillan from ordering the axing of the Civil Defence Corps in 1958, demonstrating the importance of civil defence in maintaining public support for the government's wider cold war policies.[30] The thermonuclear era saw civil defence split into two 'spheres'. One was secret, concentrating on the only real remaining priority – 'national survival'. Millions of pounds were spent on building the alternative system of government which would lead the shattered nation on the road of recovery. The other sphere, the public policy of maintaining that lives would be saved even though expenditure was relatively small, was a reaction to the success of the government's critics in undermining public faith in the survivability of nuclear war. Using the Corps to prop up public confidence in the possibility of nuclear survival, the government hoped to forestall deeper criticisms of its nuclear policy. In the late 1950s, therefore, civil defence really was, and deliberately, the 'façade' its critics had long accused it of being. The decline of 'real' civil defence was illustrated by the review of emergency planning undertaken by Whitehall in 1959 which highlighted the consequences of the sustained lack of investment in civil defence and found that little could be done in the event of war.[31]

The final, 'deterrent' phase, lasting from 1960–68 saw civil defence reach crisis point, with the Home Office and Ministry of Defence holding fundamentally different views of its importance. Officials in the Home Office had always held a genuine belief in the life-saving role. They had continually pressed for extensive measures, backing shelter provision, evacuation policy and as much equipment as possible for the Civil Defence Corps. For the Ministry of Defence, at least in the thermonuclear age, all this was essentially wasteful.[32] The money should be spent on deterrence and the public told truthfully that their survival rested, not on the post-attack activities of the Corps, but on the deterrent stopping war in the first place. The fact that the Corps would struggle to save any lives merely strengthened their argument. For the Home Office, and in the end Ministers, it was believed that the Corps did have a role to play, albeit one which involved convincing people that their lives might be saved.[33] Without it, it was concluded in 1960, public support for the government in a crisis might crumble and turn neutralist. The Corps existed in the 1960s in order to bolster public morale in a future crisis, despite the loss of official faith in it as a life-saving body.[34]

The early 1960s also saw plans to ensure some degree of 'national survival' as the government saw it – essentially the survival of the state infrastructure – reach a sophisticated stage, including the completion of wartime public advice and plans to govern under martial law. Changes in the context civil defence operated in, however, undermined these approaches. The alternative system of government could not survive the belief that it would be targeted successfully by the Soviet Union in any war.[35] The rise of cold war détente, and the decline in the influence of CND meant that the strategic and political need for civil defence lessened. By the time a final economic crisis in 1967 meant savings had to be found, civil defence had few defenders left, leading it to be placed on a care-and-maintenance basis, essentially scrapped, in January 1968.[36]

It is clear that civil defence had multiple meanings during the cold war. It meant life-saving measures, it meant misleading the public for political ends, and it meant misleading the public for strategic ends. It meant reconciling views of the 'point' of civil defence which were at times diametrically opposed. It also meant arguing for funds against a backdrop of economic turbulence, and rapidly completing paper plans for war in the midst of an international crisis. For critics, it clearly represented a heinous level of dishonesty. For Whitehall supporters of the façade theory, it meant that Britain's deterrent strategy was slightly more secure. For the ordinary people who volunteered for the Civil

Defence Corps, it meant patriotic service and, perhaps, the recreation of the 'good old days' of the war. For ordinary people, it could mean any of the above, but it certainly would have meant confronting the possibility of dying in a nuclear war. What is also clear is that this multiplicity of meanings occurred in a specifically British national context. The experience of other nations struggling to formulate civil defence plans in the face of the nuclear threat, although superficially similar, necessarily had key differences.

Anglo-American comparisons

The American and British experiences of civil defence throw up some interesting parallels but finally reinforce the importance of studying the issue in its own in-depth national context.[37] Both countries' experience can be summarised as a slow reluctance to undertake civil defence measures, with those holding the purse-strings proving markedly more reluctant than civil defence activists to commit to large-scale protective measures. Both nations undertook a review of civil defence in the light of the hydrogen bomb – and both governments rejected the call which came for a renewed effort. Finally, civil defence in both countries underwent a crisis of public faith, with sections of the population arguing that civil defence was unnecessary due to the impossibility of any defence against an all-out nuclear attack. Within this broad outline, however, there are certain differences that distinctly set American and British experience apart.

The first is essentially geographical. Its proximity to Soviet held bases meant that Britain faced the prospect of an atomic onslaught much earlier than America: as Harold Macmillan confided in his diary in the aftermath of the Cuban missile crisis, 'to us who face nearly 500 of these missiles in Russia trained on Europe, there is something slightly ironical about these 20–30 in Cuba. But, as I told the President, when one lives on Vesuvius, one takes little account of the risk of eruptions'.[38] Britain had 'lived on Vesuvius' since the start of the cold war, and if Macmillan was attempting to explain that America need not over-react to the threat, he would have also been aware that Britain had been taking account of 'risk of eruptions' much earlier than the Americans had. For example, Britain's cold war apparatus was essentially set up by the Civil Defence Act of 1948, whereas the Federal Civil Defense Administration was officially created in January 1951.[39] Britain's H-Bomb review – the Strath Report – was presented in March 1955, whereas the equivalent Gaither Committee reported in November 1957.[40]

Geography created another difference. Civil defence was more viable for much of the 1950s in the continental expanse that was America than in the United Kingdom. Certainly much larger tracts of – admittedly sparsely populated – land in America might escape the fallout peril, whereas once the main British targets were hit, there could be little escape. This led to a different attitude to the viability of civil defence in the thermonuclear era.[41] In America a public debate could take place on survivability of nuclear war, whilst in Britain, as we shall see, once the facts about fallout became widely known, people who argued that there was a 'defence' against the bomb were scarce and quickly sidelined. Thus a key element of America's civil defence history is absent in the British context. Another is fallout shelters. In stark contrast to America, there was no shelter panic, no anguished debates about 'shelter ethics', and no real doctrine of 'survivalism'.[42] Historians of American civil defence have argued that it was this 1961 public debate which in the end convinced a great many that there could be no defence against the bomb. In Britain, people had been convinced by the debates and publicity created by a mass peace movement (CND), which had reached a peak in the years 1959–61 and had quickly convinced people that Britain could not survive a thermonuclear attack, although not that the best way to prevent war was through disarmament.[43] That a sustained debate about the efficacy of civil defence can be argued to have dominated American public discourse for a short period of 1961 massively influences American work on the issue; writing on shelter-ethics, the meanings of shelters and even the basic issue of 'would it work' is inspired by those debates. In Britain, the widespread belief that civil defence would be worthless has equally influenced writing – or the lack it – on the issue.

If geographic issues affect the basic chronology of their respective histories, two other factors explain why national stories must be treated differently. One is governmental, and one is the different legacies of the Second World War. Dee Garrison in her admirable history of American civil defence argues that one of its defining characteristics was secrecy about the reality of nuclear war.[44] While information was at a premium in the United States, it was nevertheless much easier to come by than in Britain.[45] The style of government in America, where civil defence agencies bid for public money and Congress decided publicly whether to provide it was anathema to Britain. Any disagreements over the utility of civil defence, and the extent to which it was funded, were kept strictly secret. The existence of two schools of thought in America were quickly known through interested parties such as think-tanks and individual strategists and advisors publishing in a range of periodicals. The fundamental disagreement over civil defence between the Home Office and the Ministry of Defence that split Whitehall for a decade after the hydrogen bomb explosion at Bikini in 1954 remained a secret until the archives were opened.

The other factor is the very different experiences of the Second World War of the two countries. Britain ended the war with the scars of enemy bombardment, and the experience of having run (successfully, it was deemed) a large-scale civil defence operation. The memory of how the population reacted to bombardment shaped assumptions about civil defence in the cold war in a way entirely absent from the American experience. For example, Britain struggled to break free from the shackles of previous experience when planning civil defence services. Civil defence planners in London also proved remarkably uninterested in the issue of morale, assuming in early 1946 that the British public would be able to cope with the stresses and strains of nuclear war as it had dealt with bombardment by the Luftwaffe.[46] In America, in stark contrast, a great deal of time and effort was expended on wondering how the public would stand up to enemy attack. Certainly one advocate of civil defence informed his American public that a London-style spirit would be needed to pull through in an atomic war.[47] British planners would have agreed, and simply assumed that in Britain at least, the Blitz spirit had remained in place since the war.

These factors were the result of specific national context and makes the respective histories of civil defence very different, but of course there are other similarities and indeed a degree of cross-fertilisation of ideas about the effects of nuclear weapons the heavy secrecy surrounding nuclear matters in Britain meant that the key sources of information were usually found abroad. The works of Ralph Lapp, a key figure in bringing knowledge about fallout to the American public, were published in mass-market paperback in Britain,[48] and the Campaign for Nuclear Disarmament obtained much of its information from America.[49] Also, American anti-nuclear campaigners were clearly inspired by their British counterparts.[50] The American history of civil defence has been richly analysed over a number of years from a number of disciplinary angles. By contrast, this is the first full-length academic British history of the subject ever published. There are a number of reasons for this discrepancy. The cold war was more of an acknowledged part of American social and cultural life than in Britain that it was probably bound to receive earlier and more sustained enquiry; also, social and cultural history in general has yet to make the same strides in post-1945 British history as it has for the

Victorian era or the early part of the twentieth century. The main reason for this difference, however, is secrecy. Information about civil defence and nuclear war was closely guarded in Britain, and the system of government precluded the public discussion of policy which is an essential part of American political life. Vitally, the actual *facts* about these issues are only just becoming known, whereas in America the equivalent story has long been in the public domain. Kenneth Rose finds it noteworthy that the Gaither report on defence against the hydrogen bomb remained unpublished until 1976;[51] its British equivalent was not made public until 2002 and key new files are being released all the time. Truly, it is only now that the essential facts about British civil defence can be known, digested and analysed. The American literature on this issue is methodologically and theoretically advanced, and is usually based on a sound knowledge of the actual narrative framework of events. Up until now, this basic knowledge has been lacking in Britain.

This book is designed to provide such knowledge, to analyse Britain's cold war story through the history of civil defence policy. It was a troubled history, its ups and downs (more downs than ups, however) reflecting the difficulties successive governments faced in responding to the threat of nuclear war: balancing the need to prepare for the ultimate contingency with the economic requirements of the day, reconciling internal Whitehall differences about the nature of nuclear war and the role of civil defence within it, all the while attempting to project a public image of 'survivable' nuclear war vastly at odds with their own, secret, understanding of it. These were the tensions which needed to be resolved, and which ensured that civil defence policy-making was at the heart of the British state's response to the cold war.

1 The Cold War and the New Civil Defence

The explosion of atomic bombs over the Japanese cities of Hiroshima and Nagasaki caused shock throughout British government and society. In what was almost the final act of the Second World War, a powerful new weapon had been used which changed the character of the postwar world. Just as importantly the years after 1945 saw the dreams of future peace dashed as international tensions coalesced to form the uneasy co-existence that characterised the cold war. For Britain, these two factors combined to become a major threat to security. The existence of a hostile and seemingly expansionist power armed with weapons of enormous destructive force, a power following policies opposed to British national interests, decisively shaped the course of post-1945 government. It forced the British state to confront the prospect of atomic war, of Britain coming under atomic attack. In the four years after the end of the war, planners and officials developed strategies to help protect Britain in another conflict: policies to save lives and to ensure British fighting capacity could continue. Drafting such policies was immensely complex. It meant understanding and adapting to an entirely new concept of war, and preparing Britain's defence and economic infrastructure to withstand previously unimaginable levels of attack. It also meant attempting this at a time when Britain was on the brink of economic disaster: the spending of virtually every pound and the use of virtually every ounce of steel was a matter of major concern. Only policies of the utmost priority could be undertaken in the 1945–48 period. Britain's early responses to the prospect of atomic attack, therefore, remained largely on paper.

These paper plans were of doubtful utility, concentrating on enormous schemes such as dispersing Britain's industrial capacity away from the urban target areas. Such schemes were divorced from the economic and political context they would have to operate in, and came at a cost of ignoring the short-term threat of a snap war crisis. When such a crisis came in Berlin during 1948, there was no contingency plan to deal with an enemy attack. Hence we can say that civil defence planning got off to a poor start, taken unawares by sudden developments in the conflict that provided its reason for existence. Short-term crises aside, however, long-term planning did lay the groundwork for many of the most important policies of the cold war period during this time.

The shock of Hiroshima

The day after the dropping of the atomic bomb, the social research organisation Mass-Observation set about collecting the public's views on the momentous event. First reactions were mixed, the triumphalism of some mingling with an apparently more widespread feeling of foreboding. One man felt immediate fears for the future: 'I think it's awful. It gives me qualms when I think about it. Supposing they use it against us. Supposing Germany will learn the secret – and other countries. They will, you know'. Pessimism reached its apogee with a 15-year-old boy: 'I don't think I'll put my name down for hop-picking now – it's not worth while'.[1]

Fear and uncertainty characterised the early reactions to the bomb, in the press as well as on the street. On Tuesday 7 August, as the news broke in the London press, *The Times'* diplomatic correspondent wrote that the bomb's 'wider and more fearful possibilities are as yet undisclosed. The atomic bomb, more surely than the rocket, carries the warning that another world war would mean the destruction of all regulated life'.[2] The next day, the same paper cried that 'the world stands in the presence of a revolution of earthly affairs at least as big with potentialities of good and evil as when the forces of steam or electricity were harnessed for the first time to the purposes of industry and war'.[3] Letters poured into newspaper offices. In a letter to the *Manchester Guardian*, the left-wing publisher Victor Gollancz argued that the use of the atomic bomb was a 'further debasement of the human currency'.[4] The Anglican Bishop of Southwell informed *The Times* that all thinking men and women would be 'awed and conscience stricken' by the use of the bomb (the President of the Methodist Council expressed similar sentiments in the same place on the same day).[5] Public comment was so widespread that Evelyn Waugh commented in his diary that 'everyone seems impelled to make a public statement about his own opinion of the atomic bomb. Even I, left alone, began to write a note for *The Tablet* on the subject, but recovered my good sense and destroyed it'.[6]

The Japanese surrender brought about a change of opinion. The leading article in the *Manchester Guardian* of 15 August 1945 argued that 'morally, perhaps, the use of the bomb could be justified in a world which had learnt to accept the rocket bomb and the flame thrower and to applaud the slow destruction of Berlin and Cologne. But only immediate peace could prove it justifiable and quiet our concerns'.[7] This feeling was echoed by George Orwell the same day in his 'London Letter' in the *Partisan Review*: 'the prompt surrender of Japan seems to have altered people's outlook on the atomic bomb. At the beginning everyone I spoke to about it, or overheard in the street, was simply horrified. Now they begin to feel that there's something to be said for a weapon that could end the war in two days'.[8] Lionel Blackburn, Dean of Ely, certainly saw something in this, arguing that 'to me, and I think all who have dear ones in the fighting zone, all war is dreadful and anything that can shorten its horrors must be right. I confess that I feel indignant to find that those who condemn the use of the atomic bomb would have preferred a long drawn out war and a hideous slaughter of fine lives while they themselves remain in security'.[9]

But for many, the atomic bomb inspired a very real moral revulsion. One Mass-Observer wrote in September that 'such hideous destruction seems to knock the moral bottom out of life.... Ideals, hopes and principles seem to fade to nothingness'. Another wrote that she was 'too horrified to want to speak about it and yet it is seldom out of my mind. It casts a gloom over everything and its terrifying possibilities make nothing worth while doing'.[10] By far the most sophisticated moral reaction was that produced by the Catholic intellectual Ronald Knox, who felt urged to write his book, *God and the Atom* by the silence of the traditional Catholic hierarchy on the subject.[11] This anguished investigation by the nation's clergymen and self-appointed observers was not shared by the popular press, much of which exulted in the bomb and the future atomic technology would bring, indulging 'in trivialities or fantasies about atomic energy as a magic source of prosperity, with atomic-powered family cars, cookers and labour-saving devices for all'.[12]

After the atom-frenzy of the first two or three months following Hiroshima, interest in the bomb seemed to die down. George Orwell noted in October that 'considering how likely we all are to be blown to pieces by it within the next five years, the atomic bomb has not roused so much discussion as might have been expected'.[13] Leonard Woolf in

January 1946 argued that the atomic bomb was typical of those '"sensations", whose depth is measured by the height of sales of evening papers, are of their nature short-lived and in effect transient and abortive. They pass away with the last Derby or last scandal leaving much the same kind of mark upon the record of human history'.[14] Interest in the bomb, Woolf believed, 'passed away in a shiver of millions of ordinary persons at the prospect of what, some years hence, it will probably mean in misery for themselves or their children'.[15]

Orwell and Woolf certainly witnessed the decline of interest in atomic energy, but there can be no doubt of the continuing power the atomic bomb had in the imagination of ordinary Britons. Although exact knowledge of the science might be hard to find, assumptions about the awesome power of the new weapon were widespread. For example, in 1947, in the midst of one of the bitterest winters in British history, Mass-Observation asked people what they thought was causing the adverse weather. One in four named causes beyond the meteorological and most of them believed the atomic bomb to have been responsible (there had been further tests in 1946).[16] In 1950, when the Government was attempting to improve its recruitment measures for the new voluntary Civil Defence Corps, a survey reported that 10 per cent of the public sample believed they would be safe from an atomic bomb only if fifty miles from any explosion, and 15 per cent believed 'nowhere in England' would be far enough away. Around 60 per cent believed that Britain would suffer 'complete destruction' in a future war.[17] This endemic over-estimation of the power of the bomb is eloquent proof that the belief in the atomic weapon as all-powerful was firmly entrenched in the British public's mindset and that, although immediate interest in the bomb faded quickly in 1945, its devastating effects remained seared on the minds of millions. In 1945 Mass-Observation reported one woman saying: 'It seems beyond the average person to take it in. I can't judge it. It's beyond me'.[18] It was beyond most people, but as they struggled to understand the meaning of the bomb after Hiroshima, its immense power was obvious to all.

Understanding the atom

For Clement Attlee, Prime Minister for less than a fortnight, the impact of the atomic bomb was profound. Throughout that August he grappled with the meaning of atomic energy, telling the House of Commons on 16 August 1945 in his first speech to the new postwar Parliament, 'we have seen a new force, the result of scientific discovery, the far-reaching consequences of which, I think, we find it difficult to grasp'.[19] Twelve days later, Attlee had grasped some of the essential 'consequences' of the bomb and set them down in one of the most remarkable papers of Britain's cold war. His two main themes, expressed to Ministerial colleagues, were that British defence policy would have to be overhauled and that in order to avoid a future war, international control of the new weapon needed to be secured. Hiroshima had 'left much of our post-war planning out of date': bomb proof shelters and basements, the retention of ARP and fire services, and plans for 'a redistribution of industry planned on account of the experience of bombing attacks during the war' was all 'futile waste' in the face of the atomic bomb. 'Nothing can alter the fact that the geographical situation of Britain offers to a Continental Power such targets as London and the other great cities. Dispersal of munitions works and airfields cannot alter the facts of geography'. Britain, highly urbanised, highly industrialised and geographically and demographically compact, was much more vulnerable than either the United States or the Soviet Union, with their vast tracts of lands and low population densities.[20]

Britain's vulnerability meant that a future war with an atomic-armed enemy had to be avoided. It was hard, Attlee put it, 'for people to realise that even the modern conception of war to which in my lifetime we have become accustomed is now completely out of date'.

> We recognised, or some of us did, before this war that bombing could only be answered by counter bombing. We were right. Berlin and Magdeburg were the answer to London and Coventry. Both derive from Guernica. The answer to an atomic bomb on London is an atomic bomb on another great city.
>
> Duelling with swords and inefficient pistols was bearable. Duelling had to go with the advent of weapons of precision. What is to be done about the atomic bomb?
>
> The only course which seems to me to be feasible and to offer a reasonable hope of staving off imminent disaster for the world is joint action by the USA, UK and Russia based upon stark reality. We should declare that this new invention has made it essential to end wars. The new world order must start now.[21]

That Attlee found himself writing in this way demonstrated the awful shock of Hiroshima for politicians as well as the public.[22] As part of his doomed attempt to achieve a lasting settlement based on international control of the bomb, Attlee wrote to President Truman in September

1945, asking rhetorically, 'Am I to plan for a peaceful or warlike world? If the latter, I ought to direct all our people to live like troglodytes underground as being the only hope of survival, and that by no means certain'.[23] Hope for a 'peaceful world' faded over the next two years, but Attlee's belief in international co-operation over atomic energy was sincere and deeply held.[24]

Alongside Attlee's attempts to secure the future of mankind, he ensured that Britain took the first necessary steps to become an atomic power in its own right. From December 1945 until the final decision to proceed with producing the atomic bomb was taken by a select group of Ministers in 1948, it had long been understood that Britain would produce a bomb of its own.[25] Every setback for international control, every piece of aggression or obduracy by the Soviet Union and every intimation that the United States would or could not restart atomic co-operation after the passing of the McMahon Act (which in 1946 banned the American Government from such activity) only made Attlee and his Government more determined to join the atomic club.

From the autumn of 1945 what became an immense government machinery for dealing with atomic-themed issues began to grow within Whitehall. Committees such as the 'Advisory Committee on Atomic Energy' and the 'Directorate of Tube Alloys' were part of an unwieldy structure covering atomic energy (both in terms of weapons, civil energy and international control).[26] A series of key individuals who sat on the various committees meant that the findings of these disparate bodies matched up in the end. These included Sir Hastings 'Pug' Ismay, then in his final year as Military Secretary of the Cabinet and Sir James Chadwick, discoverer of the neutron, Nobel laureate, and Head of the British Mission to the Manhattan Project, and other scientists such as Sir George Thomson and P.M.S. Blackett. One such committee set about understanding the atomic bomb in relation to the needs of the present. The Joint Technical Warfare Committee (JTWC), a sub-Committee of the Chiefs of Staff Committee (the supreme military committee), especially wanted to know what the effects of the bombs were on the two unfortunate Japanese cities, what they would be if dropped on British conurbations, and how this might affect Britain's ability to fight a future global war.

To give the scientific luminaries the data to work from, a report was commissioned to look at ground-level conditions in Japan.[27] Staffed largely by Home Office scientists, the report was quickly completed, delivered to the Prime Minister in January 1946,[28] and published in re-worded form.[29] Neither version minced its words. To emphasise the power of the Hiroshima bomb (announced by President Truman as being equivalent to that of 20,000 tons of TNT), the published report contained a wartime analogy: 'the scale of destruction expected would be that which would befall a model town built to the scale of Gulliver's Lilliput, 1 inch to the foot, if there was exploded above it a bomb more than twice as large as the largest British "Blockbuster"'.[30] If such a bomb was dropped on an 'average' British urban area, they estimated around 50,000 dead from one atomic bomb, with 30,000 houses destroyed and another 35,000 made uninhabitable.[31] To put this into perspective, 218,000 houses had been destroyed and a total of 450,000 had been made uninhabitable during the Second World War,[32] but that had been spread out over six years of war. It would take six atomic bombs to cause as much housing damage, but just one would come close to equalling the 60,595 deaths caused by enemy air raids over Britain.

But the most striking aspect of the report was the descriptions of the casualties caused by the bomb. 'Flashburn' victims were vividly described, as were those who died due to radiation exposure, disillusioning those who had believed that the atomic bomb was a sort of super-sized conventional bomb, equivalent to so many tons of TNT. It demonstrated that this was a totally new force:

> Even those severely irradiated probably did not show the characteristic symptoms, nausea, vomiting and fever, for 24 hours, and rarely died in less than one week. These first symptoms were followed by bloody diarrhoea, occurring most frequently in the second week, at which time loss of appetite and general malaise also become marked. Patients began to lose their hair after the first week.
>
> Thereafter, in the severe cases, the clinical picture began to be dominated by signs of deficient blood formation.... It was apparent that the gamma rays had virtually killed the entire bone marrow.... As red blood cell formation ceased, the patient began to suffer from progressive anaemia. As platelet formation ceased, the thin blood seeped in small and large haemorrhages into the skin and the retina of the eye, and sometimes into the intestines and the kidneys. The fall in the number of white blood cells... in severe cases lowered resistance, so the patient inevitably fell prey to some infection.... Deaths probably began in about the week after the explosion, reached a peak in about three weeks, and had for the most part, ceased after six to eight weeks.[33]

Almost as chilling as the actual physical consequences of radiation was the fact that it permeated reinforced concrete buildings, killing people who were unscathed by blast or heat effects.[34]

Elaborating on the overall effects of the bomb, the report showed that 'the scale of the disaster brought city life and industry virtually to a standstill. Even the most destructive conventional attacks, the incendiary raids on Hamburg in the summer of 1943 and on Tokyo in the Spring of 1945, had no comparable effect in paralysing communal organisation',[35] and 'the larger impression which both cities make is of having sunk, in an instant and without a struggle, to the most primitive existence'.[36] Protection of the population, the Mission believed, presented 'a formidable problem',[37] and it insisted that 'planned and energetic action by central government', rather than reliance on local services, would be essential'.[38] *The Effects of the Atomic Bombs at Hiroshima and Nagasaki* is in a way the master document of British understanding of the nature of atomic warfare: it shaped and underpinned all other reviews and reports.[39] With its scientific data and belief that atomic defence was a major, but not insoluble, problem, the report influenced British policy on nuclear attack for the next eight years, until thermonuclear weapons made its conclusions redundant.

Although publication of the report aroused virtually no interest beyond Whitehall, within official corridors interest was profound. The JTWC's final report on the future of warfare drew important lessons from the Mission's data. Firstly, it formulated the Attlee-esque view that 'countries which concentrate a high proportion of the population in cities which are not self supporting, or which depend on a delicate system of transport and distribution, will be particularly vulnerable to this form of attack'.[40] This led the committee to estimate (and this remained outside the final report to the Chiefs of Staff), that 36 atomic bombs could eliminate Britain from a future war due to the concentration of industrial, transport and importing capacity in relatively few targets.[41] In a future war, therefore, an enemy 'might achieve decisive results with relatively small effort against the civil population of a nation without a clash between major military forces and too rapidly to permit either the building up of military forces or the exercise of sea power'.[42] The second, connected, lesson drawn was 'a much greater proportion of the defence effort of the country during peace must be devoted to civil defence and the dispersal of industry'.[43] Dispersal was central to the new conceptualisation of atomic defence. Although JTWC also stressed the need for revisions to, and the expansion of shelter provision, civilian medical services and the ability to store and distribute stocks of food, it was only through using the town planning apparatus to disperse essential industries and their workforce away from the obvious target areas that a nation like Britain could hope to survive an atomic attack and continue to prosecute a war.

Greatly exercised by the fear of a future British collapse, JTWC debated the extent to which public morale could withstand atomic bombardment. It was feared that as few as five or ten atomic bombs, 'with the prospect of more to follow', could cause a panic evacuation of cities on a scale 'sufficient seriously to sap the power of waging war by conventional means of any country physically and psychologically unorganised to meet such action'.[44] On the other hand, some hundreds of atomic weapons might fail to cause the collapse of a country suitably organised physically and psychologically.[45] A limited study had already argued that Britain, due to its wartime experience, would be 'highly resistive' to atomic attack (as would the USSR), whereas the USA would be much less so as an experience of bombardment was lacking.[46] The lack of British interest in public morale during the cold war is striking when compared to the work undertaken on the issue in America.[47] The assumption that the Blitz-hardened population of 1945 would see off an atomic attack as long as physical preparations were in place proved a remarkably resilient one in Whitehall.

Later, after the mushrooming of atomic committees had been regularised, and responsibility for drafting plans for defending Britain from a nuclear attack had been given to new committee of high ranking civil servants, more detailed work was completed on the effects on British cities of an atomic war. These studies, finished in 1947, argued that if no civil defence measures were taken an enemy in possession of 40 to 50 atomic bombs (the putative date for such a stockpile being available to the Soviet Union was 1956) could kill 1.25 million people and injure 1.75 million in a future war.[48] If restricting Britain's capacity to import materials (thus affecting Britain's ability to prosecute the war) rather than inflicting casualties was the enemy's primary objective then 1 million would still be killed. In addition, this 'port strategy' would destroy 1.25 million homes, reduce total importing capacity by 78 per cent and destroy 12 per cent of the electricity generating industry. Such carnage would cause a collapse of the country's ability to fight as minimum importing requirements could not be met and could, moreover, be caused by delivering just 17 atomic bombs. The concentration of so much of Britain's industrial and importing capacity in a small number of highly populated port cities (London, Liverpool, Glasgow, Bristol, Manchester) appeared to greatly compromise the nation's ability to survive a future atomic bombardment. This analysis explains why the dispersal of industry and port facilities around the nation became the central policy for mitigating the effects of atomic war in the immediate post-1945 years.

The research of JTWC in late 1945 and early 1946 was central to the formation of Britain's early nuclear strategy, as John Baylis has shown,[49] but research completed concurrently in the Home Office was much more narrowly focussed on civil defence, and especially on piecing together a new structure for the civil defence services.[50] It was quickly understood that the 1939–45 model could not stand up to the increased weight of attack seen in Germany in 1944–45, let alone in a future atomic war. Although the Home Office was quick to formulate new plans, they were only submitted to Ministers in October 1947 as part of a wider reorganisation of civil defence policy,[51] but it is worth stressing how early certain important aspects of the eventual policy were formulated. These were the necessity of centralised control over the organisation and provision of future services, that local forces should be constituted in addition to new national 'mobile' civil defence columns, and that an ethos of 'self-help' should be instilled in the civil population.[52] As we shall see, these became vital principles in the eventual formation of the Civil Defence Corps in 1949.

The work of JTWC and the Home Office continued separately, with little or no interaction. Such fractured organisation caused a minor political debate in early 1948, with the Home Office minister admitting in the Commons in March 1948 that 'the machinery has perhaps not been wholly adequate', and revealing that a new Cabinet Committee, the Civil Defence Committee, was being formed, supported by a new Civil Defence Joint Planning Staff (CDJPS) to conduct research and analysis.[53] For the *Economist*, however, this new governmental machinery was misguided, and their anonymous correspondent argued that the CDJPS should be under the direction of the Ministry of Defence, not the Home Office and that Ministers, not civil servants, should sit on the Civil Defence Committee.[54] This debate over Cabinet machinery reveals a deeper concern over the need to integrate civil defence more fully with 'traditional' defence issues. When the *Economist* returned to the issue at the height of the Berlin crisis it was to criticise the outmoded thinking that placed civil defence under the jurisdiction of the Home Office when 'there is hardly a single question of defence organisation or planning which is not affected by the capacity of this country to withstand air attack at short notice'.[55] The decision to keep civil defence within the Home Office, supported by the CDJPS and the Department's own new Scientific Advisers branch,[56] reflected the fact that organising civilian civil defence volunteers and co-ordinating wartime fire and medical services would be the central activities of peacetime planning. What is more, experience was to show the importance of keeping civil and traditional defence separate, as the Home Office championed civil defence and the Ministry of Defence eyed its budget warily. The real issue was not which department had overall control over civil defence planning, but how civil defence policy was co-ordinated across Whitehall and this was improved when a Ministerial Committee on Civil Defence was formed in August 1948,[57] but finding the most suitable governmental machinery to plan and decide policy was an abiding problem throughout the 1940s and 1950s.

Towards a civil defence policy

If the first year of peace was marked by a British foreign policy geared toward international co-operation, especially in atomic energy affairs, then after mid-1946 pessimism concerning relations with the Soviet Union caused by tensions over Germany, Greece and Persia outweighed any continuing belief in the future of genuine co-operation between the wartime 'Big Three'. After the summer of 1946 the cold war became more entrenched as a concept in the official mind of Whitehall, formally arriving at the Cabinet table in the early new year of 1948 when the Foreign Secretary, Ernest Bevin, submitted a range of papers to his colleagues, including 'a comprehensive review of the hostile policy Russia had followed towards Britain and the West since the end of the war', as Alan Bullock puts it in his masterly biography of Bevin.[58] Soviet obscurantism in virtually every sphere of international relations and the perception of the direct threat to Britain and her interests posed by Moscow-inspired international communism hardened the views of the Labour Cabinet even before the Czechoslovakian coup of February 1948 demonstrated to the world the ruthlessness with which the Soviet Union was prepared to extend its hold over central and eastern Europe.

It was in this atmosphere of mounting tension that work began on planning the large-scale dispersal of industry. Within the new civil defence planning machinery, it was hoped to complete a massive survey of the 'hard core' of Britain's war potential: those elements of industry 'which were vital in a fight for survival in this country'.[59] This hugely ambitious project, a sort of atomic Domesday book, would allow planners to identify which industrial firms needed to be protected from attack and which could be moved from the target cities to other parts of the country. But outside the narrow confines of the civil servants on the Civil Defence Committee, few in 1947 or 1948 could have believed that full-scale industrial dispersal was a viable policy, despite the approval given by the high-level Defence Committee (chaired by the Prime Minister) to the principle of dispersal contained in the JTWC report of 1946.

In fact, dispersal was still-born as a viable policy, although this fact did not penetrate the consciousness of most civil defence planners until after the Berlin Crisis of 1948. Just a week after the Defence Committee's approval of the principle, a Cabinet battle was fought concerning the building of a new power station in Poplar, East London. In strategic terms, Poplar was considered perhaps the worst place in Britain to build a power station; the docks, existing electricity generating capacity and a highly concentrated population made the area an attractive target, and a sizeable new power plant would only make it more so. But despite the protestations of the Air Minister, Geoffrey de Freitas, that such a location was foolhardy,[60] the economic case that the immediate need for new generating capacity was paramount and that the consequences of the delay and increased cost of building elsewhere were too great won the day.[61] Although after this decision the strategic advice on the location of industry was reaffirmed by the Defence Committee,[62] when another row broke out in March 1947 over a proposed power station on Bankside – with the Ministry of Town and Country Planning aghast at the effects it would have on its plans for reconstruction of the South Bank of Thames, and the Dean of St Paul's equally perturbed at the impact on the view from, and of, the Cathedral – the result was the same.[63] Poplar demonstrated the inability of defence planners to override economic policy-makers. Despite the government's real belief in the need for industrial dispersal and its acceptance of the assumptions of JTWC, the enormous importance of generating capacity to the contemporary domestic economy meant that the defence planners could not overcome the arguments in favour of building the plant. Quite simply, the short-term economic costs always outweighed the apparent long-term strategic advantages; for dispersal, as for shelter policy (as we shall see), this basic fact was crucial.

The unreality of planning for mass dispersal was not confined to civil servants, however. When the fruits of two years' planning were presented to Ministers in October 1947 it was suggested that Britain could avoid the worst consequences of war through a 'carefully planned large-scale dispersal of industry and population to the Dominions and Colonies overseas'.[64] The proposal seemed to excite Ministers and Ernest Bevin thought that dispersal could invigorate the development of the African colonies,[65] and remained on the agenda until Winston Churchill declared in a speech on 6 December 1947 that

> I am quite sure that socialism will make it impossible for 48,000,000 people to live in this island, and that at least one quarter of all who are alive today will have to disappear in one way or another, after enduring a lowering of standards of food and comfort inconceivable in the last fifty years.[66]

Unsurprisingly, the plan for a government study on the mass emigration of people from Britain was considered politically inexpedient after this speech, lest it confirm Churchill's belief that the Socialists could not support the population, and the project was quietly dropped.[67] Considering the difficulty the planners faced in influencing the location of power stations it is deeply ironic to read the lengthy discussions on the possibility of relocating industry across the globe.

Although there were some genuine results from this concentration on dispersal, such as the 'Port Emergency Scheme' for lessening the reliance on Liverpool and London in wartime by activating importing capacity in lesser ports, the overall impact of the work on dispersal was largely negative. As one insider complained at the time of the October 1947 report, too much time had been devoted to the idea of moving bits of industry out of the target areas, and not enough to whether those who were meant to stay behind and work would actually do so.[68] This criticism seemed to be implicitly understood, and when, just before the Berlin Crisis erupted in the summer of 1948, a planning document was produced to draw a line under postwar planning and elucidate a basic philosophy of civil defence, the need for dispersal was placed in the context of a broader policy containing measures such as evacuation, public shelters and wartime medical services, feeding arrangements and a fully-functioning national civil defence service.[69]

This outline policy was aimed at both protecting the population from the effects of a future war and protecting the ability of the nation to continue to fight it. The latter imperative, of course, inspired the work on industrial dispersal whilst the former led to a reappraisal of those life-saving measures so familiar from the Second World War. The vicissitudes of evacuation and shelter policy are the subject of Chapter Three, but in 1948 it was assumed that a fully functioning evacuation scheme would reduce casualties (although no scheme actually existed); equally, it was assumed that shelters would be provided for those required to stay behind and work in the non-dispersed factories (again, no shelter programme had been – or was ever to be – agreed). Likewise, plans for an emergency feeding programme, for medical services and for rescue services existed only on paper, insofar as they existed at all. On the eve of the Berlin Crisis, when it seemed as if Britain would be involved in a global war against the Soviet Union, Britain had no civil defence plan in existence. Paper plans still had a heavy sense of unreality about them. Although future shelter provision was assumed, the whole scheme for keeping British war production functioning relied on workers being willing to continue to live and work in areas subject to atomic attack, but no official really seemed to confront the possibility that this might not happen. The paper plans which did exist were geared towards a future atomic war in about 1957 – the prospect of war in the short-term caught planners totally off-guard – and long-term civil defence policy did advance along the lines envisaged in the summer of 1948. The voluntary civil defence services did come into being in 1949, an evacuation scheme was introduced in 1950, stockpiles of food and medical supplies were built up in the early 1950s, and although shelters were never built, they remained a key part of civil defence planners' policies until the mid-1950s. Of the key policies of the 1945–48 period, only industrial dispersal failed to take root. It was far too ambitious and would have had far too large an impact on the ordinary domestic economy for it ever to have been a viable peacetime policy.

The Berlin war scare

The Berlin blockade of the summer of 1948 was the first major crisis of the cold war, a genuine war scare.[70] The Soviet Union cut off the land routes from the western zones of Germany and sealed the borders to the British, American and French sectors of Berlin on 24 June 1948 as part of its determination not to see the British and the Americans succeed in establishing a separate, capitalist German state in their sectors of Germany and Berlin. The resulting crisis was the culmination of three years' fraught discussion over the future of Germany and the blockade 'dramatically exemplified' the new cold war confrontation which had grown since 1945.[71] For many, war seemed imminent. Historian Avi Shlaim has argued that 'in retrospect it is clear beyond any shadow of a doubt that this was the most critical crisis of the cold war'.[72] In Britain, as Alan Bullock put it,

> everyone with a claim to expert knowledge agreed that the Russians were unlikely to start a war to force the western powers out of

> Berlin, but the fact was that they continued to tighten the blockade and that if a war started as a result of miscalculation, there was little chance of stopping the Red Army from occupying Western Europe.[73]

Although war was averted, West Berlin being relieved through a massive air-lift operation lasting months and the Soviet Union, lifting the blockade in mid-1949, implicitly admitting defeat, the British Government certainly considered Berlin a possible step on the road to war and intensified defence planning accordingly. An emergency military plan was produced for the Defence Committee on 12 July, envisaging withdrawing from most of Germany and defending the Rhine if war came,[74] and plans for general mobilisation followed.[75] A key point in preparations was reached when the Defence Committee turned down the request of the Chiefs of Staff to suspend the releases of 92,000 trained men and women due for discharge by the end of September 1948.[76] Although retaining them would clearly aid Britain's military preparations, the proposal was rejected because, in Bevin's words, it was 'not yet necessary to abandon hope of finding a solution to the present difficulties by negotiation', and publicity for active war preparations could jeopardise talks. Attlee agreed that any suggestion of emergency preparations could prove 'highly dangerous'.[77] The paramount importance given to secrecy extended throughout that summer's debate on defence plans and beyond. Throughout the cold war, policy-making in an emergency would always be a delicate balance between the desire to undertake useful preparations and the fear of precipitating a crisis through open preparations for war. In time this fear would raise awkward questions as to whether *any* worthwhile preparations – including evacuation – could be authorised in an emergency.

A few days after this meeting the Cabinet Secretary, Sir Norman Brook, produced a report on the civil aspects of 'the defence position', distributed to the Defence Committee under Attlee's name.[78] It sought to give the facts concerning the lack of any plans to meet an immediate emergency. This was clearly a potentially catastrophic planning failure, and one that illustrates some of civil defence planning's broader flaws. Officials did actually discuss in March 1948 whether, considering rising international tension, a short-term plan should be compiled.[79] A decision was taken that the officials on the Civil Defence Committee should not be 'deflected' from their long-term planning remit. Clearly, more political and strategic direction based on sound intelligence was needed, and such an important planning decision should not have been in the hands of a relatively unimportant committee. After Berlin, with the Ministerial committee and the greater interest in civil defence taken by the Cabinet Secretary, such strategic direction was in place.

However symptomatic of problems in the direction of civil defence, this planning failure clearly represented an enormous problem in July 1948. Brook told Ministers that improvisation would be needed, and that any scheme to meet an attack 'could only be makeshift'. Moreover, any preparations must involve full publicity:

> it would be necessary to consult local authorities and numerous other authorities outside the Government; and in order to start enrolling and training the necessary volunteers it would be necessary to make it clear to the public that it was their duty to prepare themselves for the possibility of an emergency.[80]

In short, it would involve placing Britain on a full-scale war alert. Just how unprepared Britain was for any attack was made abundantly clear. Since 1945, for example, the RAF Warning System had been allowed to atrophy and in 1948 it covered only the Humber, the Solent and the Thames. Neither a blackout scheme nor evacuation could be implemented without 'several weeks' of preparations. Most of the shelters from the last war had been dismantled (including domestic shelters) and could not be replaced for many months.[81] Had global war broken out, the consequences for Britain would have been terrible. It was believed that the initial air attack would have been equivalent to that experienced in 1940–41, but civil defence preparations during the Blitz had been two years in the making. In 1948, there would have been no evacuation and no shelters, and the fire and ambulance services were no longer equipped for war. Casualties would have undoubtedly outstripped those of the Blitz. For ministers, however, concentrating on resolving the crisis rather than preparing for its escalation, any publicity surrounding civil defence preparations must be avoided.

Attlee himself ordered 'that all possible steps should be taken to prepare plans to improve a situation which was clearly disquieting'.[82] This decision set in motion a flurry of activity to prepare an emergency civil defence plan, part of which was a list of what could be done if the publicity ban was lifted. The list of 16 key subjects to be considered across various Whitehall departments gives an impression of the scale of the task facing civil defence planners. These were the mobilisation of the voluntary civil defence services, the central control organisation for this, evacuation, shelter, rest centres for homeless, food, fuel, medical services, the air-raid warning system, blackout, the communications system, gasmasks, the publicity organisation, anti-sabotage measures, accommodation, and finally camouflage and deception. Departments were instructed by the chairman[83] of the Civil Defence Committee, Sir Alexander Maxwell, to produce paper plans considering what could be done in each field and what steps would have to be taken to get them on as firm a war footing as possible.[84] The speed of activity was impressive, with a report discussing the various departmental papers presented to the Civil Defence Committee on 14 August 1948,[85] and dispatched to Ministers on the Defence Committee on 19 August.[86]

This emergency plan essentially aimed at reintroducing the successful measures of the last war, and stressed that without publicity very little could be achieved beyond paper planning. If consultation with outsiders was allowed, however, it would be possible after two or three months to 'create in advance of war the framework of an organisation which could be expanded, trained and equipped under the impetus of war itself'.[87] Concentrating on what had already been done, and what could be done once the publicity ban was lifted, this 'emergency plan' was not a final cohesive paper plan, but rather a 'living' document which detailed progress being made, and the steps to be taken if the government decided that the international crisis warranted the final implementation of a crash plan. Taken as a whole, the plan graphically detailed the shortcomings in civil defence preparations in all aspects of policy, but three key examples will suffice to illustrate the plan's recommendations.

Firstly, the civil defence services comprising wardens, rescue and the fire service. It was not possible to recruit and equip volunteers for all these services and the government would have to rely largely on improvisation. Volunteers would sign up on the outbreak of war and details were now being worked out for a scheme which would require 'in the first instance' 168,000 whole-time volunteers. 'Intensive and protracted effort' would be needed to overcome deficiencies in organisation, training and equipment and it was not expected that these services would be in any position to deal with heavy raids for some months.[88] Secondly, shelters were in short supply. Of the approximately 3.6 million Anderson and Morrison shelters provided in the 1939–45 war, 628,000 remained and the rest had been used for scrap – and publicity was urgently needed to stop even more shelters being destroyed.[89] Without publicity, little could be done in preparing public shelters (for example, the floodgates had been removed from the London Underground system). Although little could be done in terms of building new shelters, if the publicity ban was lifted the Home Office could distribute pamphlets which would, among other things, give 'advice to the public generally as to the best means of avoiding danger if they have no shelter to go to'.[90] In fact, the level of steel stocks was so perilous that it was suggested that existing stocks should be frozen in order to provide shelter in a future war. The ruinous impact of this measure on the government's housing programme was not considered by the Home Office. Thirdly, evacuation was a major problem. It had been assumed by Sir Norman Brook that some degree of evacuation from target areas 'would be expected'.[91] Evacuation would certainly have been called for by the public, and some evacuation plan, even if it was limited, would have helped bolster morale had war come. Moreover, the lack of other detailed life-saving plans would have made evacuation even more important. The plan stressed the need to learn the lessons of the last war and keep any evacuation scheme simple, and to delay announcing the plan to avoid criticism from those in areas receiving evacuees.[92] Only expectant mothers and school children from key target areas would be evacuated at first, and discussions would have to take place with local authorities and voluntary groups such as the Women's Voluntary Service and the British Red Cross, concerning billeting and feeding. These discussions, as well as the need to print evacuation timetables and pamphlets meant that publicity was both unavoidable and essential.

The other areas on the list of 16 subjects also gave cause for concern, with it being suggested that the only sources for sirens would be new production or 'possibly, the British Zone in Germany', and the Foreign Office had been asked to 'find out discreetly' whether they could obtain suitable sirens. Surely nothing, however, would suggest Britain was preparing for war more vividly than the occupying forces roaming northern Germany looking for air raid sirens to dismantle and ship back to Britain. In terms of blackout provision, care of the homeless, and disposal of the dead, materials were lacking, organisation non-existent and staff needed. Across all areas local authorities and industry had yet to be consulted. In short, the only hope for achieving a basic level of preparedness was authorising a degree of consultation which would make it clear that plans were being created to meet the possibility of war in the near future. Also, it was stated that implementing the plan would place 'a heavy load on the economy of the country.... Unless American help was made available on a vast scale well in advance of the emergency, and was subsequently maintained, we see little prospect of being able to meet these demands'.[93] Faced with a plan that would both signal to the international community that Britain was preparing for war and severely disrupt Britain's fragile and rebuilding economy, it is no surprise that Ministers refused to allow publicity when the plan was discussed on 23 August. It was felt that any announcement of plans could have a 'serious effect on the international situation', even though suspension of military releases was finally agreed to.[94]

When the Ministerial Committee on Civil Defence was finally created on 30 August, the pressure to finalise an emergency plan had lessened. Instead, the chairman, Home Secretary James Chuter Ede, informed planners that 'anything that we do to meet the possibility of war at an earlier date should be designed as far as possible to fit in with the policies we propose to adopt under the long term plan'.[95] It was intended that civil defence plans be completed in stages – the first of which would serve as the future 'emergency' or interim plan, with the final stage the completion of the long-term atomic civil defence plan. This shift was designed to elide 'emergency' plans which would soon become redundant, with building towards the long-term plan clearly designed to give some stability to civil defence planning. It was also an implicit criticism of the previous approach – instead of being too focussed on long-term planning to meet an immediate emergency, the new way of planning would build up from preparations designed to meet both immediate and long-term needs. This subtle but definite shift from the panic of late July was caused by the stabilisation of the Berlin Crisis, and Ede realised that there was little point continuing to construct a 'really effective plan' because of the problems with publicity and the shortages of all kinds of materials and supplies. Therefore, Ede concluded, 'we should accept that the outline plans that have been prepared are of limited value only and that if war comes we shall be forced to rely very largely on improvisation'.[96]

From mid-September, then, the focus of civil defence planning shifted back to looking at long-term issues. On 14 September 1948, Herbert Morrison made a speech in the House Commons revealing that the Government intended to introduce legislation to set up a new, reorganised, civil defence service.[97] Far from suggesting that Britain was preparing for war, the press greeted Morrison's speech with criticisms of the Government's previous 'dilatoriness',[98] leading Ede to conclude that preparations could be announced in the context of long-term planning, thus lessening the international implications of any announcements. This was Ede's argument when he tried to convince Attlee and other senior ministers of the need to finally lift the publicity ban to allow discussions with local authorities about interim planning strategies, to finally end the destruction of existing shelters, and to compile a census of sirens.[99] He stressed that the 'public mind' was not only ready, but actively expected, civil defence preparations to be announced, and that lifting the publicity ban would allow discussions which would aid emergency planning, especially in terms of manning the civil defence services before the long-term organisation was ready in mid-1949. This meeting took place on 1 October and did finally lift the publicity ban.[100]

The question of publicity was, at first, essentially a strategic one. It was concerned with the impact such preparations could have on allies as well as potential enemies. It was feared that civil defence preparations could signal to the world that Britain considered war likely or even inevitable, something which could have demonstrably affected the chances of a peaceful resolution to the Berlin crisis. By October, this concern had lessened. Attlee was briefed before the key meeting: 'there seems to be a good case for doing more in the way of civil defence planning and it is unlikely that the Home Secretary's proposal would lead to any deterioration in the present international situation'.[101] There can be no doubt that for Attlee and others, the realisation that great strides could be made on essential areas (such as the warning system, the mobilisation of the Civil Defence Services, evacuation, shelter, food, care of the homeless and provision of respirators) if the ban was lifted was central to the decision.

But strategy was not the only concern. An equal worry for Ministers was the public reaction to the proposal to undertake civil defence preparations. In short, they feared that the public might clamour for preparations the government could not afford. Attlee himself delivered a telling statement, that in lifting the ban 'it was, however, essential to avoid a situation in which the Government would be driven to devote resources to civil defence on a scale which would cripple the national economy, detract from our power of offence and alienate our allies in Western Europe'.[102] What Attlee said held true throughout the cold war; the economic realities faced by successive British Governments would never allow civil defence policy to develop as the planners would have hoped, and the power of offensive was seen as better guarantor of peace. As Peter Hennessy argues, 'the bomb was always put before shelters'.[103] It was a continual fear throughout the atomic age that public clamour might force a government into adopting a ruinously expensive civil defence policy, and this fear greatly influenced the government's attitude to civil defence publicity even after the ban was nominally lifted. For example, when Ministers discussed civil defence yet again on 18 November 1948 to decide on what form the consultations with local authorities would take, it was decided to postpone the proposed shelter census because, in the words of Minister of Health, Anuerin Bevan, 'nothing must be done to make the public "shelter-conscious"'.[104]

The Civil Defence Act

The meeting which postponed the shelter census also finally killed off the notion of a separate emergency plan. Henceforth any emergency would be met by adapting existing long-term plans which would, it was assumed, be in an adaptable state long before a crisis looked like escalating to war.[105] Five days later, James Chuter Ede introduced the second reading of the Civil Defence Bill. The eventual Civil Defence Act of 1948 set out the intended structure of the Civil Defence Corps and other services which were established in mid-1949. For those expecting a more detailed document, perhaps one setting out evacuation and shelter policies, or plans for wartime medical services, the Bill was a disappointment (Brigadier Prior-Palmer, Conservative MP for Worthing called it 'a flimsy Bill of nine pages' when it was debated).[106] In his speech Ede did, however outline the basic civil defence policy (such as shelter and evacuation provision) which had been produced before Berlin, the intended structure of the future civil defence organisation and the planning organisation in the Home Office, praising the work of the Chief Scientific Advisor and the Civil Defence Joint Planning Staff. Ede stated that 'the general purpose of the Bill is to enable us to take the first steps towards bringing the planning which I have described to the test of action'.[107] The Bill's purpose, then, was not designed to 'prescribe the details of the preparations to be made, but it provides flexible machinery for progressive adjustments'.[108] This flexibility was a central point of the Bill.[109]

The key provisions of the Act were to finalise the financial arrangements by which the Exchequer would reimburse local authorities between 75–100 per cent of civil defence costs, the ability to compel local authorities to undertake civil defence preparations, and allow the setting up of a new peacetime voluntary civil defence organisation. Essentially, it allowed nominated ministers to issue civil defence regulations for the preparation of civil defence plans throughout Britain. Opposition to the Bill was muted, concentrating on the lack of more detailed information. Sir John Anderson (Independent, Scottish Universities), an expert in civil defence given his wartime role,[110] was too caught up in the record and organisation of the Civil Defence Services in the 1939–45 war to be totally effective.[111] He did, however, criticise the delay in putting forward concrete plans, and argued that the new policy was the same as the one in the last war,[112] that the Government need not have bothered with a new law, and that it could have resurrected the old system by repealing the Civil Defence (Suspension of Powers) Act of 1945. In this he missed the crucial fact that Ede was deliberately evoking the civil defence structure of the last war to placate opponents and the local authorities and to reassure all that the matter was in hand, whilst introducing a flexible Bill short on details that would allow the planners to attempt to meet a scale of attack far in excess of that faced by the country in 1939–45.

The Bill was discussed in a Committee of the whole House on 30 November, and the third reading was passed on 3 December, with the new Act receiving the Royal Assent on 16 December 1948. The Act was in place, but the policy was not. This was made through the issuing of Regulations as Statutory Instruments. The first set of regulations, 'The Civil Defence (General) Regulations, 1949',[113] and 'The Civil Defence Corps Regulations, 1949',[114] were issued on 27 July 1949, and came into force on 10 August 1949. The General Regulations instructed local authorities to constitute a local planning apparatus, but it was the Civil Defence Corps Regulations, which required all local authorities to organise and train a division of the Civil Defence Corps that really saw the birth of civil defence, some four years after the Hiroshima bomb.[115] From May 1949, local authorities received a slew of Home Office circulars which set out policy in detail and led up to a national campaign for recruitment which began in the autumn.[116]

Conclusion

At the end of 1948, the British Government had a long-term civil defence plan outlined, but hardly in place. It had taken three years of slow thought, firstly to understand the implications of the atomic bomb, then to apply those implications to civil defence. As a long-term policy document was completed, the Berlin crisis forced attention to turn to emergency planning in case global war occurred. When the Civil Defence Corps was created in 1949, it ensured that a key element of the proposed civil defence was brought into existence. This voluntary body lasted until 1967 as the public face of civil defence in cold war Britain. For many, its very public nature meant that it represented civil defence as a whole, but beyond the Corps very little had been achieved in concrete terms. Evacuation and shelter policy were seen as central elements, yet no evacuation scheme had been discussed in detail, and any shelter policy would need an enormous level of government commitment for it to be implemented. Other life-saving measures were thin on the ground, and time and effort had been expended and essentially wasted on debates about the dispersal of industry. Other measures would, like shelters, be reliant on government funds. In this sense, although the philosophy of atomic age civil defence had been decided, the battle for its implementation had yet to fully begin. The experience of dispersal, and Attlee's words in October 1948, were pointers to the difficulties civil defence planners would have in securing funds for their projects in the face of competing claims.

The formative years of cold war civil defence planning are instructive in other ways, for they demonstrate the importance of coherent government machinery when dealing with complex issues that cut across traditional boundaries. The lack of adequate co-ordination and higher direction, common across nuclear issues,[117] severely impeded the formation of civil defence policy and could have had enormous consequences had the Berlin crisis turned into a hot war. Also, the distrust the government clearly felt of the public over atomic and civil defence issues was another portent of the future. Secrecy was endemic to the cold war state, but even as early as 1947–48 it was becoming clear that refusal to discuss issues in public left the government open to criticism.[118] As the cold war continued, this trend grew more serious and more damaging to the government's civil defence policy. Overall, the story of these years shows the complexity of the issues involved, and how civil defence matters had to be discussed in broader strategic and economic terms in order for a realistic policy to be formulated. A central problem with civil defence planning in these years was the inability of officials – usually from the Home Office – to understand civil defence in any broader perspective, compiling plans which would invariably be rejected due to their cost or incompatibility with other government priorities.

2
Preparing for a Third World War

After the Berlin scare, British civil defence planners returned to drafting plans to meet a long-term emergency with all short-term planning designed to make progress to that end. The planning assumption that Britain would not face attack by atomic weapons in the first phase of the war became redundant when the Soviet Union exploded its first atomic bomb in August 1949, but the advent of Stalin's bomb did not change the basic belief that long-term civil defence plans should be implemented with a view to war breaking out in 1957, not before. Although the 1949–53 period began with the assumption that Britain had a relatively lengthy period in which to implement the civil defence policies outlined in the previous chapter, these years proved tumultuous ones in Britain's cold war history. They saw a hardening of the cold war threat, the eruption in Korea of the first 'hot war' of the conflict and a corresponding commitment to British rearmament which both signalled the seriousness of the crisis and, it was widely believed in the 1950s, had a dramatic impact on the subsequent development of Britain's postwar economy.[1] The story of civil defence is inseparable from that of rearmament: a rapid increase of funds approved in 1950–51 followed by a sharp curtailment by the incoming Conservative Government in 1952. These years saw flesh put on the bones of the civil defence strategy worked out in the years immediately following Hiroshima, and if the flesh seemed wholly inadequate to Whitehall civil defence planners at the height of the Korean rearmament crisis, then it would have seemed a rich meal indeed to those who came after. Over this period a civil defence strategy was formulated and gradually implemented – one which emphasised military and economic survival as much as civilian life-saving. In these years, as we shall see, real strides were made in improving Britain's defences against atomic attack. But by 1953 it was becoming clear that any progress made in the realm of civil defence was rendered irrelevant by developments in the nuclear arms race. The enormous stockpiles of Soviet atomic bombs – let alone the hydrogen bomb – seemed to make a mockery of some of Whitehall's plans.

The next two chapters cover in depth this evolution of Britain's civil defence. The following chapter will look more closely at the development of life-saving measures and the increasingly important public discourse surrounding civil defence in the early cold war period. This chapter will look at the developments in civil defence strategy and policy within Whitehall, concentrating on the continuing efforts to understand what an atomic war would entail, and what measures could be introduced to protect industrial and military capacity and ensure Britain could play an active role in a third world war.

Korea and the escalation of the cold war

The invasion of South Korea by the Communist North on 25 June 1950 had an impact on British cold war policy far beyond the events on the Korean peninsula and the deployment of British troops under the banner of the UN to repel North Korea. It cannot be emphasised too strongly how shocking the outbreak of war in Korea was to contemporary opinion, as the invasion was widely believed to presage an increasingly aggressive stance on the part of global communism.[2] Indeed, Attlee was forced to defend in the Commons his decision *not* to issue an immediate appeal for recruits to the territorial army and the Civil Defence services.[3] It was common in the western alliance to attribute the outbreak of the war to Soviet designs, and this was part of a broader, and misguided, conception of global communism as a rather monolithic beast. Certainly within the British Government it was recognised that a new phase of the cold war had begun; and it was this belief – that the Korean war was potentially the first blow in a global onslaught – rather than the localised conflict itself, which brought about massive changes in British defence policy.

Within a fortnight of the invasion, the Chiefs of Staff informed the Defence committee that 'our present defence policy was only acceptable on the assumption that there would be a period of warning of 18 months or more' before war. Korea had shown 'that it was more than possible that there would be little, if any, warning. In these circumstances the peace-time forces maintained by the United Kingdom were hardly more than a bluff'.[4] Later the same day, Attlee explicitly linked Korea with a possible European war, telling the Cabinet that 'it was especially important at the present time that preoccupation with Korea should not divert attention from other danger-spots in these areas; and also that we should not allow the situation in the East generally to blind us to the risks to which we were exposed in Europe'.[5] Fear of a global war drove the Attlee Government to undertake a massive rearmament programme, the defence estimates rising from the £780 million agreed in December 1949 for the year 1950–51 (itself a massive increase on the previous year), to the three year plan costing £3,600 million in August 1950, and then £4,700 million in January 1951.[6] The economic and political cost of this rearmament programme was enormous. Two Cabinet Ministers, Aneurin Bevan and Harold Wilson, resigned over the cuts in welfare spending demanded by the rearmament programme; the cost in cash, and already scarce raw materials, led to a curtailment of the export-driven, dollar-earning reconstruction drive and plunged Britain back into trade deficit. The long-term consequences of this loss of momentum may have been decisive, as Peter Hennessy has suggested.[7]

Korea threw the lack of civil defence preparations into sharp focus – again. A Home Office brief on the ability of the nation to meet any attack was sent to Attlee by Ede on 4 July, who admitted that 'we should not be able to do much more than we planned to do in 1948', namely 'make the best of existing resources'.[8] The Home Office appreciation confessed that 'the civil defence organisation is in no position to cope effectively with an attack on the 1940–41 scale – let alone anything worse, and the deficiencies are such that they could not be remedied at short notice'.[9] Tardy progress was due to lack of funds: although some movement had been made with paper plans, their actual implementation had been 'precluded by the general policy of doing nothing which would interfere with economic recovery or alarm public opinion'.[10]

The deficiencies outlined would be spelt out in greater detail in the annual CDJPS report on civil defence planning which was completed in September,[11] and made it clear that there was no adequate warning system and little prospect of extending one beyond London for some months; their life-saving measures such as shelter, rescue and ambulance services would also be wholly inadequate (although some measure of evacuation would be possible); and that the fire service – though better off than the other civil defence services – would at best be able to muster around a third of its 1941 strength.[12] Had a global war broken out in 1950, Britain's industrial capacity and its ability to import vital food and materials would have been crippled, essentially destroying any hope of prosecuting a major war on continental Europe for any length of time, to say nothing of the enormous civilian casualties which would have been suffered if Britain faced major bombing raids.

Measures were, however, already being taken towards rectifying the lack of progress. In May 1950, just before the outbreak of the war, the Defence Committee had asked civil defence officials to 'submit proposals designed to enable Ministers to determine an order of priority in expenditure on Civil Defence over the next three or four years', a task completed as the Korean war broke out.[13] Conducted by the Official Committee on Civil Defence, these proposals included all the schemes designed to defend Britain in an atomic attack at the end of the planning period (1957), such as communications, due functioning of ports, industries and utilities, as well as life-saving measures. The report broke these proposals down into three categories. Category I consisted of those projects 'fundamental to the development of our civil defence measures as a whole and to their completion by 1957',[14] and which could not be improvised at short notice. (Examples were the warning system, communications generally, the training of civil defence volunteers, the command and control system, and emergency feeding arrangements.) Category II and III projects were those either less essential or most expensive (including most of the vehicles and equipment for the Civil Defence Corps, and the building of shelters), and which would require 'a reorientation of economic and social policy' to fund them. In all categories, some £936,093,000 would be needed for the years 1951–55. As it was, the report recommended funding Category I measures to the tune of £136,998,000 over the same four years. This sum was sought because it was believed it could be provided without disrupting the economy, rather than because it met estimated civil defence needs – if the £137 million *was* spent civil defence would still be wholly inadequate in 1955, but a least a start would have been made.[15]

Although these plans were agreed by the Defence Committee,[16] with the Cabinet concurring on 25 July 1950,[17] by December the strategic and political landscape had shifted. In that month the Cabinet approved a massive acceleration in defence preparations,[18] and the Chiefs of Staff issued a resultant new 'Hypothesis of Defence Preparations'[19] calling for civil defence measures 'which contribute directly to the preparedness of the armed forces' to be implemented more quickly. In short, measures such as the warning system, blackout provision, command and control operations and facilities to store and protect oil supplies would need to be completed by the end of 1952. This acceleration, coupled with the rising costs of materials and a realisation that some costs had been underestimated, necessitated increasing the £137 million civil defence programme to £180 million, excluding the cost of increasing provision for the stockpiling of food and raw materials.[20] These proposals were put to the Cabinet by the Defence (Transition) Committee (DTC) chaired By Sir Norman Brook,[21] and agreed by the Defence Committee on 23 January 1951.[22] The scale of the stockpiling effort was enormous. Ministers had approved the target of stockpiling £341 million worth of raw materials and food and £80 million worth of civil defence stockpiling (including fire-fighting equipment, uniform cloth and medical supplies) by the end of 1952. Even the £7.25 million for emergency ports counted separately.[23] In January 1951, then, Ministers essentially approved spending by civil departments designed to prepare Britain for war amounting to £610 million, with £260 million of this amounting to 'narrow' civil defence measures and their associated stockpile.[24] Although much of this money would never be spent, by early 1952 some £167 million of materials had been purchased.[25]

Of course, this increase of over £40 million to the basic programme was designed as a purely military measure, intended to ensure the fighting capabilities of British forces were up to scratch by the end of 1952. It would naturally increase civil defence preparedness on their completion, but this was seen as a happy by-product by Ministers. Over the course of December 1950-January 1951, civil defence advocates fought a doomed battle to see civil defence spending increase in line with military spending. The immediate roots of the conflict lay in a CDJPS appreciation of the possibility of defending an attack in July 1951, which was produced in August 1950 *after* the adoption of the £137 million programme and which, the report concluded, would be wholly inadequate.[26] Deeper roots included the perception, common throughout the immediate post-1945 era, that civil defence was being dangerously ignored to the extent that Britain's survival as a war-making power was in jeopardy. This had been the Home Office opinion in 1948, and they seemed determined to improve the civil defence position in late 1950.

The attempt to increase civil defence funding occurred on both the official and the Ministerial level. The former saw Sir Frank Newsam, Permanent Secretary of the Home Office, attempt to persuade DTC to recommend a broader increase when they were translating the new defence hypothesis into concrete proposals over the next year. Newsam did this on the grounds that without adequate life-saving measures 'the efficiency of the armed forces might be greatly impaired by the loss of civilian morale and, moreover the enemy might regard our lack of preparations as such a weakness as to nullify the deterrent effect of strong active defences'.[27] This argument was rebutted on the grounds, familiar from 1948, that civil defence might actually 'be considered provocative and as indicating our belief that war was inevitable by the time our preparations were complete'.[28] The actual report to the Cabinet merely flagged that the acceleration did not apply to general civil defence preparations and, borrowing from the debates of 1948, noted that this was 'presumably, to be justified by the fact that the Government are aiming to prevent war, and are not at this stage putting in hand preparations which would have to be taken if war was regarded as inevitable within the next two or three years'.[29]

The Home Office case was not left there, however, with Ede submitting a Cabinet paper simultaneously with the DTC report, stating his case. He argued that civil defence had been left behind in the recent push towards rearming, that the current plan – and the acceleration about to be approved – amounted to 'only a very limited part of the field of civil defence; as a result of the acceleration of the programme for the armed forces, civil defence preparations will lag even further than hitherto behind preparations of the armed forces'.[30] He went on, 'as the Minister charged with the general responsibility for co-ordinating civil defence measures, I feel it my duty to report this to the Cabinet and to ask my colleagues whether it is in the national interest to limit our civil defence preparations to the current schemes'. Ede informed Ministers that the newly accelerated scheme would leave provision increasingly patchy, forming but a part of the wider £936 million scheme officials had identified as being necessary to defend Britain adequately in future war. His colleagues were informed that the current programme would leave the 'broad position' as follows: there would be 'a civil warning system covering the whole country (but less efficient than that which existed in the last war)', an 'adequate system of control and communications for the operation of Civil Defence Services', and some 'formations of Civil Defence Services reasonably well trained, but with little or none of the equipment required to operate in war'. There would be 'rudimentary plans' for extending 'hospital services and... services for evacuees and the homeless, but there would be grave shortages of equipment and stores'. Furthermore, 'little or no provision would have been made for shelter for the public or industry, for emergency water supplies or for the maintenance of essential services'. There would be increases in 'the numbers of volunteers enrolled and trained' in the Civil Defence Services and 'on the assumption that the measures of stockpiling recommended for 1952 were further developed, some of the deficiencies of stores and equipment would have been remedied'. However, 'the gaps which would remain would be large and serious'.[31]

Ede firmly believed that 'an increase in preparedness... would also supplement the effect of the rearmament programme in providing a deterrent against war' as well as saving lives during war; moreover, it could be done without endangering the economy. Ede had no firm proposals in mind, just an awareness of the desirability of the £936 million programme; rather, he was asking for a broader strategic decision on the role of civil defence within the nation's cold war defence plan.[32] The Home Office believed that without civil defence any rearmament plan was hopelessly lopsided – what was the point in spending thousands of millions of pounds on 'active' defence if the country's war-making industrial capacity, its ability to feed the population, and its civilian morale, were destroyed by an initial atomic attack? Attlee's answer, during the meeting which finally approved the acceleration, showed that he considered civil defence preparations not only economically impracticable, but possibly downright dangerous. Full civil defence measures such as shelter provision, the Prime Minister argued, were to be implemented only when 'war was assumed to be inevitable'.[33] To do so in peacetime 'would create exactly that impression of apprehension which we wished to avoid, and would drive the population into a "Maginot" attitude of mind at a moment when all their powers should be strained to increase the active defence preparations which were designed to deter the enemy from attempting war'.[34]

The Committee concluded quite simply that 'the deficiencies in Civil Defence preparations should be accepted'.[35] Ede's attempt to fully integrate civil defence with the wider defence preparations had been crushed. The Home Secretary had argued that civil defence would both complement rearmament in deterring the Russians and fulfil the Government's moral duty to provide civil defence in case war broke out. Attlee, on the other hand, conceived full scale civil defence not as an insurance measure but as a last ditch policy to be undertaken when desperate. His use of the Maginot Line metaphor illustrates Attlee's views perfectly, conjuring the image of a population fearful of attack but complacent that civil defence measures would save them. This new Maginot Line, civil defence, would cause the population to rest easy, and stop striving 'to increase the active defence preparations which were designed to deter the enemy from attempting war', and actually invite the destruction offensive preparations were hoping to avoid.[36] It was the first time that civil defence measures had been rejected on strategic grounds; all previous refusals had been for financial reasons.

Of course, the financial cost of civil defence aided Attlee's decision, but this decision was the culmination of a series of statements which demonstrated the Prime Minister's embryonic deterrent strategy. In his first thoughts after Hiroshima, and in the debates over Berlin and now Korea, civil defence was given no role in deterring a possible attack. In both 1948 and 1950 he concentrated on the need for offensive measures, which civil defence preparations could only hinder by diverting resources and encouraging a defensive, and possibly defeatist 'Maginot' attitude.

Attlee stuck firmly to this line when announcing the new defence policy, costing £1,300 million in 1951/52 and up to £4,700 million over three years, in the Commons on 29 January 1951. He argued that rearmament was 'designed to deter', and therefore 'we do not propose any general acceleration of civil defence preparations'.[37] Only those 'measures which directly support the efficiency of the Armed Forces – in particular communications, the control system and the warning system' – would be implemented, although he did stress that stocks of essential fire-fighting equipment and medical supplies would also be built up.[38] Korea proved a decisive staging post in the story of cold war civil defence. In refusing to fund a major civil defence effort at a time when broader defence spending was at its post-1945 highest, it was clear that life-saving civil defence measures were not considered priority within British defence policy – for both economic and strategic reasons. Only those measures which would help the *military* position would be completed as a matter of priority. Yet although Korea showed that the Home Office's £936 million plan was dead in the water, it did ensure that civil defence became part of the cold war political and defence landscape. The sums provided for civil defence over the four years from 1951 were hardly insubstantial, and they ensured that some key civil defence measures such as the warning system, which built on the new radar system implemented in the early 1950s,[39] were completed. Moreover, much of this money was spent on quite visible preparations such as training and equipping the Civil Defence Services, especially the Civil Defence Corps and the Auxiliary Fire Service (more of which in Chapter 3).

The Conservatives and a strategy for survival

The first financial year of the new spending plan was only half complete when the Labour Government was replaced by Winston Churchill's peacetime administration in November 1951. Civil defence was hardly a party political issue in this period, with advocates for greater effort existing in either party: equally, both Governments pursued parallel policies of subjugating civil defence to more 'active' measures. As is discussed below, the split within Whitehall was far more important in framing different approaches to civil defence than any divide in Westminster. Although civil defence as such was not a party matter, it was part of Labour's wider rearmament programme, the cost of which caused acute anxiety within the incoming Conservative administration.

The discussion of civil defence by the new Government was prompted by a pair of papers by the new Home Secretary, Sir David Maxwell Fyfe, reopening the debate about the balance between offensive preparations and civil defence.[40] As he pointed out, the last government had approved schemes amounting to around £180 million over four years, and a two-year programme of stores and equipment which increased the total to around £260 million. He highlighted the basis of the Attlee Government's decision-making: that these were undertaken as *military* rather than civil defence measures. This scheme, however, had hit problems. Programmes were lagging behind schedule, in part because of production problems and in part because of the contraction in civilian demand caused – ironically – by the need to avoid inflationary pressures in the wake of the rearmament programme.[41]

Fyfe revealed that the delays and associated under-spending meant that to maintain the previous Government's policy in terms of civil defence and stockpiling would now cost some £280 million rather than the broad £260 million over the four year period – with some £198 million falling in the 1953–54 and 1954–55 financial years.[42] This only highlighted further the problem of the scheme – that it did not really enable any progression in civil defence preparedness. Delays meant that those military preparations which Attlee's Cabinet had deemed vital enough to accelerate the overall scheme would not be ready at the end of 1952 after all. Of the key military measures, only the air raid warning system would be 'reasonably adequate' by the autumn of 1954 – with communications, control rooms and oil protection schemes only 75 per cent complete at the same stage. Of the other 'Category I' measures, emergency feeding schemes would be 50 per cent ready and the Civil Defence Services were short of trained volunteers. All other life-saving measures were of course, apart from evacuation plans, hopelessly inadequate.[43]

In cataloguing the state of civil defence preparations, Fyfe was not necessarily advocating any massive increase, more wanting a statement of policy to allow civil defence planning to continue. More particularly, he wanted answers to three questions: whether civil defence preparations 'should lag so far behind military preparations', whether the money could be found to expand provision, and whether the government could afford the sharp increases needed to bring civil defence preparations up to the intended level given it would cost nearly £200 million in the following two years? Unfortunately no answers arrived to these questions. In the Defence Committee on 14 May, Churchill followed the line suggested to him by Brook – providing the consensual thread from one Government to another – doubting 'whether it would be justifiable to devote to civil defence large sums of money which would be more profitably used in active defence measures, which would be a more effective deterrent to war or, if the worst came, more valuable in the early stages of war'.[44] The Prime Minister concluded, in an echo of Attlee, that 'although it would be wise to do enough to create an impression of activity in civil defence, care must be taken to avoid spending large sums on money on measures which would pay no dividend'.[45] But although in May 1952 Churchill was clearly ambivalent at best to the prospect of an increased civil defence budget, no firm conclusions could be made until the outcome of the Chiefs of Staff's new strategic review.

The new strategic appreciation, the 'Global Strategy' paper, was completed in July and had a decisive impact on civil defence planning and strategy as well as Britain's broader defence policies.[46] It surmised that the initial stage of a future war would involve a Soviet attack on the United Kingdom 'of unparalleled intensity' which would ensure 'terrible damage'.[47] Such an attempted knock-out blow required that 'a guiding principle of the rearmament programme should be to ensure survival in the short opening phase'. In this context, the Chiefs recommended that civil defence preparations should be concentrated on 'measures for carrying on essential activities during the initial intense phase of a war'. Given the absolute need to save both money and consumption of metal, they warned against diverting enormous sums to shelters, instead suggesting efforts be limited to 'training, installing communications, planning and to those schemes which do not call for extensive building or scarce materials', with a priority on continuing the provision of alternative port facilities, although they did also suggest supplying respirators to the civilian population.[48]

More important for civil defence was the interpretation of this document by the DTC in its planning advice issued to Departments. In digesting the Chiefs' paper, Brook argued that it would be impossible to 'take all the measures necessary to minimise its effects to the extent we should like. The governing factor will in fact be our peacetime economic capabilities and not the scale of air attack'.[49] Therefore, he argued that the country must 'concentrate on those physical preparations for the initial phase of war which will pay the best dividends for the premium we can afford'.[50] Much the same could have been said about civil defence planning throughout this period, but in the second half of 1952 there was a clear effort to achieve real advances in civil defence to meet the newly conceived threat of attack on a value-for-money basis. Since the outbreak of the Korean War, planning had assumed that Britain would have around six months' warning – the build up of tension – before a war, and a period of months at the start of war during which the country would have a 'chance of minimising the air attack and mobilising our war potential'.[51] It was now assumed that the warning period could only be seven days, and that the initial attack would be on such a scale as to necessitate all preparations to be completed by the outbreak of war.

At the same time as civil defence was under review, Brook informed the officials on the Official Committee on Civil Defence that the new financial spending limit for civil defence preparations was £132 million over three years, excluding work on communications, oil defence and port emergency planning. To put this figure into context, that was an average of £44 million a year for 'narrow' civil defence purposes from 1953–54 onwards.[52] This £44 million was part of the broader civil defence budget of £77.7 million for the following year agreed in December 1952.[53] As we have seen, earlier in 1952 it had been assumed that to meet the Labour Government's original civil defence plan, around £100 million a year would have to be spent to catch up. Thus the new £77.7 million figure represented a large cut; moreover, given the planning emphasis on survival measures, oil protection, communications and ports maintained their budget – therefore 'narrow' civil defence bore the brunt of the £23 million 'cut' in provision.[54] This meant that key measures were being delayed, with spending originally planned for two years now being spread out over three. Delays were to occur in the provision of respirators, the building of control rooms and measures to ensure the 'due functioning' of essential services. Other items were simply cut, such as the incorporation of shelters in new buildings, emergency water supplies, blackout provision, food storage, and protection of railways.[55]

Such cuts were necessary because of the problematic implementation of the civil defence programme agreed in the summer of 1950. There were no real changes in planned provision made between then and

December 1952 beyond the decision to increase stocks and equipment in January 1951. The fluctuations in the budget were due to financial and administrative considerations, not policy upheaval. As the figures for the whole scheme rose due to inflation, investment obligations in the final years of the programme increased dramatically due to a lack of progress in previous years. Hence an original policy costing around £260 million over four years turned into one costing £200 million over two years. Cutting this policy back in late 1952 did involve a curtailment of intended provision, but was a necessary readjustment of the budget to more manageable levels by a Government suffering acute financial difficulties.

The Hall Report

These changes in the strategic assessment of the nature of an atomic war necessitated a rethink on civil defence. The instigator of this new work was Sir Norman Brook, whose new Home Defence Committee (HDC) was set up rather belatedly in February 1953 to ensure civil and military planning for war could meet the threat of the type of war outlined in the 'Global Strategy Paper'.[56] As we have seen, Brook, in his role as Chairman of DTC, began to take a more active role in shaping civil defence plans from 1951, with DTC taking a *de facto* supervisory role over the Official Committee on Civil Defence (CDO).[57] The founding of HDC regularised the arrangement of civil defence being co-coordinated by the Cabinet Office to ensure it adhered more closely to the government's general plans. Before 1951 civil defence had been left largely to the Home Office, which provided the chair for CDO and housed the CDJPS. This arrangement, and the general way in which policy-making bodies made bids for funds which were later decided on, allowed the Home Office to approach civil defence with a 'shopping list' mentality – witness the £936 million programme – without needing to take heed of the government's broader economic and strategic position. Brook had stepped in during the winter of 1950/51 to coordinate the subjugation of civil defence to military plans; in 1953, with the need for national survival, rather than life-saving, the clear priority to emerge from the 'global strategy' discussions, Brook finally took permanent control over civil and home defence preparations.

The first action of HDC was to commission a review designed to understand the conditions that might prevail in Britain during the initial 'survival' phase of a future war, the stage in which the nation must grimly hang on to enable later recovery.[58] This was conducted by the

National Economy in War Working Party (suitably renamed the Home Defence Committee Working Party for the duration), chaired by Robert Hall, Head of the Cabinet Office's Economic Section, and also included William Strath from the Treasury's Central Economic Planning Staff. The Hall Group worked on the basis of a Soviet stock of 200 atomic bombs allocated for Britain: 132 to be delivered on high priority industrial and population targets, 40 for air bases and 28 left over as a reserve.[59]

After three months labour the Working Party submitted their report on 'The Initial Phase of a War' in July 1953,[60] a masterly summary of the devastation which would be caused by the combined effects of 132 atomic weapons and a sparse civil defence policy. For, unlike the 1947 study on the effects of an attack on 'the Central Resources of the Country',[61] Hall's Report did take into account what civil defence measures would be in place by September 1956 (assuming plans continued and there was no change in policy), especially the high degree of evacuation and work protecting communications. Despite these measures, the effects of such an attack would have been immense: 1,378,000 people dead and 785,000 seriously injured. There would be more British casualties in the 'first days' of a future atomic war than there were, either in uniform or out, in both world wars; there would be over 10 million homeless. Nobody would know how many refugees there would be in the target areas; the effects on the morale of the population would obviously be enormous but would be largely an 'imponderable'. For the ordinary person 'it is a case of sheer survival or not, and the question is whether or not the barest mechanism of life can be maintained in the bombed areas for the first few crucial days'.[62]

The destruction of London, attacked with 32 atomic bombs, was vividly described:

> Take a half-inch map of London; put down a sixpence with its centre over each ground zero; draw a circle around it, and let that represent the area (three-quarters of a mile in radius) within which everybody is killed or seriously injured, and all the houses are completely destroyed or so badly damaged as to require demolition. Do the same thing with pennies, and you will have the ring (between three-quarters of a mile and two-miles from the burst) within which all the houses are uninhabitable, at least temporarily. What sort of picture do we get?[63]

There would be 'a practically unbroken series of overlapping penny circles' covering a massive area from Hounslow in the West to Dartford in the East, and from Enfield in the North to Croydon in the South. Although 'a few small oases untouched by bombs' would remain within the area, these would be completely cut off from the outside world. Although the 'sixpenny circles do not as a rule overlap... the ways left between them are torturous, and practically every main road into London is blocked at some point by the accumulation of debris from shattered buildings'. Some 400,000 people would die, 250,000 suffer serious injury, with little chance of the majority of the latter receiving the required medical care.[64]

The survivors' lot was also graphically imagined: 'what about John Smith of Laburnum Villa, Stoke Newington, just on the outer edge of a penny circle?' In a damaged but inhabitable house he 'would like to stay put and get on with his job for as long as possible', but there would be no power or fuel and 'apart from the tins in the store cupboard', the family would have to rely on an emergency feeding centre a mile away. 'Even worse, there is no water until a meagre supply comes through by lorry – if indeed these supplies do get through at all and are enough to go round'. He would like to 'go to his job, but he does not know if the factory is still standing. There are five sixpenny rings between his house and it, with not a chance of getting through to it above ground, and the tubes have not started running again'. He would not be able to contact the factory or even 'find out whether his mother in Acton is still alive'. As there would be 'no newspapers and no current for his all-mains receiver', he would not even be able to 'find out from the wireless what the Government would like him to do. In short, 'it is difficult to resist the conclusion that London has become unworkable and that, in particular, it is no longer possible to carry on the central administration of the country from here'. Similarly, in many provincial cities, little could be done and 'it is difficult to see how life can be carried on until the fires have burned themselves out and some sort of water supply has been arranged'.[65]

The 'mechanics of living' would have collapsed in all Britain's cities. It would be uncertain how far 'Government, in the ordinary sense of the word, has survived.... Even more important, in the early stages, is the uncertainty of what has happened to many local authorities'. Communications would have collapsed, as 'unless John Smith in his devastated area is one of the lucky few with a car radio or a portable... the BBC [operating a limited service] will be broadcasting to the empty air'.[66] Although some services might operate others will not. For example, even if there was petrol the roads would be blocked, so how would fuel and water be transported? Some emergency feeding apparatus would exist, but what if the bakers had no water supply? How could the morale of the people be sustained? Hall argued that 'without in any way underrating the British capacity for "taking it"', the social effects of the bombs would be immense. The attack 'must be a test of British staunchness, particularly if the raids are spread over several nights'. There would be 'the nerve-wracking effects of blast, the fires raging everywhere, the sight of the injured whom no help can reach – above all, perhaps, the dread of the unknown and the terror of radio-active effects'. It was 'a shattering prospect, and it is a bold man who would deny the probability of a mass flight, set off by the instinct of self-preservation, and the possibility of serious panic, especially in congested areas such as the East End of London'. Five bombs on Sheffield would produce the same result.[67]

Hall's language and his searing imagery forces the reader to conceptualise the results of atomic attack in ways no other official report does: and it is in this exposition that the importance of the report lies. It impressed on the reader that current plans for survival were hopelessly inadequate; that there needed to be more hospital beds and doctors; larger stocks of food and fuel outside but near the target areas; an adequate supply of lorries; and building supplies for repairs on a massive scale. It was stressed that the port emergency plans 'must be brought to readiness'; that evacuation would fail unless completed by the time the first bombs fell; and that the protection of communications system needed to be 'pressed forward and intensified'. Command and control was vital, and Hall believed it would collapse in war. Not just the protection of communications, but 'the necessary powers and organisation to direct manpower' were vital: first on the local level, where action must take place instantly, but next on a regional and then central government level.[68]

Unless central government could maintain control 'there will be a grave risk of a general collapse of administration and control in a very short time'. Hall recommended that 'a sufficient number of key people concerned at all levels of government, local, regional and central, must be so placed that they survive the disaster and are able to exercise immediate and effective control and leadership', and stressed that the communications between these key people, and between them and the public must survive the initial attack. As Hall put it, 'unless these conditions can be met, any detailed plans which may be made in advance are likely to break down'.[69]

This report was discussed in HDC by a glittering array of civil and military figures on 29 July 1953.[70] Brook was joined by the Committee's usual members and all three Chiefs of Staff were present (usually deputies attended). One lesson taken from the Report would be the inability to supply an army from the United Kingdom, ending the idea of 'broken-backed warfare'. Another lesson seemed to be that 'it was clear from the report that everything should be done to prevent such an attack ever taking place. This emphasised even more than before the importance of the allies building up a powerful deterrent'.[71] In civil defence terms, the most important consequence of Hall's report was the decision to substantially strengthen the wartime machinery of government. A working party under Sir Thomas Padmore, a senior Treasury official, was set up[72] – and the Padmore Committee would prove influential in the formulation of plans after the hydrogen bomb was developed. There was also a second Hall report, focussed on the period following the 'initial stage',[73] but it reported in March 1954 and its findings were lost, not to say made redundant, in the maelstrom of activity following the American thermonuclear tests in the Pacific beginning on 1 March.

As the round for planning expenditure in 1954/55 came in between Hall's reports, it had little impact on immediate provision. Instead, planners were disappointed that the three-year plan agreed the previous year was not continued, with the broader civil defence budget being cut from £77.7 million to £57 million. This was agreed on the basis 'that the general strategic picture had improved to the extent that the immediate danger of war had receded'.[74] But despite its lack of impact on the spending round, the Hall Report changed attitudes to what was considered possible in an atomic war. Before July 1953 it was believed that an army could be sustained from Britain even in an atomic war. All civil defence plans were geared towards continuing production. The maintenance of essential industries and even the ports scheme were drafted to help with the continuation of war. Now it was clear that all civil defence efforts must be geared to national survival – to ensuring government control over the population. Yet the lasting impact of Hall on actual civil defence policies was slight. The importance of policies such as evacuation, stockpiling and the Civil Defence Corps were re-emphasised, but with the need for greater effort and the prospect of diminished returns stressed.

Criticisms

The Government was heavily criticised in 1953 for its handling of civil defence policy. The House of Commons Select Committee on Estimates published a scathing report on Civil Defence in December 1953 which attacked civil defence policy-making and its implementation.[75] The

Committee accepted that both economics and strategy meant that civil defence provision was never intended to be extensive, but argued this made it all the more important to achieve value-for-money preparations. The Government, and especially the Home Office, were admonished for failing to do so. The 'loose organisation' was attacked, and the Estimates Committee considered that there 'has not been the leadership, direction and guidance from the Official Committee on Civil Defence... which those responsible for carrying out the work needed'.[76] A cause of the general problems, and a subsequent fount of many of the civil defence failings, was the Home Office's idea of a 'final plan' of civil defence: an end result which could be achieved if the Government committed to it. As sufficient funds were not forthcoming the money which was granted was being spent on a broad front – taking the whole field of civil defence slowly towards this final goal. This was a key weakness, as the Committee recognised, and it would have been a better use of resources to identify a few central projects as priorities for what money was available; a more 'compact' effort.[77]

As a result, plans were considered vague in terms of both content and delivery dates, and even these plans 'were destroyed by successive budgetary reductions and policy decisions regarding expenditure on equipment and capital works'. Furthermore, there was a systematic under-spending of the money for civil defence – only 54 per cent of the civil defence budget was actually spent between 1949 and 1953 – which was attributed to 'an unnecessary lack of precision in preparing the Estimates and failure to fix a definite plan' for civil defence. Also, preparations had been retarded due to a 'lack of drive' in building programmes and lengthy delays in basic administration. Perhaps the fiercest attacks were reserved for the handling of the Civil Defence Corps which it argued existed in 'name only', and was a 'façade'.[78] Discussion of the Corps is reserved for the next chapter, but these damning criticisms reflected badly on the Home Office and civil defence planning in general. As we have seen, they contained a great deal of truth – but only told a partial story. The Committee focussed on civil defence, and the work of CDO and the Home Office was presented and explained to them. The broader co-ordinating role, and the extent to which real civil defence preparations had been made under the cloak of military preparations, was not expounded to the Committee, undoubtedly from a reluctance to discuss such sensitive security matters in public. This meant that although the Committee identified valid points concerning the problems in direction and policy-implementation, they had no opportunity to take into account the fact that these faults had largely been addressed in the previous year. CDO had undoubtedly failed in its leadership of civil defence preparations, but it had been relieved of many of its policy-making responsibilities before the Committee reported – although, as we shall see, the Home Office remained capable of conceiving of a grand plan divorced from economic reality.

The Select Committee's criticisms were widely reported and pushed the Government onto the defensive. The *Daily Mirror*, for example, ran with 'The C.D. Muddlers Shock M.P.s'.[79] Particularly scathing was a lengthy piece in the *Economist*, entitled 'Civilians Defenceless'.[80] Press criticism focussed more heavily on the general lack of preparations than on the administrative failings highlighted by the report. The *Economist* lamented that there had been 'a master plan' for civil defence which had not been carried out, identifying those policies where no progress had been made, such as protection of industries, railways and the construction of shelters in new large buildings. Of course, these were exactly those policies which *had* been a key part of the Home Office grand plan, but were cut at the end of 1952.

Within the government, Sir Norman Brook explained the basis of civil defence policy to a Prime Minister angered by the criticism his Government had received. Reacting as much, if not more, to the press coverage than the actual wording of the report, Brook called the report 'misconceived': it had failed to understand that 'the purpose of the Government's defence policy is, not to prepare for a war regarded as inevitable, but to take all practicable measures to prevent war'.[81] Therefore, Churchill was reminded, 'the major part of our defence effort has... been directed to strengthening the armed forces; and it is reasonable and logical that civil defence should have been allowed to lag behind'. Labour had done the same. Finally, Brook argued, 'the Select Committee have used the word "façade" as a criticism; but in fact neither this Government nor the last have ever intended to build more than a façade of civil defence'.[82] The Select Committee had actually accepted that civil defence should lag behind military preparations – it just assumed that the government's actual civil defence policy should be implemented as it had been formulated. It was the press which focussed more strongly on the lack of actual preparations, and that was because the government had left the Home Office to present all the evidence to the Committee – and they emphasised what they would have liked to be done and failed to adequately put across policy as it had actually been decided in 1952–53. Nothing illustrates the lack of direction the Estimates Committee were so critical of than the fact that the actual basis of policy was not adequately portrayed. There was little point Brook complaining about the

Committee misunderstanding the basis of civil defence planning if no-one with responsibility for co-ordinating that policy – such as himself – was willing to present the policy to the Committee. Furthermore, the events of late 1952 showed that Ministers, as well as Brook himself, were far from satisfied with the implementation of policy up to that point. In 1953, however, the government would not risk admitting that civil defence policy was based on military and economic survival in the face of an atomic onslaught rather than saving lives. Given that the Committee assumed life-saving was the priority of civil defence, how could it be other than critical?

The criticism wounded the government's pride, and the Home Office's initial reaction to the report was to consider rushing out a White Paper outlining in full the rationale behind the Government's civil defence policy. The idea was abandoned because it would 'focus too much public attention on the question of Civil Defence, and might lead to a public demand that greater sums of money should be spent'.[83] The Government's response, when it arrived, came on 28 January 1954 by Fyfe via a written question, in which he defended the Government's record and criticised the Select Committee's 'misapprehension' of the Government's civil defence policy, which he stated was 'to build up the nucleus of an organisation with a view to its subsequent expansion if necessary'. He also stressed civil defence's 'secondary role' in the wider defence strategy compared with the Government's priority of deterring the enemy.[84] The next day the *Times* criticised the Home Secretary with some severity. It argued that 'obviously something is very wrong with the nation's civil defence', and attacked Fyfe for his statement, suggesting he had placed 'the bruised feelings of Ministers and civil servants' above the issue of whether civil defence was being pursued with adequate vigour.[85] The *Economist* called the statement 'evasive and vague' and noted correctly that the Committee was not complaining about civil defence's 'secondary role' but that 'it was not being carried out'. Criticism was valid because 'the stark facts are that there is still no civil defence worthy of the name, that it cannot be produced out of a hat when it is needed, and that its absence might powerfully encourage the potential aggressor'.[86]

Was there 'no civil defence worthy of the name'? If we survey the successes and failures of civil defence planning at the point when atomic-age civil defence was about to become obsolete, we can see that the Estimates Committee had identified areas where preparations had fallen behind, as well as areas which had been well served. As we have seen, work on the warning system, communications and the ports scheme had been given special priority since 1950. The Estimates Committee discussed only the last of these, and commended the fact that much of the work had been 'under direct Cabinet supervision and not subject to the control of the Official Committee on Civil Defence or the Civil Defence Joint Planning Staff'. Also, 'a clear decision on priorities has enabled the work to proceed with reasonable expedition'.[87] The ports scheme was one of the key spending priorities of the period, with plans to ensure that Britain could maintain importing capacity by improving facilities at smaller ports and anchorages around the coast – negating the effects of a major attack on the main ports such as London and Liverpool. Planning for this was substantially complete by 1951,[88] and although delays in acquiring steel throughout this period meant that the target of having all mooring gear and 558 mobile cranes completed by 1952 was missed, they were virtually all in place by the time the Estimates Committee reported. This success was only possible because a concerted effort had been made to implement it, based on a widespread understanding of its importance. For example, Robert Hall helped resist the move to cut back on the scheme in order to save steel in November 1951, arguing that 'it is quite wrong to save money on this. It is no good spending dollars, or spending our own resources, on building up a defence structure if we allow the whole basis of the economy, our importing capacity, to be undermined'.[89]

The port scheme was a clear success, a physical measure that by 1954 had demonstrably improved Britain's chances of surviving an atomic attack. Another was the warning system, which was improved in two phases, the first being a system to recognise that an attack was coming, the second to turn that tactical warning into a general alert for the population. As we saw in Chapter 1, Britain was incapable of alerting its population to an enemy attack in 1948. Even by September 1950 only a skeleton warning system existed in South-East England, meaning it could be easily outflanked, only in London had sufficient sirens.[90] By February 1954, however, as a result of the concentrated effort on the system, an adequate warning and siren system covered virtually all urban areas. In fact only 15 out of 6,300 sirens had yet to be issued to local authorities, and three quarters of sirens had been installed. Moreover, plans were afoot to improve the system to deal with the increased scale and speed of the estimated attack.[91] On communications, progress was slower but still impressive: protected communications links had been installed in London – in underground works in Holborn – and were proceeding in provincial towns, designed to ensure that the vital communications network would survive an atomic attack.[92]

These three schemes had been given priority in 1950 and progress had been made, but they proved that a real political and official commitment was needed if the programmes were to be completed – as the ability to resist the deepest cuts to the ports scheme testifies. Of course, these measures were supported on a primarily *military* basis, and the history of other physical preparations for civil defence tells a very different tale. One key example can suffice, and that is the lengthy debate about installing shelters in new buildings. The story of shelter provision is told in the next chapter, but the debate about new construction illustrates the problems civil defence planners had in making any real strides towards their 'grand plan'. The Estimates Committee told how the Home Office had admitted that providing strengthened basements into new buildings was a 'special priority', but that 'the London County Council had been waiting for over two years for permission to proceed with one experimental scheme'.[93] It wasn't strictly true that the policy had 'special priority'. The policy was rejected by Ministers in 1949 as being too expensive,[94] and although in April 1951 it was agreed to in principle,[95] at no point was the Treasury committed to supplying the extra expenditure. In March 1953 those erecting buildings were 'encouraged', without any financial assistance, to 'embody structural precautions', e.g. basement shelters.[96] Although the policy may have been a Home Office priority, it was clearly never a government one. Although the protection provided would have been small in scale, had buildings been required to offer protection since 1948 some progress would have been made for relatively small sums. But at a time of acute shortages in building materials, the policy was relegated in the pecking order.

Conclusion

The precarious state of civil defence had of course been identified by the Estimates Committee, but the whole basis of the policy which they were judging had changed when the Hall group pieced together just what Britain would look like after an atomic war; it was to change again, even more radically, less than eight months after the Hall report was finished. Given this, how do we assess the five or so years of civil defence planning surveyed in this chapter? We can see that flaws in the decision-making process and an inability to implement agreed policies hindered preparations. Also, the Whitehall machinery which saw policies adopted first, and then joined battle to secure the funds afterwards, rather than the other way round, meant that the civil defence planners' schemes were always under-funded – a process also in evidence in the Government's debates surrounding National Service.[97] A financial decision was needed, with civil defence priorities settled afterwards to ensure real physical preparations were completed. The difficulty in implementation – whether the fault of Whitehall or of broader difficulties within the economy – badly short-changed civil defence, guaranteeing that the 1950 four-year plan was not implemented. The strategic re-evaluations of 1952 and 1953 ushered in a period of uncertainty, characterised by yearly budgetary debates and an inability to plan ahead. Little did they know that the period of uncertainty was only beginning. Real progress had been made on a few fronts, with many other worthy plans left by the wayside. But the paradox at the heart of civil defence remained as intractable as ever: was it worth spending money on civil defence when that cash could be devoted to 'offensive' measures to actively deter war? What was the worth of spending such sums if Britain could be crushed by an initial all-out atomic attack? Between 1949 and 1953 money had been spent on the warning system, emergency ports, communications and stockpiling precisely to avert such a disaster – but developments in the cold war meant they gave planners little solace at the very moment they were coming to fruition.

3
Protecting the Public

The last chapter concentrated on measures designed to ensure the survival of Britain as a war-making and economically viable state. As we saw, the government prioritised such measures to the exclusion of others. But to many within Whitehall, and to all those volunteers who took part in it, civil defence was about one thing: saving lives in an enemy attack. It was this desire to help one's family, neighbours and community which drove many members of the public to serve in the government's civil defence services. It was this desire also which ensured that evacuation was a policy priority for civil defence planners throughout the atomic age and which inspired the Home Office to repeated attempts, always doomed, to commit successive governments to undertaking a programme of shelter building. It is these three policies, shelter, evacuation, and the voluntary services which underpinned life-saving measures in the cold war. The government's, and the public's, fluctuating attitudes to them illustrate the limitations of civil defence as well as the role it was expected to play in Britain's defence strategy. These policies had of course formed the bulwark of Britain's attempt to save as many lives as possible in the Second World War when the nation came under heavy attack. All three policies formed a major part of the Home Front story, and it was widely assumed they would provide the backbone of civil defence policies during the cold war.

In putting forward these policies, planners did not rest their case solely on the humanitarian desire to save lives. They also argued that cold war military plans would be jeopardised by the lack of vigorous life-saving measures. Without them, the *will* to fight would collapse as surely as the nation's *ability* to fight would collapse without measures to secure imports. Morale was a sketchy term for planners, with the ability to maintain 'good' morale assumed as long as civil defence measures were taken.

Not much thought was given to the impact of atomic bombing on morale, with planners assuming that the Blitz-hardened British people would see it through. Morale, then, was seen as a rhetorical stick to beat Ministers rather than a troublesome concept to be evaluated. In general, public measures to save lives had been neglected in favour of plans of military worth which of course remained secret. Radars and warning systems, emergency ports and control rooms were important measures, but had little impact in terms of 'selling' civil defence to the public. To convince the ordinary people that they, and the nation, could survive an atomic war required strong and public measures. Shelters, evacuation and civil defence volunteers: these were the visible signs of a 'successful' civil defence policy, and the absence of any of them from the government's plans would lead to criticism, and all three provoked widespread debate both within and outside Whitehall.

Shelter

The provision of domestic and public shelters was a cornerstone of the British government's response to enemy attack in the Second World War. Although Londoners in the Underground system created iconic images, it was the provision of domestic shelters in homes and gardens which enabled everyday life to proceed with a degree of normality.[1] It was a cast-iron assumption that shelters would be provided in the cold war; indeed, Attlee himself told Parliament in November 1947 that it was one of the 'essential elements in an overall plan for Civil Defence'.[2] Throughout the atomic age, civil defence planners sought to turn that general assumption into concrete policy in the face of an economic position which demanded restraint in financial expenditure and the use of steel, not to mention a burgeoning strategic landscape which raised questions about the desirability of building shelters.

Shelter policy was discussed several times within Whitehall from 1946 onwards, with decisions pivoting on three issues: the lives it would save, its economic cost, and its possible cold war impact. The Home Office undertook research on shelter provision throughout the second half of the 1940s and argued that shelters could be built to save lives – whether as in domestic steel shelters, surface concrete ones, or protected accommodation in large buildings.[3] In October 1946, the Home Office sought £260 million to provide shelters for 11 million key workers who would remain in the urban centres.[4] As this figure was some £32 million more than the entire National Health Service estimates for 1949–50,[5] one can see why it was so quickly dismissed as a viable plan by senior civil servants.[6] The new shelters were needed as the vast majority of old ones were used for scrap in the acute post-1945 steel shortages – a stop was only put to the practice in 1948.[7]

Home Office policy-formulation was based on the premise that the case for shelters was obvious, but that economic concerns were over-ruling the need to implement this vital policy. Attlee's admission in late 1947 fitted this general trend. More importantly, however, when Ministers began to discuss shelters the following year, it became clear just how unlikely it was that shelters would be built. As we have seen, Ministers postponed a proposed census of existing shelters in order to avoid possible publicity – to avoid the public becoming 'shelter-conscious'.[8] Fear of public clamour decided this, as the cost of shelters in money and scarce raw materials was so high as to jeopardise the economic security of the nation. When detailed plans were finally submitted in early 1949, Home Office insiders admitted that economic realities ruled out full-scale shelter building; but, they argued, the fact that 'only a little can be done at present is not in itself an argument for inaction. On the contrary, the less we can do, the more important it is that we should start early'.[9] It was clearly hoped to commit Ministers to shelters in the short-term at relatively little cost, with provision being slowly built up. To that end, they requested £890,000 to build 50,000 'Anderson'-style domestic shelters (which cost four times more than their Second World War equivalents) which would cover 225,000 people, and to conduct studies on adapting old buildings and ensuring new buildings afforded protection.[10]

That this was merely making a start on the problem highlights just how costly it was. This £890,000 would cover just under 1.5 per cent of the population protected by shelters in the last war, yet it would use up nearly 4 per cent of annual domestic steel production – the lack of which was already crippling the government's housing programme. To build shelters for everyone necessary would take almost three years' worth of total steel production. No wonder crafty Home Office civil servants suggested that 'as a matter of tactics... endeavour should be made to secure the general approval of the scheme by Ministers without mentioning particular quantities of steel'.[11] No wonder Ministers rejected it.[12] Officials tried again in October 1950, this time proposing a twin track approach to limit costs – atomic 'Grade A' shelters would cut casualties by 80 per cent whilst even 'General Standard' shelters (of Second World War specification) would cut atomic casualties by 60 per cent. Building 'Grade A' shelters for 7 million people and 'General Standard' for 9 million would cost £290 million in 1950–51 prices and use 100,000 men and 160,000 tons of steel per year for five years.[13] Central to their case were the consequences if shelters were ignored – very heavy casualties and a possible collapse in morale. Planners argued that it was 'difficult to see how civil defence can be taken seriously – whether by the Civil Defence Corps or by the local authorities – if the commencement of shelter construction is long delayed'.[14] Although ruled out for economic reasons, the Ministerial Committee – chaired by Ede – agreed that the plan was sound in principle,[15] and Ede himself outlined the policy in the Commons that atomic defence was possible, but that at the present moment planning only must suffice due to other calls on resources.[16]

Ede's statement, along with Attlee's in 1947, was as close as cold war Britain ever came to shelter provision. As we have seen, when Ede sought to increase civil defence provision in 1950/51 he was crushed, with the whole strategic worth of civil defence questioned by Attlee – and shelters in particular on the receiving end of the prime ministerial disapprobation. This was not the end of attempts to provide shelters, with officials instead focussing on the need to provide protected accommodation in newly-constructed large buildings. This made scant progress in this period – its impact on costs and materials always holding it back.[17] Throughout this period measures which aided 'active defence', such as the warning system and even importation measures and stockpiling, were also given priority over measures purely designed to save civilian lives.

Evacuation and dispersal

Evacuation was a central plank of civil defence plans during the early cold war. Its efficacy and price made it so; the ability to get millions out of danger areas whilst incurring no cost until an actual emergency ensured the policy was a high priority. The importance of evacuation to any civil defence plan went beyond its seeming simplicity, however – for a nation who had experienced evacuation in the Second World War removing vulnerable people from target areas had a remorseless, virtually moral, logic.[18] As had happened during 1939–40, the apparent simplicity of evacuation as a life-saving measure was complicated by the need for the policy to fit in with broader requirements concerning the economy and industrial manpower.[19] The conflicting pressures of life-saving and production created a tension within policy-making which was still unresolved when the hydrogen bomb made all previous plans redundant and imposed a revolutionary set of new problems.

In the atomic-age evacuation plan developed in depth during 1948–49, the main concern was ensuring that those who needed to be removed from the urban centres could actually be billeted in less dangerous places.[20] The scheme kept the previous division of evacuation, neutral and reception areas and much the same 'priority classes' to be evacuated: children of school age, expectant mothers and under-fives accompanied by their mothers or other guardians. The CDJPS had considered excluding the latter category on the grounds that mothers with their children 'caused more dissatisfaction in reception areas' than the other two classes, but concluded that opinion in the evacuation areas would demand their inclusion in the plan.[21] The plan was published in 1950, and stressed that priority classes had been retained to stop 'the indiscriminate transfer of the general population of large industrial towns' having a 'crippling effect on the economic life of the country'.[22] It emphasised that it was 'essential in the national interest that in wartime all persons with work of national importance to do should remain at their posts unless the Government advised them to move'.[23] This was an explicit reminder that civil defence preparations would be undertaken within the context of a national war effort, and that although the role of evacuation was humanitarian, it was vital to continue war-production. Children would be evacuated because it was 'in the national interest that all possible steps should be taken to preserve the youth of the country and the future generation',[24] and it was implicit in all Whitehall discussions of civil defence that the evacuation of children and the mothers of young families would be the key way of maintaining the economy. If the government did not want workers leaving their posts in order to protect their families, then the state would have to protect them instead.

The published plan set out little but an outline of the policy – and much planning and consultation work was required to ensure any scheme would be workable. The exact numbers each reception area would receive had to be agreed, and only 70 per cent of areas had settled this by the end of 1953.[25] Intricate transport plans had to be drafted to ensure the projected five million evacuees could leave the cities. To do so, it was intended to initiate the massive evacuation of London (two million people) as soon as war was deemed 'imminent', and to stagger the evacuation of other centres, allowing the railway system to cope under this enormous strain.[26] The basic railway planning was complete by the end of 1953, meaning detailed consultation could take place on the fate of evacuees once they arrived. At the start of the hydrogen bomb era, it seemed that the evacuation plan was close to completion and if a crisis came, priority classes *could* be evacuated and billeted in reception areas. It was certainly the one area of planning David Maxwell Fyfe was satisfied with when reviewing civil defence for his colleagues in April 1952.[27]

This picture of success pays little heed to the enormous strains the policy would be under in an actual war emergency. It is almost certain that the reality of evacuation would be very different from the rather calm, quick evacuation of London portrayed in the Boulting brothers' *Seven Days to Noon* (1950).[28] Could the reception areas cope with any large influx of 'unofficial' evacuation? That male and female workers would remain in the target zone was a basic assumption of the plan published in 1950. Would the government be able to provide the necessary additional food to areas with swollen populations in the post-attack period? These were imponderables. In order to address some of the flaws of the basic evacuation plan, which had been formulated when it was assumed a Soviet atomic capability was a more distant prospect, new plans were drawn up which would save lives of essential workers and, vitally, ensure continued production. Drafted as the 1950 evacuation plan was being published, the new 'Phase III' scheme, as it was called, planned to leave priority-class evacuation pretty much alone, but instead to 'disperse' essential industries and their workers from the strategically vital but undefined 'central key areas' – sort of super-evacuation areas – and send them to less dangerous neutral areas rather than the crowded reception areas.[29] The neutral areas could absorb 3.5 million people, with half a million places allocated to those over 70, the blind and the disabled ('we want them out of the way', as the planning document put it), and 3 million others. Essential industries in the key areas would be moved to neutral areas with their workers, and non-essential firms shut – with their employees either finding work with those undertakings in neutral areas, or finding work and commuting in to those essential industries unable to relocate away from the target areas. It was therefore hoped that the areas most vulnerable would be empty of people and stripped of as much industry as possible – with people and firms relocating to neutral or 'outer key areas' which would still be in target areas. This would save lives and maintain production; it also increased the chances of people remaining in their place of work.[30]

Although no areas were identified, it is clear that those places with a heavy concentration of key industries would be completely evacuated or dispersed – the dock or industrial areas of East London, Liverpool, Glasgow and Sheffield were prime examples. The planning assumption was approved by Ministers in May 1950,[31] but the proposed plan was too complex to actually implement.[32] It suggested identifying areas on a small-scale basis, as well as designating individual firms as essential or non-essential. It would have involved liaising with the local authorities of neutral areas and admitting that many inner cities were unworkable in atomic warfare; moreover, just how many 'essential' industries was it possible to relocate at short notice? The questions of which industries and their workforces stayed or left, and which workers were given 'safer' accommodation outside the target areas would have been complex and divisive. 'Dispersal' was a linguistic sleight of hand, and once the principle of evacuating only uniform classes of population was broken it would surely have been difficult for the government to rather arbitrarily disperse certain workers and not others without dire consequences for industrial production and social harmony. Although discussion on the plan proceeded throughout 1951 and 1952, it was clear by 1953 that the sheer scale of an atomic attack on British cities meant that the dream of major population dispersal to continue essential war production was merely illusory.[33] Once detailed dispersal was ruled out, planners turned to attempting to disperse the parts of those services 'essential to the life of the community' they could. But as the Hall Report concluded, planners had to face the consequences of the fact that no production would be possible in the main urban centres – which would naturally have a massive impact on both war production and on the long road to post-atomic war recovery.[34]

The Civil Defence Corps

From the beginning of the postwar period it had been a central tenet of civil defence planning that a voluntary civilian service would be resurrected. Initial plans were evolved in 1947 for a tripartite service involving civilian static units (essentially the ARP services of the last war), civilian mobile services and lastly military mobile groups.[35] The aim was for a highly mobile service controlled on a regional rather than a local authority basis which would be able to move resources into the worst hit areas, and Attlee announced in November 1947 that services would proceed along these lines, although recruitment would be restricted to civilians serving on a part-time basis in the first instance in order to build up a trained nucleus.[36] The proposed mixture of static and mobile civil defence workers remained official doctrine throughout the atomic age, but although the first recruits for local static services were signed up in 1949, the first 'experimental' mobile column was only founded in January 1953,[37] and that was staffed by national servicemen rather than civilian volunteers as intended.[38] For civilians, then, voluntary service was restricted to 'static' service in the Civil Defence Corps. Those volunteering could join either the Civil Defence Corps, Auxiliary Fire Service (AFS), the National Hospital Service Reserve or the Special Constabulary. To join the Corps, women had to be aged over 18 whereas men had to be over 40, reflecting the fact that those younger were liable to be called up for military service in the event of war. There were six sections: headquarters, warden, welfare, ambulance, rescue and pioneer, although the last two were amalgamated in 1952.[39] Women could only join the first four sections, although they were not officially barred from the more physical sections.[40] Once signed up, volunteers undertook basic training one evening a week before progressing to sectional training. In wartime those trained were expected to provide part-time service in civil defence. Courses also existed to turn more experienced recruits into instructors.

Recruiting, when it did begin, was initially very reliant on veterans of the civil defence services from the last war. This is unsurprising as there was at first little publicity to attract the general public, and the extensive network of local civil defence associations, comprised of veterans, seemed a potentially rich source of recruits,[41] not least due to the rhetoric of their officials. When initial recruitment proved distinctly underwhelming – just 21,477 had joined up to the end of January 1950 – the finger was apparently appointed at the associations for exaggerating the keenness of (their by now obviously largely paper) membership.[42] Of these recruits, 80 per cent had served in civil defence during the war and only 26 per cent were women, perhaps reflecting the masculine nature of the associations. The differing responses to these poor figures, by the government on one hand and by outsider civil defence opinion on the other, is illustrative. Ede announced in a speech to the National Federation of Civil Defence Associations in early 1951 that he considered the results 'disappointing', promising a major recruitment drive in the future. Intriguingly, given the audience of veterans, he stressed that 'we cannot rely exclusively on those who served in the last war… we cannot ignore the brutal fact' that everyone was a decade older than they were in 1940, and that 'we must get a good response to our appeal from a generation ten to twenty years younger than those of the old brigade. We want to get in men of forty and just over and women of under forty, for it is upon these "youngsters" that we shall have to rely more and more in the future'.[43] This illustrates that many of the civil defence veterans who rejoined the colours were much closer to 60 than 40.

To attract these new 'younger' volunteers, Ede suggested answers to two negative responses that had been encountered: the views that civil defence was unnecessary and that it was no use. In response to the former, Ede argued that there could be 'no doubt that enrolment in the Corps should be regarded as a duty by able bodied citizens over the military age and that time should not be lost in fulfilling that duty. Such action is a needed insurance against a future national risk against which experience shows it is wise to be insured'. The latter response was 'hopeless defeatism', and although 'it may not be possible to avoid grave loss of life under atomic attack, proper measures of civil defence which include, of course, a highly trained, organised and disciplined body of civil defence personnel, can prevent a very high proportion of the casualties that would otherwise occur'.[44] Ede's views represented the government's approach to recruiting volunteers in the early 1950s: people had to be convinced that it was their duty to volunteer, and to volunteer was to be part of a modern, useful civil defence service which would make a real difference in war. The response of the magazine *Civil Defence*, published quarterly from 1949, and then monthly from 1954, was quite different. It partly blamed the boasting of the unofficial civil defence associations, and partly blamed the Home Office for not appreciating the slowness of local authority bureaucracy and thus giving very little notice of recruitment, and lastly partly blamed the local authorities who were yet to appoint the Civil Defence Officers required under the 1948 Act.[45] *Civil Defence* was a periodical dominated by relatively senior civil defence workers – exactly the sort who became Civil Defence Officers or instructors. Throughout its life, the publication was the organ of these people, and they usually blamed the government for any civil defence fallings, whether it be the Home Office for administrative errors in this instance, or – almost constantly – the government for its lack of commitment to civil defence.

Ede's recruiting stance was reflected in the national campaigns which followed. When the national campaign began in April 1950, it featured messages strong on patriotism and duty, such as the advertisement featured in the national press which portrayed a potential recruit arguing that 'Of course I'm patriotic. I'd join at once, but...'. The advert thundered that 'patriotism is not enough, unless you back it up with action', and that 'the job that's left to someone else never gets done'.[46] The same sort of message was given in a companion advert, which argued 'don't leave it to someone else. Training only takes a few hours a month. Join today and your friends will too'.[47] At the bottom of both adverts the logo '**CD**' was juxtaposed with the unambiguous slogan 'A Call to Duty' (see Figure 3.1). At the same time as the press effort, the government commissioned a public survey to aid recruitment, which was conducted in Spring 1950, and concluded that those with previous civil defence experience and with a 'sense of duty' were most likely to join. Impediments were a lack of spare time, 'having no interest' and 'having had enough in the last war'. It also concluded that greater public awareness of the civil defence services and of the effects of the atomic bomb would encourage participation.[48] In the spring of 1950 the government was attempting to reach beyond civil defence veterans with a message of duty and patriotism, hoping to attract those of over 40 who were veterans of a different sort: combat veterans too old to be recalled to the military whose patriotism would drive them to cold war voluntary service. This message had only limited success, with membership numbering just 31,809 on 30 June 1950, although the proportion of those new to civil defence had risen to 40 per cent.[49]

Figure 3.1 Civil Defence Corps Advertising, National Campaign, Early 1950.[50]

The Korean war saw a massive rise in recruitment. This was for a number of reasons: the fear that a general war was close was the main one, exploited by recruitment propaganda. The cumulative effect of propaganda also played a major part in convincing people that civil defence was a worthwhile pursuit, as did a new effort to explain to people the true nature of atomic war. In late July Attlee called for volunteers in a radio broadcast which stands as one of the most interesting cold war statements produced by a British statesman. In it he linked Korea with the communist 'banditry' in Malaya and denounced global communism's attempt to 'mould the whole world to their pattern of tyranny'. He stressed that sacrifices were needed to protect British freedom and called on people to serve in the civil defence services.[51] Attlee's cold war rallying cry was based on the lesson of the Second World War – the aggressors had to be resisted he told the public, or they would never stop. 'This is why what is happening in Korea is of such importance to you. The fire that has been started in Korea may burn down your house'.[52] Attlee's rhetoric inspired a series of recruitment advertisements which highlighted the threat of war. One used the above 'fire in Korea' quotation, and another implied only a hopeless optimist would suggest there would not be a war in five or less years.[53]

Attlee's speech came just days after the publication of the government's pamphlet, *Atomic Warfare*,[54] which gained a lot of press interest and sold some 74,000 copies in a few months.[55] Reaction to the new publication was very favourable, with the *Economist* stating that it 'provides the kind of facts and arguments which should convince the ordinary citizen that civil defence training is worth having'.[56] The *Manchester Guardian* was particularly fulsome, praising it for tackling the 'fatalistic attitude' of those who believed nothing could be done, and arguing that this was all the more effective for its refusal to 'suppress any of the hard facts which might seem to encourage an impotent pessimism'.[57] The positive reception of the pamphlet's honesty and realism helps explain why civil defence recruitment improved, as it aided the atmosphere in which civil defence could flourish – that of assuming the atomic bomb threat could be met and survived. As important as the belief that atomic attack could be defended against was the belief that the Civil Defence Corps was a body which could do so effectively. This came more slowly, and like belief in atomic defence was far from universal, but gradually the weight of propaganda through a variety of media helped establish it.

The year following the outbreak of the Korean war saw recruitment increase nearly fivefold with members numbering 147,464 in June 1951, with 100,000 joining in the nine months up until 31 March 1951.[58] This was still far below government targets, and a second opinion survey conducted from January 1951 highlighted that although people now accepted the need for civil defence, much more needed to be done to convince individuals that, however war-weary they were, *they* needed to respond.[59] This emphasis on the individual became a key theme of the new recruitment campaign which began in late 1951. Press advertisements focussed on one individual and outlined his or her motivations for joining.[60] As male recruits had to be aged over 40, representations of men invariably focussed on their wartime experience, be it civil defence-based or on active service (see Figure 3.2). Portrayals of women enabled more flexibility, from middle-aged housewives with ARP experience to a twenty year old receptionist training to be a ambulance driver. All appeared above two key slogans: 'join your neighbours in civil defence', or 'you can't be certain – you can be ready'. A central plank of recruitment was short films to be shown in the cinemas. One was *The Waking Point*, shown from late 1951. This showed a man tempted to join, but dissuaded by his wife, before finally being convinced of the need for volunteers when local members rescued his son in an accident, reinforcing the message that civil defence couldn't be left to others and that it helped neighbours as well as one's own family. The portrayal of the wife being resistive to patriotism ignored the fact that from a slow start female recruitment began to overtake male, the quarterly returns showing that more women than men joined in the first three months of 1951. This pattern continued throughout the rest of the atomic age, and by the end of 1952 women formed a majority of the Corps.[61]

By the summer of 1952 active civil defence recruitment had been ongoing for more than two and a half years and had attracted some 201,349 members, with the 1951–52 recruitment campaign

Figure 3.2 Civil Defence Corps Advertising, National Campaign, 1952.[62]

adding more than 50,000 members.[63] As this was still around 300,000 people short of the peacetime target a special Advisory Committee was established by the Home Office, chaired by William Mabane, to advise on boosting recruitment.[64] The Committee concluded that the worth of civil defence needed to be more firmly established in the public mind as a permanent peacetime organisation rather than as a contingency body. In short, to increase participation a greater effort was needed to demonstrate the worth of civil defence to the ordinary member of the public. The main way of doing this, it was argued, was to place more emphasis on local recruitment.[65] This advice was followed and built on an existing trends in recruitment. The 1952 and 1953 campaigns thus saw recruitment being driven locally, with the national campaign very much supporting local efforts rather than the other way around.

Local campaigns often had various elements. Most successful was house-to-house canvassing – approaching people directly while dressed in uniform was apparently an effective means of persuading people to join. Another key element was the local pageant or demonstration. These saw volunteers give a demonstration, or a series of them, of activities such as putting out fires, or staging a rescue, often with elaborate rubble and featuring volunteer casualties.[66] Such displays often took place at county or town shows and allowed the more efficient elements of the Corps or the AFS to display their up-to-date machinery and present a very positive image of civil defence to the public. The AFS' new water-pumps, the now-legendary 'Green Goddesses', were a case in point. Of course, many members of the civil defence services were not sufficiently fit or well-trained to perform such tasks as were demonstrated, nor was there much machinery beyond that on display – but the overall impact of such staging, as the local press clippings dutifully dispatched to the Home Office suggest, was to show civil defence as a useful, efficient service equipped with the modern machinery needed to confront atomic war. The actions of volunteers in a series of real civil emergencies, such as the Canvey Island floods of early 1953 or the gruesome Harlow train crash in October the previous year helped cement the image of an able, effective Corps.[67]

Nationally, propaganda continued to emphasise individual responsibility for civil defence, this time with profiles appearing of smaller portrayals of civil defence in operation, showing in particular its vitality in action and the modern nature of its equipment.[68] The 1952–53 period also saw a number of civil defence related speeches and appearances by the Home Secretary which added to the impression that civil defence was being taken seriously and was a valuable force.[69] A boon to the impression was the eventual setting of the first – and only – civil defence mobile column at Epsom.[70] These columns had been envisaged as being staffed by civilians during war, but the actual column was staffed by conscripts to save money. Launched in January 1953, it toured the country making public appearances and demonstrating what could be done by a well-equipped mobile reserve in war. Its tour was a genuine part of the experiment to see how such a column would function in war, but its part in strengthening the positive image of civil defence was no doubt most welcome. A major boost to recruitment was the decision to allow men aged between 30 and 40 join, and those aged between 18 and 30 who were not going to be called up immediately on the outbreak of war.[71] This freed up a million potential recruits and undoubtedly aided recruitment in late 1952 and 1953.

When the Estimates Select Committee reported in December 1953 some 302,922 had joined the Corps, 60 per cent of its target.[72] We have seen the Committee's criticisms of civil defence planning in general, and it did not spare the Corps. Of particular concern was not the number of recruits, but the number who completed – or even turned up for – training. They estimated that between 20 and 25 per cent of those enrolled failed to turn up for training but remained registered as members, and noted that many rural areas had exceeded targets whereas urban centres were below strength: Sheffield, for example, had 2,200 volunteers out of a target of 7,300 (30 per cent).[73] Noting that nearly £5 million was spent annually on the Corps, they questioned whether it was worth continuing with the 'façade' of national civil defence, suggesting that the money should be devolved to local authorities. Although Ministers and officials reacted angrily to the report, especially lamenting the impact the Committee's disparaging remarks might have on recruitment, the Estimates Committee had obviously identified some grave flaws. There were very few fully trained recruits: and the Mabane Committee's second report broke down these figures and found that throughout the UK 19 per cent of volunteers had not undertaken any training, and that although 34.5 per cent had finished basic training, only 7.4 per cent had completed their section training – meaning only 24,000 fully trained civil defence volunteers, including less than 150 in Scotland.[74] As a defence force, the Civil Defence Corps in 1953 was pretty poor: had an unexpected war broken out, it would have been understaffed by willing but largely untrained volunteers. But, as Fyfe pointed out in response, the policy was to recruit a nucleus of volunteers – 500,000 members – which could be expanded to meet the wartime requirement of 1,500,000, and the Corps was progressing towards that target.[75] The magazine *Civil Defence* joined Fyfe in attacking the report's 'sweeping generalisations', although it agreed that the mobile organisation needed to be fully implemented.[76] It argued that 'after four years' effort it is high time that some part of the organisation is able to function', and stressed that the government needed to provide

> buildings, vehicles, and equipment sufficient to enable practical training and exercises to be carried out. These should include a control centre for each area, a certain number of warden's posts, one or two fully equipped rescue vehicles, ambulances and wardens' practice equipment for first aid and rescue. Such buildings, vehicles and equipment will enable a nucleus of people to operate in the event of a sudden attack.[77]

As we can see, contemporaries perceived the grave flaws in the Civil Defence Corps – in terms of recruitment, training and provisions – but perhaps we should pause and consider some of its achievements. Its main achievement was its size; although falling short of expectations, we need to assess not why the government's target was missed, but why so many people volunteered to train to fight an atomic war.

At the start of the cold war it was assumed within Whitehall that those who had served in the Second World War would sign up virtually immediately as they 'feel the loss of responsibility and leadership and local recognition of authority. They miss the comradeship and friendly association in a common cause'.[78] But by the summer of 1952 (the last time figures were broken down in this way) only 89,474 former civil defenders had signed-up, compared to 111,875 without previous experience.[79] Who were the 300,000 volunteers who had signed up by March 1954, and why did they join? Such questions need a full scale social history to provide adequate answers, but we can provide some broad conclusions. They included around 160,000 women compared to 142,000 men.[80] Well over half the women belonged to the welfare section, which would care for evacuees and those made homeless by enemy attack in war, whereas two-thirds of men belonged to either the warden or rescue sections (women were excluded from the latter). The appeals for volunteers were strongly gendered, with one poster for the heavily under-strength and all-male rescue section declaring unambiguously 'this is a man's job', with another from the same campaign (1952–53) crying 'there's a job for women too!'[81] (see Figure 3.3) – seemingly oblivious to the actual gender make-up of the Corps. The Corps' image was more masculine than its actual membership, perhaps reflecting the fact that the male preserve of rescue was presented as being of much higher status than the female domain of welfare – not to mention that the higher echelons of the Corps such as the instructors or the local civil defence officers were usually men. Only the ambulance section was not overwhelmingly gender imbalanced, with women outnumbering men by a ratio of 3:2. Furthermore, whereas 55 per cent of these men who had volunteered by mid-1952 had previous civil defence experience, only 33 per cent of women had, a result perhaps of age differentials.[82] In addition to the gendered make-up of the Corps, it was largely rural in character. Few towns came near to meeting their peacetime establishments, although Coventry came close reaching 95 per cent by the end of 1953,[83] a legacy perhaps of the city's wartime experience. So, broadly speaking typical recruits would be a relatively young woman in the welfare section in a rural community, and a middle-aged male warden in the same area.

These people joined in their hundreds of thousands because they wanted to do their bit, but certain elements had to be in place before volunteers could be attracted in such numbers. As outlined above, these included a belief that defence was possible in an atomic war and that the Corps was a body which could provide it. The history of the Corps in the 1949–53 period shows that although progress was slow, both elements were largely in place – although never undisputed – by 1952/53. The publication of *Atomic Warfare* helped create the impression of the defendable atomic war. Criticism of the government's handling of civil defence throughout the period also reinforced this belief – critics reproached the government for not taking civil defence seriously enough, for not spending enough money, but never for lying to the public about the nature of atomic war. Maligning the government's civil defence record, then, reaffirmed the fact that civil defence itself was a viable and responsible response to the threat of atomic war. On the Corps, although recruiting and equipping members was slow and inadequate in terms of a future war, there were enough men and women – and machines – to present an image of a functioning Corps capable of making a difference. Once the Corps was up and running it established a place itself in national, but especially local, culture and this greatly helped the sustained recruitment that saw numbers double between June 1951 and the end of 1953. This is not to downplay the Corps' undoubted flaws as an actual life-saving body, and it is true that those elements which underpinned its success were destroyed by the advent of the thermonuclear era in 1954, leaving it exposed to increasing criticism and even ridicule. It is, however, important to recognise

Figure 3.3 Civil Defence Corps Recruitment Poster, National Campaign, 1953.[84]

that the Corps was an example of how significant civil defence was in early 1950s Britain, and it both reflected and simultaneously reinforced how important civil defence was in the British government's cold war strategy, and how engaged with this policy at least some sections of the public were.

Conclusion

How did these measures fare in convincing people they could survive atomic attack? The public displays of the Civil Defence Corps and AFS encouraged such views, as did the general tendency of propaganda to limit the consequences of atomic attack, falling back on a rhetoric of the Blitz which implicitly emphasised the continuities with the last war. Both factors probably did much to contain discontent with civil defence, but it was far from a risk-free strategy: if atomic destruction could be discussed within the smothering framework of the war against Hitler, then the hydrogen bomb certainly could not. Such an approach only went so far, as the *possibility* of defence was not the pressing issue; rather, the fact that the government needed to do more, that it was not achieving what was possible, was the criticism which had to be faced. Both Labour and Conservative Ministers had the same approach in explaining why civil defence preparations were relegated far below those for 'active' defences – that government policy was to avoid war, not to prepare for it as if it was inevitable.[85] This placed successive governments in the position of emphasising again and again that defence against atomic war *was* possible, but that funds for it were dispensable compared to money for active measures which would deter aggression. These positions were not mutually exclusive, but they did rely on visible measures such as the Civil Defence Corps taking the strain of promoting atomic survival.

4
The Hydrogen Bomb Revolution

When the United States tested its thermonuclear weapons in the Pacific between February and May 1954, they were hardly breaking new ground. An American hydrogen bomb had first been detonated in November 1952, with the Russians following with a disputed 'hybrid' bomb in August 1953 and a 'true' bomb in November 1955.[1] Yet it was the 1954 tests which sparked off a global panic about the destructive power of the bomb and its deadly legacy of radioactive contamination. In Britain, public, press and parliamentary opinion reacted strongly to the bomb. If no-one knew quite what to do about the weapon, everyone knew that all Britain's defence policies had to change. In Whitehall, a great deal of effort was expended attempting to understand the full implications of the hydrogen bomb and to implement the necessary plans, an effort which was to last a year. While central government was drawing, tearing up, and re-drawing new civil defence plans, a battle was being fought to save the reputation of civil defence as critics attacked it as useless and wasteful. The consensus which had characterised civil defence in the early cold war was fractured by these claims. As the year wore on and 1954 became 1955, it was clear that bold strategies would be needed both to implement worthwhile policies and to convince the public that they could survive a future war.

Panic

The 1954 tests galvanised the British state, inspiring Churchill to mount an attempt to end, or at least ease, cold war tensions and driving the Government to approve the building of Britain's own hydrogen bomb.[2] The shock was palpable, comparable to that of Hiroshima nine years before, as the reaction mounted in late March and early April. The *Daily*

Mirror christened the weapon 'the monster' and 'the horror bomb'.[3] Harold Macmillan noted in his dairy that 'it is obvious there is tremendous interest, almost panic, in many parts of the world, about the hydrogen bomb'.[4] Focal points were the realisation that Japanese fishermen had been contaminated with radioactive fallout despite being some 82 miles from the explosion,[5] and the statement by a senior advisor to Eisenhower that the new weapon could be made 'as large as you wish' and could certainly wipe out New York City.[6] This emphasis on its sheer power and destructiveness characterised discussion of the bomb, and it is no surprise people that questioned the consequences of attack and the possibility of nuclear survival. This fear of the bomb coalesced later in the 1950s and saw the founding, and spectacular rise, of the Campaign for Nuclear Disarmament. If it is possible to give one response as 'typical' of many intelligent people's reaction to the H-bomb in 1954, perhaps Nesta Pain, a BBC radio producer can provide it. She wrote to her head of features, Lawrence Gilliam, and explained that 'I think we ought to do a programme on the hydrogen bomb and its implications for the human race.... It seems clear that in a war in which hydrogen bombs are used, England would quite clearly be finished'.[7] Her motive was simple: 'like many people, I have simply avoided thinking about these bombs and their implications during the last ten years. Now that I have been obliged to do so, I feel very strongly indeed that... [we] face dangers which might conceivably engulf the whole of the human race'.[8]

In civil defence circles, the most important reaction to the bomb came from Coventry City Council. On 5 April the Labour controlled local authority passed a resolution declaring that 'in view of the recent reports in regard to the explosion of the hydrogen bomb and its devastating effects', it would inform the Home Secretary that 'it is a waste of public time and money to carry on with the Civil Defence Committee: therefore, it is the Council's intention to take steps to terminate its existence'.[9] Alderman Stringer, leader of the Council, and his 'Socialist' colleagues, were attacked in scathing terms by the *Daily Mail* on 8 April 1954, which called them 'conceited little men who, because they have been elected to a local council, think they have a mandate to run the world. The socialist councillors of Coventry have no moral right to decide whether a life-or-death matter for the people shall be subject to their whims and fancies'.[10] The newspaper also reported a planned protest march by the 3,000 Civil Defence Corps volunteers in Coventry.[11] Coventry had, after all, had seen the highest levels of recruitment to the Corps out of all urban areas.[12] On 30 May there were remarkable scenes in the city when the experimental mobile column staged a demonstration with the aid of faked casualties; opposed by the council, the event descended into farce with some councillors trading insults on the street with the Home Office regional officer on the spot.[13]

The row rumbled on and was only brought to a conclusion on 24 July 1954 when the Home Secretary, Sir David Maxwell Fyfe, exercised his right (enshrined in regulations made under the 1948 Civil Defence Act) to appoint three commissioners to undertake the civil defence functions in Coventry 'in the name and at the expense of the said Council'.[14] The summer of 1954 saw a series of left-wing councils threaten to follow Coventry's lead. Opposition to civil defence reached such levels that the magazine *Civil Defence* was moved to allege a conspiracy: 'there seems little doubt that Civil Defence is being carefully, systematically and deliberately attacked by a welter of organisations many of them of a political character'.[15] Responding to the attacks on civil defence, Ministers such as Fyfe and the Lord Privy Seal, Harry Crookshank made a series of speeches attacking critics of civil defence. Fyfe spoke in Bristol and Birmingham as well as on the radio and in Parliament. Crookshank weighed in at Skegness. In these speeches, it was attempted to rein in the worst excesses of the panic by admitting how terrible the truth was. Fyfe's springtime Bristol speech serves as the exemplar: 'we must not lose our nerve in the face of this fresh potential horror. To suppose that one such bomb could destroy the world or even kill everyone in this country is a sign of ignorance, hysteria and panic. What it can do is sufficiently horrible without indulging in unreasoning exaggeration'. With actual policy statements thin on the ground in the summer of 1954, and with the government keen to stall for time as its reviews were conducted, Fyfe rested on the logic that the increased scale of destruction made trained civil defence volunteers more, not less, necessary.

> The radius of the area affected by the bomb would be bigger. But not so big that in the main concentrations of built-up areas – for example, in London, the Midlands, Merseyside and Clydeside – there would not be a very large areas indeed in which trained civil defence services must be ready to operate. And this situation might be reproduced in any of the smaller built-up areas if the bomb were exploded away from the 'town centre'.[16]

This may have been scant consolation for the two-thirds of the population living in towns of more than 50,000 people in 1950s Britain.[17]

With these speeches Ministers were attempting to ensure that people believed there was a possible defence against the hydrogen bomb – there was a tendency to downplay the effects of radiation, for example.[18] They were also attempting to defuse political strife by emphasising the bi-partisan nature of civil defence planning since the 1940s. Certainly, the 1954 recruitment campaign steered clear of political controversy with its emphasis on 'neighbourliness', a stance which highlights the difficulties the civil defence authorities were in: the advertisements mention 'working for peace' and 'commonsense', but not nuclear weapons or destruction (see Figure 4.1).[19] But by presenting vague assurances rather than policies, it was impossible to fully counteract the belief that thermo-

Figure 4.1 Civil Defence Corps Advertising, National Campaign, 1954.[20]

nuclear war signalled utter destruction. Perhaps it was impossible any way. Civil defence had attempted to convince people of its efficacy in the atomic area by establishing links between the world war and the cold war: such links, tenuous in many respects as they were, were utterly shattered in the public mind by the pictures and descriptions of the H-bomb.

The first reviews

The first internal Whitehall attempts at providing a convincing response were necessarily tentative, and focussed on understanding what this new weapon could do. An early meeting was called by Sir Norman Brook on 12 March 1954 to thrash out what advice would be given to Chiefs of Staff. Sir William Penney, head of weapons development at the United Kingdom Atomic Emergency Authority (UKAEA), and one of the truly great British physicists,[21] outlined to all the graphic consequences of the hydrogen bomb:

> A [five megaton] bomb dropped on London and bursting on impact would produce a crater 3/4 of a mile across and 150 ft deep, and a fire-ball of 2 1/4 miles diameter. The blast from it would crush the Admiralty citadel at a distance of 1 mile. Suburban houses would be destroyed at a distance of three miles from the explosion, and they would lose their roofs and be badly blasted at a distance of seven miles.[22]

The committee concluded that it was clear that the nation faced potential attack, 'the intensity of which far exceeded our previous assumptions and the plans which we had based on them'.[23] Whitehall had to re-evaluate the whole nature of warfare: its likelihood, what form it would take, and the policies, both active and passive, needed to meet the challenge. These discussions, Brook revealed, would take place within a 'small Ministerial' committee assisted by the Chiefs of Staff on 'active' defence and the Home Defence Committee on 'passive'.

This meeting was the starting point of two separate sets of assessment by the military and civil departments. The former came to fruition in June 1954 in a Chiefs of Staff document called 'United Kingdom Defence Policy'.[24] A massively important paper, it argued that the bomb's destructive power was such as to enable Britain to effectively deter aggression whilst allowing much needed cuts in conventional forces. It was then a precursor of the 1957 Defence White Paper, setting in train the discussions which led to the decision to built the British hydrogen bomb.[25] For civil defence purposes, its importance lay in its discussion of destruction. In demonstrating that Soviet delivery of thermonuclear weapons would be possible very soon, the paper emphasised the danger Britain was in. For the Chiefs, such destructive power – and Britain's ability to build it – 'puts within our grasp the ability to be on terms with the United States and Russia'.[26] Later problems with the method of delivering such weapons, however, meant that such parity proved chimerical.

For David Maxwell Fyfe, discussing the report in the new Defence Policy Committee – Brook's 'small Ministerial Committee' made flesh – of greater concern than British power's improved fortune was the fact that the Chiefs ignored civil defence. Despite the report arguing that, depending on the size of the weapons, an attack on just ten cities would kill 5–12 million people, the Chiefs did not consider public reaction. As Fyfe put it, 'the policy [of deterrence] outlined... could not be sustained unless the British public were prepared to accept the risks which it involved. If those risks were to be run, public opinion must be carefully prepared'.[27] Public support, he argued, was undermined by 'left-wing politicians', such as those in Coventry, 'who believed that it was useless to try to protect the civil population against the effects of nuclear attack and that this justified the adoption of a "neutralist" attitude in international relations'. Thus announcing a deterrent policy and admitting that Britain would suffer such casualties *without* securing 'public understanding and support' beforehand would be to court disaster, with a mass rejection of the policy and the rise of neutralist opinion throughout the country. He stressed that civil defence would still have a role to play providing aid 'on the periphery' of any explosion, not to mention the importance of evacuation and regional controls. Civil defence would have to form part of the policy presented to the people.

Fyfe had clearly been rocked by the Coventry episode, and the fear of a public revolt underpinned the parallel revision of plans occurring in the civil defence planning structure.[28] Officials in the Civil Defence Committee were fearful that without a lead being given to local authorities, morale would be damaged. Yet, as we shall see, they were in no position to offer any new solutions. Caught in this way, all they could fall back on in May were the reassuring platitudes offered to Parliament by Fyfe.[29] On actual policies, it is clear that much work needed to be done preparing the nation for the 'sheer struggle for survival' which would follow attack.[30] The guidance planners so clearly wanted was provided by Ministers in the Defence Policy Committee on 6 July, who agreed to the principles put forward by Brook:[31] that plans had to be revised with regard to the threat of thermonuclear attack, that war was relatively unlikely in the next five years, that money was in short supply, and that 'civil defence programmes should be concentrated upon the measures essential to building up public confidence in civil defence and sustaining the efficiency and morale of the civil defence services'.[32]

This advice represented a step-change in civil defence thinking: all current preparations were suspended and life-saving measures were officially relegated below public confidence that life-saving measures existed. The distinction is not so fine as it may first appear: it meant that inefficiencies in the Civil Defence Corps or the existence of a doubtful evacuation plan did not matter as long as the public believed effective measures to be in place. Fyfe had called for public education concerning the 'conditions of life they may have to tolerate',[33] but Brook's policy of bolstering the public face of civil defence gained precedence. It meant doing 'enough in civil defence to reassure the public that the civil defence services have a useful job to play in a future war'.[34] It was also vital, argued Brook, to stop treating civil defence and active defence separately: at a time when Government expenditure on Civil Defence was decreasing, it was necessary to link civil defence with the broader defence position. If this was not done, Brook warned, the public would expect the civil defence effort to increase. This argument – that only through linking the two policies together could the lack of civil defence preparations be defended – grew in importance over the following two and a half years, but in the summer of 1954, efforts were still being made to consider a more positive response to the thermonuclear challenge.

But for all this emphasis on public morale, there was little real guidance for planners, who set about *revising* existing plans throughout 1954, when they needed to be torn up and started anew. From the initial discussion in the Official Committee through to the major report on plans by the CDJPS in October, the Home Office planners were operating with a relatively sketchy understanding of the new weapon.[35] They saw the problem mainly in terms of increased blast power, neglecting the importance of radioactive fallout. An illuminating example of this work is their review of evacuation. This advocated an enormous expansion of the population to be evacuated (and some degree of shelter provision) to save 90 per cent of casualties. The expansion of evacuation would involve extending the evacuation areas to swallow up most of the old 'neutral' areas and provision to include all 'children of school age or below, accompanied by their mothers' as well as adolescents, which would mean the numbers in the priority classes rising from 4.6 to 12 million people. It was thought that evacuating families together would appreciably simplify the movement of the population and eliminate some of the social strains attendant on separating children and mothers.[36]

It was also envisaged that there would be 'central areas' from which non-priority classes would be evacuated – essentially the main cities and ports. Those evacuated might include: 'persons not employed; non-essential workers; and possibly also certain people whose special abilities or skills make them essential to the continued life of the nation, and who cannot be replaced, but whose continued presence in the central areas is not absolutely necessary'.[37] Who these essential workers would be was not discussed, and in later years proved to be a thorny and unanswerable question. Obviously the scale of the final scheme would rest on the extent of such 'non-priority' evacuation (who and where from). If billeting was extended to a density of 1.5 persons per habitable room, 15 million people could in theory be evacuated, doubling the population in reception areas and representing, due to the resulting 'severe social strains', the 'maximum absorptive capacity of the reception areas before attack'. If such strains were acceptable, it might be possible to evacuate the 12 million 'priority' and 3 million 'additional' people.[38]

The CDJPS admitted that 'it must be recognised that the magnitude of such an evacuation plan may impose serious difficulties on its execution', especially the issues of transportation and the ability of the reception areas to sustain a population of double their peacetime size.[39] Despite these reservations, CDJPS' revisions to evacuation policy served as a sort of 'statement of intent', and it was swiftly despatched to Ministers who agreed it as a basis for further planning and investigation.[40] The CDJPS plan was attacked within the Treasury, however, as hopelessly unrealistic. Richard 'Otto' Clarke, an Under-Secretary at the time, received the papers of the CDJPS Working Party on Evacuation, and he provided perceptive criticism of its work to Sir Alexander Johnston.[41] These plans were being worked out, but, as Clarke put it, 'I would really have hoped that someone was occupied in thinking rather than in working out paper plans'.[42] This statement could be used to criticise much of the planning going on throughout the second half of 1954. Clarke went on to argue 'in order to get a proper basis for civil defence plans, I think one has to devote a lot of thought to the making of assumptions for working purposes'. One of these assumptions must be which areas were to be regarded as 'safe'. The second was an issue which had been largely ignored throughout the whole cold war: would people stay in the areas the attack was expected? As Clarke put it, 'it is important to know whether anybody will be willing to stay in London under imminent threat of annihilation, and there is something faintly comical about dividing the population into classes, some of whom are told by Home Office officials that they are to go and others to stay'. A realistic appraisal was needed: 'we want a clear idea of whether people will remain in those areas or not. The standard work on the subject is by Mr H.G. Wells, written, I think in 1896 – "The War of the Worlds" – which is much better than any piece of Home Office paper that I have yet seen'.[43]

Clarke had pinpointed an enormous flaw in the Home Office preparations for civil defence: there had been no analysis of the human element. The dry paper plans took no account of how people might react in wartime – nor did they grasp that the evacuation areas would be far from safe. His espousal of *The War of the Worlds* is prescient. Wells' portrayal of the 'swift liquefaction of the social body' caused by the hysterical flight from London in the face of enemy attack was far from the arid Home Office plans and, for Clarke, amply depicted the essentially unknowable behaviour of the public.[44] It was unrealistic for civil defence planners to routinely assume a pliable public adhering to announcements and corralling by the authorities. By contrast, in early 1950s America, the Federal Civil Defense Administration (FCDA) had worked with the secret Psychological Strategy Board and received a study on civil defence by an Ivy League cold war think-tank 'Associated Universities' which contained significant research on panic, and how to prevent it.[45] The contrast can probably be explained by a combination of cost and the belief that such studies were of little use in the British context. In the early postwar years, as we have seen, studies were made on the issue of civilian morale, but the conclusion – drawn from the lesson of the Second World War – was that the British public would be able to stand up to the rigours of atomic war. It is possible that such a conclusion became an entrenched and probably unspoken assumption. The same factors which saw Home Office officials ploughing on through paper plans and incrementally revising policy, rather than taking a step back to review a strategic reality which had radically changed, might have been responsible for taking morale for granted.

Although in mid-1954 General Sir Sidney Kirkman was appointed as the first Director-General of Civil Defence in order to ginger up policy,[46] we can argue that civil defence planners had become stuck in a groove of drafting papers which were related to and developed from existing papers which had been drawn up years before. Evacuation was a case in point: the policy was there in outline, it just had to be modified. Had they been capable of stepping back and analysing civil defence afresh, they would have seen the flaws in their plans, and certainly would have understood that the issue of morale and public control was central. Not for nothing did Clarke ask Johnston 'whether there is, in your view, any chance of getting any real thought done on these subjects, preferably by fresh minds'.[47] From the Treasury's point of view, he was worried that under current planning 'an awful lot of money will be wasted on civil defence', because although the budget was then limited 'it will not be long before people are sure to ask for quite considerable sums of money to handle the very large casualties which are to be expected. And I don't at that time want to be confronted with something really half-baked'.[48]

To be fair to the civil defence planners, they felt the want of basic strategic guidance. In October, the CDJPS was lamenting that 'Departments feel the need for a more clearly defined picture of conditions likely to prevail in the first weeks of a war'.[49] Planning was effectively stalled as the full implications of the hydrogen bomb had not been understood.[50] There can be no doubt that a greater appreciation of the effects of hydrogen bomb warfare on Britain should have been conducted before any revision of civil defence plans was undertaken. The 'advice' of Brook in July was simply not enough in terms of scale: it did not lead the Departments anywhere. Although the revision of plans within the civil defence structure continued throughout the rest of the year,[51] they were dead letters, with the attention of more senior Whitehall figures now focussed on a fundamental review of defence plans which occurred over the winter of 1954–55.

Although short-lived, we can see within these 1954 plans trends of thinking which were to re-emerge after the Strath Report: the realisation that there were severe limits on the possible extent of evacuation; that thermonuclear war meant that the atomic-age physical preparations to ensure survival were no longer effective, and equivalent ones for the thermonuclear era either impossible or cripplingly expensive; that this meant that money could be saved at the same time as the public would be desirous of *increased*, not reduced, effort; that the only way to reconcile the two would be to firmly patch discussion concerning civil defence into the wider debates over deterrence and defence policy; and that to bolster the image of a workable civil defence policy the burden must be borne by its most visible aspect – the Civil Defence Corps. So at the time when the volunteers' ability to save lives in wartime was being fundamentally undermined, their importance as representatives – ambassadors even – of the government's faith in nuclear survival meant that the Corps was more important than ever. It was a recipe for failure: the government was counting on the Corps to present the illusion that lives would be saved, but who could fail to realise that it was a rapidly depreciating asset?

The monstrous gestation

This inconclusive, rather meandering revision of plans was sharply suspended in December, when it was finally decided that the dangers of fallout meant the Government's defence plans needed to be comprehensively overhauled. The catalyst for this new review was a meeting of the Chiefs of Staff Committee held on 8 November which included the Chiefs, Brook, Sir John Cockcroft (Director of UKAEA, Harwell), Sir Fredrick Brundrett (Scientific Advisor, Ministry of Defence) and officials from other Government Departments, including William Strath from the Treasury, who had previously served on the Hall Committee.[52] The meeting concerned the 'latest scientific estimate of the facts' on fallout received from the United States, and it was clear to all that fallout 'will have a revolutionary effect on all our war plans – military and civil'.[53] Urgent action was needed, not least out of fear that Washington might announce their fallout findings before the UK was ready to respond.[54]

Over the course of November and early December 1954, the senior operatives of Britain's nuclear community mobilised to provide Ministers with the devastating new advice concerning fallout. Brook was instrumental in forming a small new group of civil servants, headed by William Strath, to provide co-ordination within the Cabinet Office on war planning. Before the group, the Central War Plans Secretariat (CWPS), was set up, co-ordination between military and civil war planning had largely rested on the shoulders of Brook himself. Given the increasing co-dependence of such planning, the new group would provide not just secretarial support, but would actively aid the co-ordination of plans.[55] The CWPS' first task was to co-ordinate the drafting of the fallout document, written by Sir Frederick Brundrett,[56] with Strath and Sir Edwin Plowden (Chairman, UKAEA) casting an eye over it before it was dispatched by Brook to Harold Macmillan. When finished, the paper went not only from Macmillan to the select group of Ministers, but also to Churchill and finally the full Cabinet.[57]

The Cabinet paper contained Brundrett's masterly annex on the effects of the hydrogen bomb, explaining in detail the destructive force of the weapon in terms of heat and blast and outlining the phenomenon of radiation.[58] On the former, it told Ministers that 'blast and heat are more intense from an air burst than from a ground burst'. The heat and blast from the explosion of an-air burst 10 megaton weapon would cause 'surface devastation to ordinary brick houses' 7.5 miles away, and cause fires up to 12 miles away (these figures would be revised in the new year). Beyond the areas affected by heat and blast, radiation would be a major concern. 'Fallout', radioactive particles sucked up by the (ground-burst) explosion, carried by the wind and deposited over a potentially huge area killing people and contaminating crops, was explained to Ministers. From a single 10 megaton device, fallout 'would cover an area of 5,000 to 6,000 square miles'. Also,

> There will be an inner zone of approximately 270 square miles in area (larger than Middlesex), in which radiation will be so powerful that all life will be extinguished, whether in the open or in houses. Because of the persistence of the radio-active contamination in this inner zone, general relief measures would be virtually impossible for some weeks, and possibly months. People in especially deep shelters with their own supply of uncontaminated food and water would have some chance of survival, provided they were not entombed by other effects of the explosion. Even so, for at least a week it would not be safe for them to emerge and leave the area. Fires in this area would have to be left to burn themselves out.[59]

Outside this area, the danger would progressively lessen with distance, but within an area of about 3,000 square miles, (around 170 miles long in the direction of an average wind and over 20 miles wide in places), 'exposure in the open on the first day might easily be fatal'. Some rescue operations could commence on the outer fringes of this area by the second day 'but the greater part of the area would be immobilised for several days. Survival in this area depends on cover'. Suitable shelter in ordinary houses would 'reduce the dosage rate by a factor as high as 20'. Outside this would be an outer area of 2–3,000 square miles 'in which there is a danger of radiation sickness if no precautions are taken. In general, it would be sufficient for people to stay indoors for about 12 hours after the onset of contamination'.[60]

The annex, therefore, left Ministers in no doubt of the true effects of fallout and its 'revolutionary' impact on all war plans.[61] To fully understand this, a full scale review was needed, and this is what Macmillan proposed in the Ministerial meeting which followed his paper. Prompted by Strath and Brook,[62] Macmillan proposed that a small group of officials – led by Strath – be appointed 'to examine the broad consequences of fallout on our war plans as a whole and indicate the guidance which

Departments responsible for detailed planning would require',[63] which the Prime Minister approved three days later.[64] The group was to be kept small to 'enable work to proceed without disseminating widely knowledge about the nature of fallout'.[65] Fear of the public reaction to the government's plans was marked, and Macmillan himself noted that the issue of selling the new policy to the public would be a thorny one.[66] Under Strath would be General Brownjohn, secretary to the Chiefs of Staff, Sir Richard Powell (Ministry of Defence), Sir Fredrick Brundrett and General Kirkman.[67] Days later Philip Allen (Home Office) was added to the list,[68] and Strath also had authority to co-opt Sir Robert Hall, Mr Patrick Dean (JIC Chairman) and a scientist to be nominated by Plowden.

At the end of these five weeks of frenetic activity, Brook sent a note to his Permanent Secretary colleagues informing them of the founding of CWPS, emphasising that a 'special effort' was needed to update war plans, and stressing that high level officials should be placed on the work. 'The intellectual problems presented by the latest strategic advice are such that we cannot hope to get our plans on the right lines unless senior people are enabled to give some thought... to the framing of the outlines of the new policy'.[69] Although the Strath group was too secret to reveal to all his colleagues, we can see in Brook's note a criticism of the conduct of war planning previous to November 1954. It had not been taken seriously enough, and the best people were not given time to investigate it. In fact, the whole foundation of the CWPS and the Strath Group was a criticism of previous war planning. The CDJPS had attempted to investigate the civil defence implications of the hydrogen bomb, just as it had probed civil defence problems since 1949. The bypassing of the CDJPS was in part due to the desire to investigate the problem in the round, bringing civil and military planning together, but only in part. The whole official civil defence planning structure centred around the Home Office and Official Committee on Civil Defence was weak and the Home Office representatives on the Strath group were more senior than those usually working on the subject. But if the CDJPS' reactions to the hydrogen bomb had been poor, this was largely due to a failure in the central planning machinery. It was not the job of the Home Office machinery to analysis strategic assumptions or formulate plans for civil and military departments. CDJPS itself bemoaned the lack of guidance.[70] It was a failure in the central machinery that strategic advice had not been given sooner, and it was in recognition of this failure that the Strath group was set up free of any 'tramlines' affecting the direction of planning.

While the Strath Report was undergoing its 'monstrous gestation' as one official put it,[71] the government was presented with a more immediate political problem: the annual Defence White Paper was due to be published in February, before any review could hope to be completed. The 9 December Ministerial meeting had approved the idea of an interim document presenting a public 'middle course', stressing the evolutionary nature of the plans, to be steered until the final policy could be announced.[72] This paper was published on 17 February and its civil defence importance can be seen in three areas. Firstly, it frankly admitted the destructive power of the new weapon, declaring that 'if such weapons were used in war, they would cause destruction, both human and material, on an unprecedented scale'.[73] The fatal effects of fallout were explained, and the description ended by informing the public that post-attack life 'would be a struggle for survival of the grimmest kind'.[74] Secondly, it stressed the commitment to meeting the threat faced: the Government 'thought it their duty' to build a British hydrogen bomb[75] which would help reduce the chances of war; although there was also the 'determination to face the threat of physical devastation, even on the immense scale which must be foreseen' rather than adopt 'an attitude of subservience to militant Communism, with the national and individual humiliation that this would bring'.[76] Thirdly, it emphasised the part civil, or rather home, defence would play in this: on the one hand measures which would, 'by demonstrating the country's determination to resist aggression in all its forms, buttress the resolution needed to sustain an effective deterrent policy';[77] on the other hand, although there would be 'interruption' of services and 'serious problems' encountered post-attack, it stressed that much could be done to save lives.

On civil defence, it flagged that the new plans were not complete, but stressed the continued need for 'rescue, fire-fighting and welfare operations', and outlined how the Civil Defence Services would be supplemented by the training of the armed forces in civil defence and the formation of 'The Mobile Defence Corps'. Planned to amount to some 48 reserve battalions, these would be made up of Army and RAF reservists who would receive a month's training, and were to represent the fruition of the long-cherished dream of a rapid, well-trained mobile force which could be deployed 'in support of the local civil defence services wherever the need is greatest'.[78] The importance of evacuation and stockpiling was reaffirmed, and a future shelter policy was hinted at by explaining the efficacy of a simple 'trench with overhead earth cover' as a way of protecting against fallout. The total defence budget for civil Departments was estimated at £69.66 million for 1955/56.[79] Most of the money was to be spent on increasing the strategic stockpiles of food, oil and medical supplies. Further measures were promised and the public were informed that although there was no 'simple or immediate solution' to civil defence problems, the Government was 'confident that the people as a whole will be ready and willing to play their part in building that will to resist which is an essential part of the deterrent to aggression'.[80]

The interim nature of the section on civil defence was criticised by the *Times*, but its leader did stress civil defence's importance: without it 'the new deterrent may only be a test of bluff'.[81] The *Economist* declared that the White Paper 'inspired real confidence' that Ministers had at least realised the problems facing the nation,[82] whilst the *Daily Mirror* applauded the creation of the Mobile Defence Corps, if little else in the policy paper.[83] The Mobile Defence Corps policy continued the trend set with the previous year when RAF reservists were assigned fire-fighting duties, but was designed to provide the military mobile forces which had been envisaged as back-up for the Civil Defence Corps from the beginning of the cold war. The ending of national service meant that the scheme was short-lived, but its intent was to provide a large cohort of national servicemen who would be trained in rescue and fire-fighting. Macmillan's aim in introducing the new body was to provide a link between the Civil Defence Corps and the regular military, and to 'refresh the spirit' of the civilian services and 'combat the attitude of mind which had displayed itself in Coventry'.[84]

The ensuing Parliamentary debate on the White Paper was more memorable for the internecine warfare within the Labour Party than any penetrating look at the hydrogen bomb or civil defence.[85] Churchill began his opening speech by stating that 'there is no absolute defence against the hydrogen bomb',[86] but there was no outcry to match that which followed a similar statement by Duncan Sandys as Minister of Defence in 1957. Manny Shinwell, a former Minister of Defence, did attack the Government for what he considered the paltry provision for the protection of the public,[87] and Gwilym Lloyd-George, Home Secretary since October 1954, made a spirited defence of the need for a civil defence policy. He explained that the complexities of fallout meant that the Government's full plans 'have not yet reached the stage when they could be made public'.[88] He did stress that the Government would pursue an evacuation policy and he ruled out the provision of 'deep-shelters', although the Government was 'considering how [protection against fallout] can be given'; he also announced that all national servicemen would receive basic civil defence training.[89] Lloyd-George was also praised for taking the issue more seriously than his predecessor, whose apparent glibness the year before still rankled with some.[90] Overall, however, Parliamentary interest was focussed on the actual weapon, rather than the measures for mitigating its effects.

The Strath Report

'Mr Strath's Group', as it was called within Whitehall, officially began work on 1 January and reported on 8 March 1955. The strategic basis of the group's work was provided by a Joint Intelligence Committee (JIC) report on 'The "H"-Bomb Threat to the UK in the Event of a General War'.[91] The intelligence message was mixed: although the JIC's analysis largely discounted the threat of a global war until at least 1960, it added what Peter Hennessy has called 'a bone-chilling addendum' on Britain's fate should war occur.[92] Firstly, it believed 'that the Russians will regard the UK as such a threat that they will aim to render it unusable for a long period, and will not hesitate to destroy great parts of the UK to achieve this aim'.[93] In wartime, the 'simplest and most effective form of attack' to knock Britain out of any war would be to detonate hydrogen bombs at ground level 'in suitable meteorological conditions', thus maximising the effects of fallout. The paper went on:

> We are advised that something like ten 'H' bombs, each of a yield of about 10 megatons, delivered on the western half of the UK or in the waters close off the western seaboard, with the normal prevailing winds, would effectively disrupt the life of the country and make normal activity completely impossible.[94]

This knowledge underpinned Strath's work, as did a belief that the public needed to 'have a clear and complete understanding of the problem before the outbreak of war' and to have 'taken all precautionary measures that are possible', in order to aid recovery.[95] Success would depend 'on the confidence which the Government has engendered due to the measures it has carried out'.[96]

The final report began by outlining the power of one ten megaton hydrogen bomb.[97] An air-burst device (maximum immediate devastation), would destroy everything within a two or three mile radius, ordinary brick houses would be destroyed or be irreparable up to six miles away, and the same house uninhabitable 16 miles away. In average meteorological conditions fires would occur in houses up to 15 miles away. If ground-burst (for maximum fallout), the figures for destroyed and uninhabitable houses were reduced to five and 12 miles respectively. Overall, 'though the zone of major damage by blast and heat would not extend more than some 12–16 miles from the point of burst, widespread minor damage would be done to roofs, windows and light structures at much greater distances'.[98] With fallout, 'there would be fatal consequences and considerable sickness over an area of some 400 square miles even if people remained in their houses and this might extend to some 50 miles downwind'. Those outside this zone would be in grave danger in the open up to 140 miles downwind. In short, 'hydrogen bomb war would be total war in a sense not hitherto conceived. The entire nation would be in the front line'.[99]

If Britain were attacked with ten of these weapons 'life and property would be obliterated by blast and fire on a vast scale'.[100] It would represent an explosive force 'forty-five times as great as the total tonnage of bombs delivered by all the allies over Germany, Italy and occupied France throughout the whole of the last war'. It would leave

> No part of the country... free from the risk of radio-active contamination. A single attack with ten 10-megaton bombs could deny us the use for varying periods of thousands of square miles of our agricultural land and the standing crops from a much greater area. Open water supplies for sections of the population would become undrinkable for weeks. The risk of starvation in the period immediately after the attack would be high.[101]

Each bomb would create a zone of contamination covering some thousand square miles in which 'local inhabitants would at best be able to lock themselves in their houses and in the inner part of this region [200 square miles] some would not be able even to do this'. It would leave survivors 'isolated not merely from the less contaminated areas outside but from one another. The household would become the unit of survival. Individuals would have to subsist on such stocks of food and water as they had got ready in advance in their individual places of shelter'. For each survivor, 'life in the contaminated areas would demand a high degree of self-discipline... in the observance of elementary precautions to reduce the risks from exposure to radiation until it had subsided to an acceptable level. Clearly such discipline could not be secured unless the need for it were widely known and the basic precautions thoroughly understood by everyone in advance'.[102]

Without preparations, 12 million would die, and 4 million would be seriously injured. Four million of those casualties would be caused by a single bomb on London. A major cause of casualties would be fire: 'the fire hazard from nuclear attack dwarfs all previous experience to insignificance. The heat flash from one hydrogen bomb would start in a built-up area anything up to 100,000 fires, with a circumference of between 60 and 100 miles'.[103] There would be over 13 million people 'pinned down in their houses or shelters for at least a week' within the fallout zones – and evacuation would increase this number. There could, at first, be little hope of rescuing them or ensuring all those who needed medical aid received it: 'it would be quite unrealistic to hope to maintain anything like normal medical standards. There would be grave problems of priority in dealing with a wide range of casualties some of whom would have no hope of recovery'.[104] The 'chief difficulty' would be deciding who among the injured and burnt 'had also been exposed to a lethal dose of radiation and who would therefore ultimately die, and on whom it would be wasteful to expend scarce medical resources'. Even relatively minor radiation cases would probably prove fatal as the 'good food, good nursing and rest' needed for recovery could not be provided.[105]

The 16 million dead and injured amounted to nearly a third of the population. Most of the 12 million deaths would result from heat and blast – more than 9 million as opposed to less than 3 million caused by radiation. To prevent such horrific casualties, and to ensure that Britain could somehow survive as a nation and recover from such an attack would take an immense planning effort. Strath stressed that 'this attack would fall with devastating suddenness. All preparations would have to be ready in advance and brought to a high state of efficiency. It would be folly to trust to improvisation. The price of unpreparedness would be catastrophe. Inefficiency and indecision in the execution of plans would be hardly less costly'. To reduce casualties, evacuation, 'local dispersal of those not evacuated to a distance from areas of greatest risk', and shelter provision were all recommended. Strath argued that 'these measures are not alternatives. In practice a combination of all three would be required'. Evacuation, especially, was important: 'levelling out risk wherever the bombs might fall', could 'reduce the figures very substantially'. For example, of the 4 million estimated casualties in London, evacuation might save 3 million, and providing shelters would save still more'.[106] Shelter, it was believed, 'should in principle be provided on a nation-wide scale', for defence against fallout; those 'on the outskirts of likely target areas' should be constructed 'to give some protection against blast and heat', but there could be no protective shelters in the inner 'target areas'. Strath stressed that 'effective protection against fallout can be secured by a shelter of reasonably simple construction', and recommended that further investigations should be made to see what types of trenches or refuge rooms, and what stockpiling measures, would be needed. He also stressed the need for protected basements in government buildings (an old chestnut) and that 'guidance should be prepared for issue in due course to householders and others concerned on the construction and equipment of shelters'.[107]

Public information, for Strath, would be a key element of any life-saving programme. Deterrence relied on the 'determination to resist aggression even at the risk of having to undergo nuclear bombardment', but such 'determination can be real only if the public understand what is involved'.[108] Public education was therefore needed to ensure that everyone fully understood the effects of the hydrogen bomb, particularly the threat of 'radio-activity about which people are still largely ignorant'. If people understood the dangers and what they could do to maximise their chances of survival, it would save thousands of lives at no cost to the government. But how could people be encouraged to stock up on food and to be aware of the absolute necessity of staying under cover in any attack without provoking panic? Any 'process of indoctrination' would take some time, and need to start at once, *and* 'be done in such a way as to avoid spreading despondency or causing panic demands for unwarranted expenditure on protective measures'.[109] This was the great difficulty at the heart of British civil defence. Once it was explained why such measures needed to be taken by ordinary people it would soon become clear how little chance of survival people in urban centres, for example, had. Unless Strath's life-saving measures – evacuation, dispersal, shelter, not to mention vigorous rescue and feeding services, and a massive purchasing of food and medical stockpiles – were undertaken, how could people hope to survive? Honesty with the public was only really possible as part of a wide-ranging and expensive programme. If Strath's measures were decided to be too costly, then public openness would be literally something the government could not afford.

To ensure the survival of the nation and to save lives in any attack would require a massive effort controlled by a robust government machinery. The relief effort, mobilising all remaining civil and military resources, would be in danger of collapsing unless government control could be maintained post-attack. Strath stressed that such control might be impossible: 'in some parts of the country, particularly if several bombs fell in the same area, there might be complete chaos for a time and civil control would collapse'. If this happened, the local military commander 'would have to be prepared to take over from the civil authority responsibility for the maintenance of law and order and for the administration of the Government'. He would need to 'exercise his existing common-law powers to take whatever steps, however drastic, he considered necessary to restore order'. All civil agencies, including the police, the civil defence services and the fire service would fall under his control. Even in less badly hit areas, civil authorities would require military aid to retain and maintain control.[110] In planning terms, the Strath Report recommended 'that a flexible system should be devised which would allow the military authorities, where required, to support and, where necessary, to take over control from regional or local authorities'. The problem of control meant 'very heavy responsibilities would fall on the police and arrangements should be made to strengthen their numbers in an emergency'. There would need to be strengthened central and regional war rooms to aid the maintenance of control, which would also 'require the use of drastic emergency powers. A complicated series of Defence Regulations, providing for detailed controls, as was used in the last war would be quite unsuitable. Much more rough and ready methods would be needed to cover the period when the nation would be struggling to survive'.[111]

The struggle for survival would characterise post-attack Britain. Recovery would be slow and painful. 'Rough and ready' methods of control, military government and the severe rationing of medical services leading to the non-treatment of radiation casualties would be the stark reality of post-nuclear British life. Even with these plans, 'it would still be impossible to forecast how the nation would react to nuclear assault. The effect of this on dense populations would remain beyond the imagination until it happened'.[112] Yet Strath believed that the nation could recover from such devastation. Immediately following an attack there would be 'a critical period during which the surviving population would be struggling against disease, starvation and the unimaginable psychological effects of nuclear bombardment'. Food and water would be in short supply, and at least half of Britain's industrial capacity would have been destroyed. Food stockpiling would be an absolute priority in order for recovery to be achievable. As long as 'what was left of the nation could get through that period and the survivors were able to devote their resources to the work of reorganising the country, they should eventually be able to produce a wide enough range of goods to meet ordinary civilian needs'. Although substantially reduced, 'the standard of living... would still be above that of the greater part of the world'.[113]

The Strath Report provided some fundamental lessons that could not be ignored: all plans had to be ready before attack; large-scale preparations were necessary to save lives and aid recovery, including evacuation, shelter and stockpiling; the population had to be ready to face an attack; and efforts were needed to ensure civilian control of the country. If the necessary policies were implemented, thermonuclear war would still be a catastrophe: but it would be one where millions of lives could be saved and where those survivors had a chance of pulling through in a nation determined to recover. Without them, there could be 16 million casualties from the initial attack and 13 million people trapped in radiation zones with little or no chance of rescue or medical care from a society which had collapsed in on itself. This was the stark choice emerged from the group's complex and unparalleled study: implement these measures or risk a thermonuclear war destroying Britain as an organised society.

Conclusion

The Strath Report remained the central document for understanding thermonuclear war in Whitehall. It defined the limits of the possible and proposed strategies that could possibly have aided Britain's recovery from the abyss of nuclear destruction. It capped a year's worth of work attempting to understand just what the thermonuclear bomb meant for the future of British defence. Preliminary work before Strath had recognised that the bombs presented an unprecedented level of destruction, but not just how radiation would affect such plans. For CDJPS, the H-Bomb seemed to mean more evacuation and shelters on the atomic model, more fire-fighters and more members of the Civil Defence Corps. There was no sense that such volunteers would be impotent in the face of the huge zones of contamination which would dominate the British landscape. Nor was there any sense of what Britain might actually look like after an attack: how would these people be fed, cared for, ruled even? It took a group dedicated to looking into the prospect of utter destruction to answer these questions. In doing so, Strath managed to provide a hint of the unknowable brutality of life in post-attack Britain. As Jeff Hughes puts it: 'in constructing their imaginary space of the thermonuclear apocalypse and after, the planners literally reached the limits of language – not just the indescribable, but also the *unthinkable*'.[114] The language of nuclear attack was unremittingly bleak from 1945 onwards. Words and phrases such as 'destruction', 'catastrophe' and 'survival' littered planning documents, and the Hall Report of 1953 had discussed the threat of national oblivion. Few discussing nuclear attack in atomic age Whitehall could be accused of hyperbole – the language used understandings of potential destruction, and the ability to articulate what such destruction meant, to its limit. The hydrogen bomb went beyond such limits. The Strath Report had to utilise the same words, but they now meant different things. Looking into the abyss of nuclear war was a difficult and painful business: Philip Allen, later Lord Allen of Abbeydale, always declined to revisit the memories of that 'terrible committee on a terrible subject'.[115] How politicians reacted to this picture of the abyss and its call for a substantial civil and home defence effort will be seen in the next chapter.

5
Years of Decision

The two years following the Strath Report of 1955 saw fundamental change in civil defence. Strath had concluded that to save lives, and to recover as a nation, in a nuclear war wide-ranging measures would need to be implemented. Officials and Ministers initially seemed positive towards Strath's recommendations, with many specific policies approved in principle. When the time came to approve the measures supported in the report, however, the money was not forthcoming. Caught at a time of financial difficulty, Ministers baulked at approving the first tranche of money towards its implementation. As this first year's cash was less than would be needed in following years, it became clear by the end of 1955 that it was very unlikely that Strath would be implemented. Once it became clear that the government would not be able to afford to fund the measures needed, the pro-Strath Home Office was exposed to a re-drawing of strategic needs to meet economic realities. In 1956, civil defence was cut and this was justified on the twin grounds that expensive 'recovery' measures could not be afforded and that civil defence would not really save many lives in the increasingly unlikely event of a global war. The 1955–56 period, then, saw civil defence reach crisis point. It was then that it was finally and decisively decided that civil defence was too expensive in relation to the chance of war and its efficacy in saving lives.

The implementation of the Strath Report

A month after Strath had reported, the incoming Prime Minister, Sir Anthony Eden, was being briefed about its conclusions ahead of the Defence Committee meeting which was to approve them.[1] Sir Norman Brook, who produced the brief, left Eden in no doubt about the effects of an attack. Under enemy attack Britain faced 'human and material destruction on an appalling scale'.[2] The old assumption that Britain could serve as a supply base for forces on mainland Europe was gone. Eden was sternly informed that there were no alternatives to these facts despite 'a natural temptation to shrink from applying them stringently and to hedge against the possibility that war may take a different form'. The limited funds had to be dedicated to dealing with 'the most likely and most dangerous possibility'. The Prime Minister was informed that 'it would be possible to contain its effects and enable the nation to survive if adequate preparations were made in advance'. These preparations, Brook informed him, included the 'most difficult and politically sensitive' policies: shelter and evacuation. Brook himself told Eden that some form of evacuation was 'necessary' as was some 'simple construction' to protect against fallout.[3]

Brook was clearly profoundly affected by the Strath Report. In previous debates over civil defence, Brook had advised that shelters were financially prohibitive and that, strategically, they were unnecessary. His views had now changed, and his advice to Eden reflected the belief that the power of the hydrogen bomb and the devastating potentialities of fallout demanded some sort of protection. This did not represent a conversion to full-scale civil defence provision on Brook's part; rather it reflected the fact that although British defence strategy must continue to rely on the power of offensive, the risk of utter destruction seemed to demand some degree of shelter provision.

Eden's brief was a distillation of the initial reactions to Strath formed in various Whitehall meetings.[4] As well as providing Prime Ministerial information these meetings set the planning agenda for the next few years in three key ways. The first, as Eden had been informed, was that Britain could no longer pursue a policy of broken-backed warfare, meaning that many of the measures paid for in the atomic age to aid the military were no longer worthwhile as, post-attack, there would be no way of physically supplying mainland Europe.[5] The second was the decision to adopt for planning purposes the assumption that 'the Government would be able to detect a serious deterioration in the international situation some six months before war came and would know, say, seven days in advance that an attack on this country was to be expected'.[6] Such an assumption was very useful for planners – it meant that many costly or detailed preparations could be left to the last moment to be completed in the six months' warning period. A week-long attack warning would fit in nicely with the need for a structured evacuation of the big cities. Despite the fact that the military always stressed the uncertainty of any such warning period and that

Strath had warned that preparations had to be firmly in place before a war, this assumption remained in place for the rest of the decade.

The final key element was the conclusion that there was no point in Ministers and officials attempting to explain to the public the dangers of thermonuclear war 'until they could tell them at the same time what measures could be taken'. Otherwise, such knowledge 'would breed despair... and encourage the view that civil defence preparations were a waste of time and money'.[7] In one of these meetings Strath himself had argued that 'he had been struck by the tremendous difference between what would happen if people know what the hydrogen bomb could do and what preparations could be taken against it, and what would happen if the public were left in ignorance'.[8] The decision that knowledge about the bomb and knowledge about mitigating measures should advance hand-in-hand was a sound one, but rather rested on the twin assumptions that the government would both be in a position to announce such measures relatively speedily, and that it would be confident that the public would like what it heard. In the event, policy discussions progressed very slowly and ended by refusing to countenance expensive measures, meaning that the public learned through other sources about the true effects of the weapon and the government was in no position to sweeten the bitter medicine with the honey of civil defence.

Such consequences were of course in the future when Whitehall, under the leadership of Brook, began to piece together the policy implications of Strath. One of the first jobs undertaken was the re-structuring of the machinery of government, part of a wider attempt to streamline decision-making in the defence sphere.[9] The Ministerial side was agreed by Eden after it was thrashed out between Selwyn Lloyd (the new Defence Minister) and Gwilym Lloyd-George, in the summer of 1955. A new committee, the Home Defence (Ministerial) Committee would co-ordinate the military side of home defence (chaired by Lloyd). 'Under that committee', Lloyd suggested, would be the existing Ministerial Committee on Civil Defence under Lloyd-George. On the official level, Brook's Home Defence Committee would report to Lloyd's committee (despite Lloyd contradicting himself in the same paper, saying it would 'normally' report to the Ministerial Committee on Civil Defence) whilst the Official Committee on Civil Defence would report to either the Ministerial Committee on Civil Defence or, through Brook's committee, to the Home Defence (Ministerial) Committee sitting on top of the planning tree. Overall, Lloyd believed 'that this arrangement would clarify the chain of responsibility'. As may be guessed, the opposite proved true.

Rather than supplying the proposed 'high level co-ordinating body for the military and civil sides of home defence' it just led to a replication of work and the tendency of successive Ministers of Defence to regard themselves as *de facto* overlords of civil defence planning. The respective names of the two Committees implied a distinction between civil and home defence that did not really exist. In an age in which the nation's post-attack aim was survival, how could there be? All civil defence policy decisions went to the Lloyd's Ministerial Committee, except evacuation, and this only because the Department actually responsible for the policy – Housing and Local Government – was unrepresented on the more senior body. In fact Lloyd-George's body was essentially relegated to a sub-committee on evacuation, meaning that the majority of Ministers with an interest in civil defence were placed on an emaciated civil defence committee but excluded from its home defence cousin, never participated in the top-level decision-making.

This confusing hotch-potch only lasted until Macmillan became Prime Minister in January 1957 and placed home defence more firmly within the purview of a heavyweight Home Secretary, R.A. Butler. But the reforms of 1955 did have more positive implications on the official level: Brook transferred the chairmanship of the Official Committee on Civil Defence from the Home Office to the Cabinet Office, and made the CDJPS a Cabinet Office group, now renamed the Civil Defence Planning Committee (CDPC). These changes greatly loosened the Home Office's stranglehold on civil defence policy-formulation and meant that draft plans would be produced with a greater awareness of, and sensitivity to, wider government aims and strategies. Far from being arid technical matters, these machinery of government reforms shaped the Whitehall response to Strath. Placing the Minister of Defence in a prime co-ordinating role would have decisive effects on the future of civil defence, and alongside the changes to the official committee structure, weakened the strongly pro-Strath Home Office and increased the influence of those more likely to argue that the deterrent made high levels of spending on civil defence unnecessary.

When officials actually settled down to draft and cost Strath-inspired policies in May 1955, Brook informed them they were working to a timetable. New plans had to be completed by the end of September in order to finalise the civil defence budget for 1956/7 and to enable Ministers to announce any revised civil defence policy.[10] The main policy areas for revision were shelter, evacuation, fire-fighting, medical services, water supply, communications and broadcasting, stockpiling and the 'due functioning' of essential industries. Discussions on these topics took place over the summer.[11] All were vital, although evacuation was less immediately pressing given the lack of cost implications. Shelter was also handled separately, a testament to its political and financial importance. The report Brook sent to Ministers on 11 October, then, was one of a series of 12 papers passed around the now labyrinthine committee structure dealing with the future civil defence budget, *excluding* shelter, in the last months of 1955.[12]

The figures were enormous. Brook informed Ministers that it was believed the stockpiling of vital food, oil, medical and other essential supplies in order to prevent 'people dying of starvation, exposure or disease' in a future war would cost some £383 million, including the construction of storage facilities, and an additional £30 million a year to maintain.[13] Stockpiling was vital, Ministers were told, 'although this part of the Home Defence Programme is not one which attracts much public attention'. It was these measures which would determine the manner of Britain's recovery from nuclear attack. Only by stockpiling fuel, medical supplies and food could people who endured the initial attack also hope to live through the grim struggle for survival that would typify life in thermonuclear Britain. The civil defence services needed £78 million of capital expenditure, which included £11 million for radiation-measuring instruments and some £40 million for fire-fighting equipment, and £7 million per year for upkeep. More than £38 million was needed to provide protected accommodation for the central and regional government headquarters as well as police and civil defence local accommodation. Although 'no preparations can prevent extremely severe dislocation of public utilities' in war, Brook believed a programme costing £80 million would be needed to secure electricity supplies.[14] Including the 'Home Defence' share of the Post Office's defence spending on communications, this amounted to capital expenditure of £628 million, with a recurring cost of about £50 million a year on completion.[15]

Brook defended such levels of proposed expenditure by stressing that although 'active' defence preparations to meet a global war were being scaled back in favour of measures to meet limited emergencies, the measures were 'essential, not only to support the deterrent, but as minimum insurance' in case deterrence failed. A further reason for adopting such a programme, Brook argued, was that 'public opinion was naturally expecting some increased emphasis on these measures' both from 'general reasoning' and the government's own stance in the 1955 Defence White Paper. The proposed £628 million plan envisaged a seven-year programme ranging from £78 million in 1956/57, rising to £150 million in

1960/61, and then falling to £128 million in 1962/63. Selling the now strategically redundant stockpiles of industrial war materials that had been accumulated since 1950 would bring in £20–25 million a year over the course of the programme – meaning that in the coming year planners were asking for around £50 million *net*, with much heavier calls to come.[16]

When Ministers debated the expenditure the argument that 'it would create a deplorable impression on Parliament and the public if the effect of the review of home defence policy in the light of the hydrogen bomb was seen to be expenditure appreciably lower than in 1955–56, and considerably lower than in earlier years'[17] was a powerful one. People would expect the budget to increase. It had been cut dramatically over the previous years as Ministers and officials put together successive budgets in an atmosphere of strategic uncertainty. It was a long time since the Attlee Government had put together a three-year plan in 1950/51. Since the decision in late 1952 that civil defence expenditure could be cut as previous post-attack measures were unlikely to prove effective, it had suffered severe year-to-year downward pressure as a succession of reviews curtailed the limits of what was possible for civil defence to achieve. So after three years of annual deliberations and cuts, 1955 was a chance to settle policy for the rest of a decade. The future direction of policy could be decided at this point.

Policy was not decided at this moment, however. Although the whole Strath-derived plan called for a seven-year programme, the economic difficulties being experienced by the government – a result of the economy being allowed to overheat in the build-up to the 1955 election – meant that attention was focussed on next year's expenditure only.[18] Once the Defence Committee decided that stockpile sales could not be used to offset new expenditure, the first instalment of the plan was in danger. Instead of £78 million, the Treasury insisted – and economic imperative agreed – that the budget be restricted to under £50 million. The final figure of £44.66 million allowed for some £16 million to be spent on stockpiling (as opposed to the planned £40 million) with the food stockpile taking the brunt of the cuts. The remaining £28.4 million was declared to be the 'minimum needed to maintain public confidence'.[19] Over £33 million was cut from the proposed civil defence budget, and at the same time Strath was scuppered. The original £78 million plan had been the first, relatively small, instalment of a seven-year plan. Economic crisis in 1955 cut year one, and the legacy of yearly expenditure crises made the Treasury loath to agree to burdensome commitments in years ahead. The home defence budget would have to face the yearly gauntlet, and with little optimism: the Defence White Paper announcing the new policy was designed to avoid any suggestion that that expenditure would rise appreciably from the level set in late 1955.[20]

Given the outcome of the general war planning measures, perhaps shelter provision was always doomed. It did not stop the Home Office and its Minister, Gwilym Lloyd-George, staging a sustained campaign to have shelter policy adopted. Strath had argued that shelters 'should in principle be provided on a nation-wide scale',[21] and Brook had suggested the same to Eden in the summer of 1955.[22] We can see that there was real support within Whitehall for the provision of fallout shelters *in principle*. Whereas the officials debating the intricacies of policy got weighed down in an acrimonious dispute over the worth or otherwise of providing shelters in newly-built housing, principle played a large role in the Ministerial debates over shelter, and Lloyd-George kept to his case that shelters were necessary to save lives.[23] Officials were debating the new-build option as a way to ensure some provision if Ministers rejected full-scale provision – with some arguing it would provide worthwhile protection and others stressing that such provision would be so-haphazard as to be worthless.[24] These debates were based on awareness that shelters for all would cost £1,250 million in total – whereas new build only would amount to £30 million a year.[25] But whereas officials were attempting to provide a fall-back provision, Lloyd-George was interested in the full Strath.

The shelters in question were trench-style affairs, covered with earth in gardens or cellars, likened to an inspection pit in a garage. They would provide fallout protection but nothing else. They would, however, save many lives and Lloyd-George ensured the casualties were at the forefront of everyone's mind when Ministers met to discuss the policy. He argued that 'radioactive fallout would cause a very large number of casualties unless some form of shelter was provided for the population',[26] outlining the Strath analysis of the need for shelters – that, unprepared, Britain would suffer 12 million deaths from a hydrogen attack with 3 million injured and 13 million more trapped in their homes, many suffering from radiation sickness.[27] The Home Secretary noted that evacuation was essential to reduce deaths, but it could not replace shelters as it increased the numbers pinned down by fallout and, without shelters in addition, 'the numbers who will be sick and who will die from radiation' would rise. He also tackled the cost issue head on: although providing all houses with shelters would cost £1,250 million, or £62.5 million a year for 20 years starting in 1957/8, 'alarming as these figures are they would not appear so to the man in the street while we are spending some £1,500 million a year on defence'.[28]

Lloyd-George pressed home the obvious need for shelters. The heavy casualties estimated could not be kept secret: 'any intelligent person in possession of a population density map of this country and details of the effect of thermonuclear weapons, which have been officially given to the public in America, and indeed to civil defence authorities in this country, can forecast comparable casualty figures'.[29] Simply, 'it is in my view the duty of the Government, by planning evacuation and by the gradual provision of shelter, to reduce the possibilities of casualties on this scale'. Without shelters, morale would be endangered, and there was little point 'keeping forces for the "hot war" if the morale of this country is to collapse and we lose the will to fight'. The Government would be 'politically vulnerable' if no shelters were provided, given that they had been in 1939–45 and 'casualties would be immeasurably greater in another war'.[30]

Lloyd-George's plan that the Government should announce in Parliament its intention to build shelters in new houses and embark on a long-term plan of shelter building for existing housing was fiercely resisted when the Ministerial Committee on Home Defence met on 27 October 1955.[31] Although he argued that 'if the Government are to announce that any expenditure on the provision of shelter was impracticable the consequences were difficult to predict but would certainly be very serious', the Committee stood against him. General Brownjohn 'said that he was sure the Chiefs of Staff would be seriously alarmed at a proposal that a sum of the order [proposed]... should be spent on what was a purely passive measure. It would be a sum comparable to what was being spent on the primary deterrent to war'. Selwyn Lloyd admitted 'that the problem was an extremely difficult one. He fully realised the force of what the Home Secretary had said. On the other hand, the primary objective was to prevent war, and a sum of this order spent on medium bombers would be much more likely to influence the decision of the aggressor than the same sum spent on shelter'.[32]

Thinking inside the Air Ministry, as evidenced by a brief for George Ward, Under Secretary of State for Air, agreed with this – £62.5 million a year was too much to pay for the deterrent value of shelters. It was also felt that in the long term 'expenditure on shelter policy is likely to compete with the amount of money spent on the active deterrent'.[33] Its impact on morale was doubted: 'is it really true that the public would feel comforted by the knowledge that a house in the London area had a shelter of the "inspection pit" type?' Finally, it was 'difficult to see that shelters... would make a great deal of difference to the number of casualties' in London and other target areas.[34]

When the Defence Committee met on 7 December 1955 – the same meeting which also rejected the seven-year plan – Lloyd-George attempted a final push to convince his colleagues of the need for shelters but found it impossible to overcome the financial objections.[35] One consideration was that he was calling for spending on shelters for homes at a point when the Government had reduced the housing programme on economic grounds. It was quietly decided that 'the financial and economic situation precluded a programme for the construction of domestic shelter at public expense'.[36] Shelter policy was effectively dead. Never again would it be seriously investigated as a pursuable policy: its economic ramifications were too enormous to countenance.

Evacuation

Pushed back by the discussions over budgets and shelters, evacuation was discussed between November 1955 and February 1956. A central policy in the Strath Report, evacuation had always held pride of place in war planning for its cheap, effective way of saving lives. Strath argued that the priority classes – children, mothers and the elderly and infirm – should be removed from large evacuation areas. Non-essential workers from the 'central target areas' should be 'dispersed', while the remainder who needed to stay dispersed locally as far as possible. The first post-Strath scheme put forward by planners in November 1955, the first of a series of proposals and counter-proposals over the following months, ran along these lines.[37]

By excluding smaller areas previously designed to be evacuated but deemed unlikely to be hydrogen bomb targets, such as Brighton and Grimsby, the plan amounted to 11.25 million people in the priority classes within the evacuation areas. To be dispersed were 2.8 million non-essential workers and 1.8 million essential workers in the inner 'areas of highest density of population' (no longer called the High Risk Areas, as the term was apparently 'liable to misinterpretation' – the term 'Target Area' was also discouraged), namely London, Birmingham, Liverpool, Manchester and Glasgow, which all had over 1 million people living within a five mile radius of the city centre. This plan to evacuate or disperse these people raised difficult questions: how to define these inner areas, how to define those 'essential' workers who would not be evacuated but only dispersed to the edges of such areas, how to enforce the distinction, and how to justify excluding the five other areas with central populations of over 500,000 from the scheme?

Limited dispersal was intended to keep people at work; industrial workers and their essential office staff in plants which were impossible to move, virtually all transport workers, and the workers needed to maintain essential utilities and services, all were to stay. For this scheme to work, planning would have to proceed 'on the assumption that the Government of the day would not delay putting into effect some measure of evacuation until war seemed certain', because it would take 11 days to complete the evacuation of London. Even that was a best case scenario. Given this requirement, it was also necessary that the scheme catered 'for the possibility that the outbreak of war might be delayed for some time after the evacuation has been carried out, or might indeed never come at all'. For this reason, 'plans must not therefore bring the life of the community to a stop merely on a threat of war'.[38]

When the plan came before Brook's Home Defence Committee, the dispersal issue was earnestly debated.[39] Were all these workers needed? Wouldn't economic life be disrupted anyway by such a mass evacuation? If war came the extra economic dislocation would not matter, and if it did not people would be so relieved as to soon forget. So why not just let police, fire-fighters and essential utility workers remain? This view was attacked as a dangerous 'counsel of despair'. Measures to reduce economic dislocation were vital on two counts: first, if evacuation was ordered at the sign of war 'the Russians would be able to ruin us by frequent threats of war'; second, without measures to minimise economic disruption a government might be dangerously reluctant to order evacuation until war was certain, in which case 'it would almost inevitably be ordered too late'.[40] These issues were not resolved when Ministers on Lloyd-George's Civil Defence Committee met to discuss the plan. Just before they did, the Treasury Minister involved, Henry Brooke, received a brief which cast serious doubts over the whole scheme.

Penned by Sir Alexander Johnston, Brooke's brief clearly felt the plan was neither coherent nor plausible.[41] The complete disruption to production that an attack would undoubtedly bring would leave those men 'asked to let their families go and to stay because their work was vital to the country... hanging about without enough to do'. Johnston argued that the planners 'seem appalled by the idea of a 95 per cent or 98 per cent evacuation of these high density areas and they look round for some way in which to reduce the commitment they are undertaking'. He thought that 'there would in fact have to be almost complete evacuation of these areas, certainly of Central London', and that 'every attempt to interest people in civil defence by painting the full horrors of the hydrogen bomb makes it less likely that people would be willing to remain behind in areas where certain destruction seemed to await them'.[42]

Yet despite this, Johnston attacked the basis on which the Home Office and the Ministry of Housing and Local Government planned to evacuate those they had earmarked: 'it is all very well for officials to lecture Ministers... on the need to order the evacuation of priority classes at an early date; but Ministers will not take early decisions on this, nor will the public accept evacuation until things are looking pretty dark'.[43] He went on: 'we are not dealing with pawns who can be moved across the chess board to the whims of officials'; families would stay together in an emergency, and it would be difficult to persuade fathers to remain behind. A compulsory, rather than voluntary scheme might be necessary. 'One is dealing with an unprecedented risk, whereas the Ministry of Housing still cling to the idea of a glorified Sunday School picnic'. Finally, he attacked the two arguments against mass evacuation of the areas of 'high density' population: firstly, 'that it would be impossible to get workers to remain in places like Coventry and Sheffield if workers in the five main areas of population had been allowed to go'. Johnston believed it 'quite impossible... that large numbers of highly-skilled workers are to be left to certain death in Central London solely because it was thought undesirable that workers in Coventry or Sheffield should leave these towns'. Secondly, on the lack of billets in the reception areas, Johnston argued that more people could be put in the same number of rooms: 'the problem is not the physical impossibility of billeting much larger numbers in the reception areas, but the degree of discomfort which can be tolerated'.[44]

Johnston's paper demonstrates the enormous problem of formulating a sensible evacuation policy. There was no official agreement on the policy to be pursued, and an analysis of Johnston's penetrating but contradictory paper explains why. Here was a Treasury Minister being briefed that the evacuation policy did not go far enough and that it should plan to evacuate the whole of the five designated areas, and others, but also that it was unrealistic in believing that evacuation could be started before war was deemed inevitable. Johnston clearly did not take into account the constraining factor of the limited capacity of the transport services. The 11 days plan was essential because that was the fastest London could be evacuated. It was clearly impossible to evacuate more people than the plan envisaged in less time than originally allocated. Although Johnston was correct in questioning the possibility of an early evacuation, as well as in arguing that London would probably need to be evacuated wholesale, he seemingly failed to understand that such a policy was impossible: the population of these cities would not be magically evacuated from the cities on the say-so of a senior Treasury civil servant.

The contentiousness of the plan was further demonstrated when Ministers finally debated the issue on 11 January 1956.[45] Peter Thorneycroft, the President of the Board of Trade, argued that 'he did not attach any weight to the importance of keeping industry going once the Government had decided to start evacuation.... Any plans that were approved ought to be for evacuating as many people as possible on the basis of an orderly and phased programme'. Iain Macleod, the Minister of Labour and National Service, also 'thought it important to define objectives. We could either plan to save life to the maximum possible extent, or to keep industry going. We could not plan to do both at the same time... the principle should be to save lives'. This seemed to be accepted, and it was clear that Ministers disagreed with the original plan, believing that 'the plan should provide for the evacuation of virtually the whole population of all the evacuation areas'.[46] Although the length of time such an evacuation would take was realised, a phased plan starting with the priority classes and leaving the essential workers until last would at least 'have as its stated objective the virtually complete evacuation of all evacuation areas (though it was admittedly unlikely that time would be available for so large a move)'.[47]

These conclusions were fleshed out by Lloyd-George for further discussion – the virtual complete evacuation of the evacuation areas (some 97 per cent) amounted to 24 million people, more than double the original number planned. The Home Secretary admitted that 'such a plan is never in fact likely to be carried through to completion, but we feel that it is essential to make it, to announce it and to put it into operation if the situation ever called for it'.[48] He conceded that substantial criticisms of the policy would have to be faced: it would cripple production in an emergency; the decision on which necessary skeleton key workers would stay would be a difficult one; there was the danger of inducing panic; it would entail breaking up the family unit; it would destroy civil defence recruitment in the evacuation areas. These were acknowledged by Lloyd-George, but he argued that none were decisive, and the policy of saving as many lives as possible should be paramount.

The new 24 million policy was much simpler and in a way more realistic than its predecessor: industrial production would have been impossible to maintain once evacuation had begun. The comments on Lloyd-George's paper bore this out, although a couple of Ministers seemed uncomfortable with the new policy.[49] Patrick Buchan-Hepburn, the Works

Minister, argued that such a scheme would immediately cripple the nation's industrial production, and he doubted 'whether the decision would ever in fact be taken; but if it were it might mean that we had lost the war before a single bomb had been dropped'. Aubrey Jones, Minister of Fuel and Power, argued that such a scheme would be seen as 'manifestly impossible' to implement and would destroy public confidence: 'we should in effect be proclaiming that practically every urban area in this highly urbanised country would be uninhabitable'.[50]

In response to these comments, Lloyd-George presented his colleagues with two alternatives which would substantially alter the new evacuation policy: 'to divide the evacuation areas into two classes, from the first of which there would be virtually complete evacuation of the whole population, and from the second, evacuation of the priority classes only' (the former areas would now be the ten most densely populated areas); or 'to limit evacuation to the priority classes in all the evacuation areas roughly defined as at present, and to make no organised plan for the evacuation of other classes of persons'.[51] The first option, Lloyd-George conceded, might lead to unauthorised total evacuation in other areas not selected. The second alternative would 'avoid the objection that by closing down production we should be planning to eliminate ourselves from the struggle before a blow is struck', as well as avoiding over-congestion in the reception areas. No mention was made of the fact that in a nuclear war it would leave millions in central London, Birmingham, Liverpool, Manchester, Glasgow and other cities.

Duncan Sandys, Minister of Housing and Local Government, made a final plea for the 24 million scheme, calling for a variegated policy of evacuation for the priority classes, and then workers, from all evacuation areas as the Government saw fit in an emergency. When Ministers met to discuss it on 6 February 1956,[52] however, support for the maximum evacuation scheme fell away. The scheme re-imposing a division between high density and other evacuation found no supporters. Sir Walter Monckton, the Minister of Defence, 'had no hesitation in ruling out the proposal for discriminating between different classes of evacuation area..... It followed, in his view, that a scheme based on the priority classes only would constitute the right approach at this stage'.[53]

In an impressive retreat from what must have seemed the fevered atmosphere of the previous month, Ministers lined up to knock the full scheme down, praising the 'women and children first' doctrine, and stressing that full evacuation would 'undermine the country's will to resist'. It was clearly felt that a priority-classes-only policy would be manageable and that refusing to evacuate any workers would have less disastrous consequences than evacuating some. Only Macleod stood up for Sandys. He 'regretted any withdrawal' from the original scheme, and 'failed to see how any plan could secure public support and confidence that might leave the working population to feel that they had been disregarded in the official plans'. But it was to no avail. Lloyd-George summed up on the basis of planning only for the evacuation of the 11.5 million priority classes. Although the intention was to plan only for the priority classes, it was hoped in an emergency to remove 'as many as possible of the rest of the population' from the evacuation zones, 'to the extent that facilities were available and time permitted'.[54] In the space of a few weeks Ministers had rejected a scheme to evacuate and disperse 16 million people, replaced it with one to evacuate 24 million, and then torn up their own scheme in favour of evacuating under 12 million.

There would be enormous logistical barriers to the success of any evacuation scheme. It was clear that everything rested on the Government ordering evacuation with enough time to evacuate London, meaning before war was deemed unavoidable, but it was open to debate whether such a policy would ever be carried through. Equally unknowable was the impact evacuation would have on the ordinary population: would it have caused panic, unauthorised flight, a crippling of production and a collapse of the public's will fight? So much of any evacuation policy, and therefore civil defence policy in general, rested on little more than partially educated guess-work on how millions of individuals would react in that final, unthinkable emergency. These imponderable questions, which went to the heart of civil defence policy and Britain's capacity to wage nuclear war, remained unanswered. In the end pragmatism ruled. The simple fact of the unlikelihood that anywhere near 24 million people could be evacuated probably did most to kill the policy off, and the fact that the 12 million 'women and children first' would be simpler, both logistically and 'morally', ensured it was favoured.

The 1956 Defence White Paper announced that the Government 'have reached the conclusion, which they are sure will find general support, that first attention must be given to the evacuation of "priority classes"'.[55] After this had been agreed, a meeting of the Ministerial Committee on Home Defence was called to clarify the extent to which Monckton, in his Commons speech, would indicate that evacuation could be extended beyond the priority classes.[56] Lloyd-George warned against any indication 'that they regarded wholesale evacuation as a desirable objective, to be secured as transportation etc., permitted'. It would lead to 'chaos'. Sandys argued that 'he had only agreed to the more limited statement about evacuation in the White Paper on the understanding that something more would be said during the defence debate'. It was essential, he believed, 'that during the course of the debate at least a brief indication should be given that evacuation would not stop with the priority classes'.[57] Sandys was again defeated, however, and in Monckton's speech the stress was laid on the enormity of the plan to move 12 million people rather than on the need to move more.[58] Reaction to the Government's new civil defence policy was dominated by Monckton's announcement of the 12 million evacuation scheme,[59] rather than the White Paper's argument that the civil defence budget be cut because thermonuclear weapons lessened the risk of an all-out global war.[60] The *Daily Mirror* used the lack of detail to criticise the government's policy, declaring that 'the public demands facts, details and reasons' and that the basic questions 'Where? How?' had been left answered.[61] For the *Observer*, however, the emphasis on evacuation directed attention from the major issue: ensuring the continued nuclear protection of the United States.[62]

The end of Strath

The government's economic crisis deepened throughout 1956, and successive waves of belt-tightening profoundly influenced civil defence provision for the rest of the decade. Indeed, the policy decisions made rapidly in an unpleasant economic landscape proved more durable than the policies so painstakingly put together after the Strath Report was completed. They put to bed all talk of saving lives after attack and allowed policy some stability for the first time in a turbulent half a decade in British nuclear history. The immediate context for the policy reappraisal was Chancellor of the Exchequer Harold Macmillan's quest – and that is an apt word – for savings throughout 1956. In his diary Macmillan stated that he sought 'to save the economy from a complete collapse'.[63] In fact, one of Macmillan's first acts as Chancellor was to stymie the Strath-inspired seven-year plan, keeping expenditure below the proposed £70 million to an agreed £55 million.[64] That was on 3 January 1956. Twenty-three days later, he shaved £10 million off the civil defence budget down to the £44.66 million announced in the Defence White Paper.[65] In his 17 April Budget, Macmillan promised £100 million of further government savings, and the next months saw agonising within the government about how this could be achieved.

Civil Defence took an early cut of £5 million in May, achieved by slowing down construction of the Royal Observer Corps posts designed to monitor fallout, reducing outlay on radiation-measuring and fire-fighting equipment, and postponing the third Mobile Defence Corps training depot.[66] In complaining about this cut, Lloyd-George expressed 'serious concern at the singling out of home defence for this quite disproportionate cut'.[67] Home defence was being cut by 11 per cent, compared to 3 per cent of active defence and 4 per cent off the civil vote. Even worse was to come for the embattled Home Secretary. Reacting to the cut, he had asked Walter Monckton, the new Defence Secretary, for his support if departments were pressed to go further than this reduction.[68] The events of the following month were to show Lloyd-George just how little support would be forthcoming from Monckton.

Concurrently with these debates a select group of Ministers were discussing the future strategic direction of Britain in a 'Policy Review Committee' (PR).[69] The review did not really question Britain's wider economic and political strategy, only 'the demands placed on it'.[70] Instead, PR descended into a vehicle for delivering Macmillan's £100 million cuts and petered out as Ministerial interest was diverted by the erupting Suez crisis. In defence terms, however, it can be seen as an antecedent of the Sandys White Paper,[71] a point when, according to Macmillan's diary, the military were 'gradually beginning not only to talk about the Hydrogen Bomb strategy but to contemplate putting it into effect'.[72] Moreover, the review had grave implications for home defence.[73]

The Ministers on PR included Eden, Macmillan, Monckton, Selwyn Lloyd (now Foreign Secretary) and Lord Salisbury (Lord President of the Council). No Ministers who had responsibility for civilian preparations for war were part of the group, meaning that its policy on home defence was instigated and shaped by Monckton. On 7 June 1956 he submitted a paper proposing a radical rethink of home defence policy. He argued that 'we should discontinue expenditure which is designed to enable us to "survive" a war and to "recover"'.[74] All that should be continued were 'those home defence preparations the absence of which would be liable to undermine the deterrent'. These were: 'measures for the continuity of government and the control of the population under attack; communications for air defence and for air-raid warning; and the maintenance and training of civil defence forces and of military forces allocated to home defence'. These three policy strands were needed because without them 'all central command would come to an end and complete chaos would ensue the moment the first bombs fell'. The pace of preparations should be slackened in line with 'the fact that we do not think war is very likely in present circumstances'.[75] This meant that the stockpiling programme could be run down, and the construction of government control centres eased.

Monckton had given thought to the public impact of such a scheme. The reduction of civil defence 'should not be so abrupt as to cause a shock to our allies and our own public'.[76] This meant not ceasing stockpiling immediately. It also meant 'we must be prepared to explain publicly... that in the present circumstances we are concentrating our efforts on the level of home defence preparations which is necessary to enable our deterrent to continue to work: that within these limits, our home defence preparations will be realistic and not a façade'. Monckton was advocating coming clean with the public over civil defence: admitting it was for deterrent purposes only, and not life-saving. This stance created some ambiguity over the role of the civil defence services. Monckton argued that they should continue, along with the armed services devoted to civil defence, in order to avoid 'all central command coming to an end', suggesting that Monckton saw their role as a part of the command chain that could gather information and direct the civilian population.[77] It can be assumed that Monckton believed that the Corps was one of those measures which, if cancelled, would 'cause a shock' to the public.

Monckton's new policy would provide immediate savings on stockpiling, allowing the budget to be cut to just £30 million, with it falling to £25–30 million in 1957/58 and then less than £20 million thereafter. When discussed by other Ministers in PR on 9 June, Monckton's colleagues clearly felt uncomfortable with the prospect of entering into a war without sufficient food supplies. It was concluded, however, that even *with* stockpiles war would still be catastrophic for the human race as well as the nation, and given the cost involved – more than £100 million a year for the full Strath preparations – it was preferable to cuts elsewhere. Stockpiles could be increased later, and much quicker than munitions production.[78] Just four days later, Monckton met Lloyd-George, James Stuart (Scottish Secretary) and Derrick Heathcoat-Amory (Minister of Agriculture) in an ad hoc meeting.[79] Monckton told them, rather disingenuously, that there was a defence review going on, the longer term consequences of which were to be discussed later in the Ministerial Committee on Home Defence: the purpose of the ad hoc meeting was to discuss Macmillan's new paper seeking stockpiling cuts. There was certainly no intimation that the impetus behind these cuts came from Monckton himself, and that the future direction of home defence had essentially been settled by senior ministers days before. Forced to acquiesce in the £11.5 million cut, Lloyd-George noted that barely six months previously, the Ministerial Home Defence Committee was recommending a budget of £70 million – it was now

£30 million.[80] The Home Secretary worried that the reduction 'would make it increasingly difficult to convince the local authorities and the public that the Government were taking any serious interest in civil defence preparations and there was a risk that a defeatist attitude would become prevalent'.[81]

Monckton had assumed the role of civil and home defence overlord. In PR he admitted that 'in view of the especial secrecy of the Committee's discussions at the present stage, he had not consulted the Home Secretary or other Civil Ministers concerned in the preparation of his memorandum'.[82] In his ad hoc meeting with Lloyd-George discussion had been based on how the Ministers would 'handle' the Treasury pressure for extra cuts.[83] This dual role could not last, and when Lloyd-George received Monckton's paper outlining the Defence Minister's future policy plans on 18 June,[84] his reaction was fierce. Monckton's policy was due to be discussed only two days later, so Lloyd-George sent a personal minute outlining his concerns.[85] Monckton wished to cut provision to around £20–25 million in future years by reducing expenditure on stockpiling and equipment. Lloyd-George, however, insisted that more thought be given to the issue; he believed stockpiling was necessary and that any decision to abandon it must be based on sound strategic grounds. On equipment, Lloyd-George argued that promising, and then providing, more and better equipment 'has done more than anything else could do to improve morale' of both civil defence volunteers and the local authorities who organised them.[86] Without proper equipment, the civil defence services would indeed be a façade'; with it, the government would avoid 'any further "coventrys"'. The Home Secretary also suggested that the deterrent forces would be undermined without measures to reduce casualties.[87]

Lloyd-George concluded that any workable civil defence policy must cost more than £20–25 million as equipment was essential if it was not to be a sham. He was clearly perturbed about the speed of decision-making. Ministers, himself included, had spent a large part of 1955/56 debating and deciding the policy response to Strath; that carefully-wrought set of policies was now being torn up in very short order. Unlike Monckton, Lloyd-George was not privy to the strategic discussions of PR – and he wanted policy based on a genuine review of civil defence needs, not on short-term pressure to push the home defence budget down. To this end he refused to endorse Monckton's policy when Ministers met, and it was decided to set up a review of 'the possible levels of expenditure on which a coherent home defence policy could be constructed'.[88] The basis of future policy on home defence was entrusted to Brook's Home Defence

Committee. Brook, of course, had been present throughout the deliberations of the Policy Review meetings, and was thus more seized with the necessity of reducing home defence expenditure than the outcast Lloyd-George.

This review was speedily completed – in just nine days – and, unsurprisingly, backed Monckton's 'preservation of the deterrent policy'.[89] It argued that a coherent policy could be provided for £25–30 million, although it was stressed that provision would need to rise if the threat of war increased as without stocks of food and oil and the means of distributing them, 'deaths from starvation in global war might well exceed those from bombing'.[90] Also, HDC made it clear 'that the absence of an insurance against the failure of the deterrent could not be concealed'. If more money was available then stocks could be maintained, but Brook did not probe the option deeply – covering it in two short paragraphs whereas he devoted two and a half pages to Monckton's policy. At this point in the proceedings, Eden sent Monckton a remarkable minute 'to make it clear that your responsibility for the balance within our defence effort covers the defence programme as a whole and not only the programmes of the Services'.[91] This included civil spending on home defence, but that did not 'mean that your relations with the Ministers in charge of these Civil Departments in respect of their defence tasks are the same as your relations with the Service Ministers'. Monckton had over-stepped the mark in his handling of home defence, treating Lloyd-George and Stuart as subservient Ministers, as he did the Minister for Air. Moreover, there was clearly an impression in some quarters that Monckton had used his position not only to exclude other Ministers but to safeguard his own budget at the expense of home defence. Of course, Eden had acquiesced in this as far as he had allowed it to be discussed in PR, but the current dispute meant that the final decision was removed from the Committee chaired by Monckton and taken to the Policy Review Committee – now swelled by the inclusion of Lloyd-George and Stuart, and chaired by Eden himself.

Before Ministers debated the report, Macmillan weighed in on 12 July seeking even more savings. He declared that 'I do not think that we should spend more than £15 million in 1957/58 on defence expenditure by the Civil Departments'.[92] He believed half of this could be spent maintaining existing stores, and the rest on measures which would either 'take a long time to complete, are relatively inexpensive' or which 'would give us a foundation on which we could build a more adequate structure of defence, if the need arose'. This would mean 'a decision to stand down the local civil defence volunteers and have nothing locally except a nucleus organisation which could be expanded – along with other preparations – if the risk of global war came above the horizon'. Macmillan believed 'that there is sufficient in this programme to show the people of this country and any potential enemies abroad that we are prepared to face a hydrogen bomb attack in the unlikely contingency of global war'.[93]

When it met to take the final decision, the Prime Minister was briefed by Brook that PR had 'agreed that we should maintain the minimum element of home defence required to support the deterrent', and that this minimum level had been outlined by Monckton and fleshed out by officials and amounted to spending about £25 million a year.[94] Macmillan's proposal to stand down the Civil Defence Services 'would have to be justified on the basis that we can see no prospect of an attack on this country for many years to come. It would not be consistent with our defence policy generally'. It would 'at least appear to undermine the deterrent', as well as being difficult to defend publicly; 'it would involve admitting Coventry was right'.[95] In the meeting, Macmillan's proposal was savaged by Monckton and Lloyd-George. Monckton explained: 'though the risk of global war in the near future might be remote, the possibility of global war could not be ruled out altogether', and the new policy maintained 'a sufficient level of defence preparations to ensure that the deterrent could operate and that the Russians were not led to believe that they could destroy this country in one attack without being destroyed themselves'.[96] Monckton believed that 'it would be inconsistent to provide the necessary fighters for the protection of the bases, and not to take comparable precautions to maintain the essential civilian infrastructure of the country without which operations could not continue even for the short period now envisaged'. This meant the Civil Defence Services had to be maintained. 'Moreover, if the Civil Defence Services were stood down it would be impossible to conceal the fact, which would be likely to have a disturbing effect' both on 'public opinion and on Britain's allies'.[97]

Lloyd-George, converted to Monckton's plan by the necessity of defending civil defence from Macmillan's even more devastating cuts, weighed in by arguing that £25–30 million a year was 'the lowest level on which it would be possible to maintain a successful home defence programme'.[98] It was his belief that some civil defence preparations were 'essential to the preservation of the deterrent, for example the warning and monitoring system for radioactive fallout'. Also, 'widespread casualties among the civilian population would affect the willingness of the Services to continue active operations'. The continuation of the Civil Defence Services was vital: 'if the volunteers were stood down, the whole organisation would be likely to disintegrate and it would be difficult to build it up again if it were required'. The local authorities 'were already beginning to lose interest in civil defence activities because of their doubts about the Government's attitude' and the steady decline in civil defence spending 'since the development of thermonuclear weapons' had left the 'growing impression that the Government had accepted that nothing could be done about civil defence in global war. There was a risk that a defeatist attitude might spread throughout the country'.[99]

These arguments triumphed, and Monckton's policy was confirmed. Some months later, a three-year plan based on this policy was produced. The report, presented as a Policy Review paper, made it clear just how limited provision would be even in the areas covered by the new scheme.[100] For example, 'no further progress will be made with the long-term plan... to build up stocks of vehicles and equipment' for fire-fighting purposes. The previous policy, to have emergency supplies of water available 'on an operational scale' had been abandoned. The lack of due-functioning measures meant there would be virtually no electricity, and all communications and 'in particular the operation of the warning system would be drastically impaired; wireless communication with the public might become impossible'. There was to be no scheme to decontaminate, or indeed protect, water supplies. Measures on emergency ports – that key policy of the atomic age – would also be stopped. There would only be enough food stockpiled for two weeks post-attack.[101] Although the central alternative seat of government would receive priority, not a single regional headquarters would be finished by 1960.[102] In terms of saving lives, civil defence in the years after 1956 rested on the idea of self-help, aided by a warning system which would at least give the public the chance of survival. In the areas of peripheral damage, it was hoped, the Civil Defence Corps would have a rescue role. The Royal Observer Corps (ROC), and the new United Kingdom Warning and Monitoring Organisation provided the structure for the warning system and fallout monitoring.[103]

The debate over civil and home defence policy in the summer of 1956 was the death-knell to the conception of civil defence as a life-saving programme. Throughout the Second World War, the atomic era, and the early thermonuclear years, planners had sought to save lives in an enemy attack. As the cold war wore on, the limits of civil defence became ever more sharply defined and the possibilities for saving lives were reduced as the costs of doing so were increased. To save lives on the scale envisaged by Strath would have proved hugely expensive. When the Government's finances came under pressure in 1956 a line had to be drawn: gone was any planning for aiding ordinary people in survival or recovery; instead, civil defence was to be subordinated to the deterrent. Two trends in strategic thinking allowed this line to be drawn in such a way. The first was that the threat of global war was seen to have retreated significantly from the early 1950s, meaning that the 'insurance' premium of civil defence could be reduced without undue risk. We can subsequently argue that savings on civil defence – close to £15 million in 1956/57 alone – can be seen as a small 'peace dividend' arising from the de-escalation of cold war tensions in the 1950s.[104] The second was the increasing confidence in nuclear deterrence within British strategic circles. For Monckton, at least, civil defence had little value beyond aiding the credibility of the British deterrent force. Only offensive force would prevent war, and if deterrence failed, then an extra £15 million or so on civil defence would hardly make enemy attack less catastrophic. What the events of 1956 did was push Strath-type civil defence back into a concept. Civil defence logic had previously been clear: the perils of the cold war meant that measures *had* to be taken to mitigate a potential attack. Thermonuclear weapons and early détente had overturned this view; now it seemed more pertinent to argue that war was much less likely and so the countless millions that were needed to fund civil defence properly were better spent elsewhere.

Of course, the new policy had to be announced to the general public. Civil defence advocates believed the reduced policy entailed a large risk. When the new three year civil defence plan had been drafted, planners had stressed 'the difficulty of defending a home defence programme which makes no significant provision for the survival of the country in the event of nuclear attack', suggesting that 'that it might be easier to justify this programme by reference to the general financial and economic conditions than by reference to any revised appreciation of the risk of global war'.[105] In his last civil defence-related act as Home Secretary, Lloyd-George delivered a remarkable valedictory Cabinet paper on 7 January 1957. The new policy, he argued, would cause people to conclude that 'the real reason for the reduction is not so much the reduced risk of war as a Government decision that civil defence preparations are of little value'.[106] He believed that if this view became widespread existing civil defence preparations would be jeopardised, thus undermining the deterrent. Evoking the 'widespread defeatism' felt after knowledge of the hydrogen bomb became public, Lloyd-George warned that only 'reiterated assurances that the Government was still convinced of the value of civil defence' could avert a calamitous collapse of confidence and discourage local authorities following the example of Coventry and abandoning civil defence.[107] Two days later, Eden, broken by Suez, resigned and Lloyd-George was removed by Macmillan, the new premier. This paper was a last roar from a Minister who had devoted much of his time since becoming Home Secretary in October 1954 to dealing with civil defence, and whose humane attempts to secure adequate finances for the protection of the public had been continually brushed aside by colleagues concentrating on economic circumstances.

These warnings were significant. Home Office ministers and officials believed that the public would not accept the view that the deterrent would indeed deter and that the declining prospect of war meant that civil defence preparations could be eased. They believed that people *expected* civil defence plans and that without them they would feel exposed, with the abstract concept of deterrence providing but a thin blanket. Without more protection confidence in any sort of civil defence would collapse, and even Monckton argued that civil defence was needed to maintain the effectiveness of the deterrent: hence the belief that money, rather than strategy, should be used as the justifying cause for the cut. These fears illustrate the enormous divide that had opened up between Home Office and Ministry of Defence on civil defence. Ministry of Defence thinking had won the day in 1956, but the Home Office knew that the proof of the policy's efficacy would lie in the public reaction.

Conclusion

The two years between William Strath completing his report and the new three-year plan were ones of fundamental change in civil and home defence. In March 1955 few people would have expected the 'interim' civil defence budget of £70 million to be cut back so drastically, to less than £22 million in 1957/58. For civil defence planners, the trend of spending had appeared to be upwards. The scale of attack which faced Britain, and the enormous consequences of a lack of adequate measures seemed to demand hefty spending on stockpiling, control measures and life-saving equipment – to say nothing of shelters. All pointed to a budget of over £100 million a year. Yet it became clear during 1955 that such money would not be forthcoming. Financial concerns meant that cash was tight – and immediate need will often trump future contingency. When the Chancellor of the Exchequer sought savings of £100 million, he found 15 of those millions in the home defence budget: there can be little doubt that it was sacrificed to meet more pressing concerns. But there is much more to the reduction of provision than being caught at the wrong point in stop-go cycle. Throughout these two years there was clear and growing concern that the Strath Report's recommendations entailed an enormous commitment over many years. Monckton's actions in the Policy Review Committee need to be seen as the end point of a process which saw expensive life-saving measures as lacking in value – the prospect of war had receded, and worthwhile measures were very expensive. It can be argued that the strategic grounds for the cut masked the fact that Monckton was selling home defence short to protect his own budget, or equally that it masked the view that civil defence would be worthless in a war anyway – a view which would most certainly not have been shared by those in the Home Office. How Whitehall viewed the exact 'worth' of those civil defence measures which remained after 1957 is difficult to judge. The Home Office believed that they could help save lives if a bit more money was spent on them; the Ministry of Defence cared only that they would aid the control of the country; both probably believed that they were politically necessary to avoid controversy. The exact role of civil defence was left ambiguous, testament to the nature in which decision-taking had evolved: the reduction of the civil defence budget *was* ambiguous, a largely financial decision justified on strategic grounds which masked the fact that there was no agreement over what civil defence was actually for.

6
Separate Spheres of Civil Defence

Between the Sandys White Paper of 1957 and the Berlin Crisis of 1959, civil defence policy-making lost its volatility. These two events book-ended a period in which policy was settled, but public debate increasingly fierce; it saw on one hand the announcement of a radical new policy, and on the other the potential problems which a policy created in a period of international tension. The mid-1950s had been tumultuous years for civil defence policy; the cost and possibility of saving lives and planning for recovery had been extensively debated and, in the end, regretfully sidelined. This left civil defence planners in a quandary. What measures *were* going to be taken, and how could the lack of real life-saving measures be explained in public? Over the course of 1957–60 a strategy which had been evolving throughout the 1950s came to fruition: civil defence policy essentially separated into two distinctive spheres. The first was the public one of the Civil Defence Corps. In 1956 the future of the Corps had been guaranteed due to its rather ill-defined role in physically maintaining the nuclear deterrent and because the shock of its immediate axing might prove controversial. In the years after 1957 it became more and more obvious that public civil defence measures were being undertaken mostly to avoid political strife. The rise of the nuclear disarmament movement ensured lengthy public debate about the survivability of nuclear war, which naturally focussed attention on the government's civil defence plans. By 1960, the Corps and its recruitment activities stood in opposition to the nuclear protesters, each presenting different views of nuclear survivability.

If the public sphere of civil defence was concerned with presenting an image of survivable nuclear attack in order to deny the Campaign for Nuclear Disarmament the easy propaganda victory of official recognition of the impossibility of nuclear survival, then the private sphere of civil defence had very different aims. This secret sphere was constructing a control system, from central government down to street-level (it was hoped) which would be able to maintain control of the country after a nuclear war. Only through an alternative system of government, with protected accommodation and communications, could the central tasks of the post-attack phase be undertaken, whether they be launching nuclear retaliation or co-ordinating national recovery. There was no element of façade here: the policy was deadly serious, absolutely top secret, and vital to Britain's chances of postwar survival. In the knowledge of what hydrogen bomb warfare really meant the state felt it could do little within economic reason to save lives, but it knew it could work to ensure that some semblance of government was maintained after an attack; without it, there would only be anarchy.

Presenting deterrence: the Sandys Defence White Paper

As we have seen, Ministerial discussions during 1956 had led to a massive cut in civil defence provision. Gone was the concentration on survival and recovery, and in its place was a policy designed solely to protect the deterrent, based on government control systems, including the civil warning system, and a barely-equipped civil defence force. Despite these discussions, there was still fundamental disagreement between the Home Office and the Ministry of Defence about the utility of civil defence in cold war Britain. Defence officials believed that civil defence needed to be subjugated to the active deterrent, and that the public would accept that the deterrent would preserve peace and thus make expensive civil defence measures unnecessary. Support would be secured only by boldly stating that civil defence cuts were warranted by the decreased likelihood of war.[1] Whereas the Home Office, perennial advocates of thoroughgoing civil defence measures, continued to argue that civil defence had a role to play in saving lives. More importantly, they disagreed with the view that the public would be convinced by exhortations to believe in the value of deterrence, arguing that the lack of life-saving measures could undermine morale and lead to the disintegration of the civil defence forces, undermining the deterrent.[2] Indeed, it was argued in late 1956 that the crises in Eastern Europe and the Middle East hardly suggested war was unlikely; therefore, curtailment of expenditure needed to be justified on economic grounds.[3] The Suez crisis itself, despite the threats of Nikolai Bulganin that rockets were pointed at Paris and London,[4] had little impact on civil defence policy aside from some relatively low-level emergency planning within the Home Office which would later influence government war planning more generally.[5] Although in early 1957 both departments believed that some civil defence was needed for 'insurance' purposes and to prevent political controversy, the extent of that provision – and the justification for reducing it – was bitterly contested. Both stances also raised the prospects of expenditure going back up: in the 'deterrent' way of thinking, this would happen if global war became more likely; for the 'civil defenders', this should happen when economic circumstances allowed.

The fragile nature of the 1956 policy compromise can be seen from the manner in which the policy was announced in the 1957 Defence White Paper – usually called the 'Sandys White Paper' after the new Minister of Defence – where the strategic justifications for civil defence cuts were unclear.[6] Original drafts made it plain that civil defence was being cut for strategic reasons, just as they made it clear that Fighter Command was being scaled back as it could not provide blanket protection against enemy attack.[7] As a result of heavy redrafting, however, the final White Paper deviated from its original intention.[8] Firstly, it stated 'it must be frankly recognised that there is at present no means of providing adequate protection for the people of this country against the consequences of an attack with nuclear weapons'.[9] Whereas such sentiment had originally been designed to illustrate the impossibility of stopping the delivery of bombs,[10] the removal of the original reference to Fighter Command suggested that the government believed that there was no defence at all from the effects of nuclear weapons – which was contrary to all stated civil defence policy. This naturally impacted greatly on the meaning of the section on civil defence, which obviously contradicted it by arguing that 'it would be wrong not to take some precautions to minimise the effects of nuclear attack, should the deterrent fail to prevent war. Civil Defence must accordingly play an essential part in the defence plan'.[11] The redrafted deterrence section undermined civil defence, and the insistence of the new Home Secretary, R.A. Butler, that the White Paper provide a more positive picture of civil defence had the effect of undermining the case for deterrence.[12] The original drafts might have lacked nuance, but the prospect of deterrence failing was barely raised. In the final version, the possibility of its failure and the costs of this happening were dangerously heightened.

Therefore the hugely delayed White Paper actually presented a rather distorted picture of home defence and the deterrent, and the 'no defence' statement would haunt the Conservative government for many years. The initial press reaction, however, was relatively muted, with newspapers understandably more concerned with the defence cuts and the end of conscription. The editorial of the *Daily Mail*, in summarising the White Paper's rationale, echoed Stanley Baldwin's famous comment made a quarter of century before: 'the H-bomber will always get through'.[13] Neither the *Times* nor the *Daily Telegraph* mentioned the 'admission' outside of summaries of the document. The *Manchester Guardian* had it in bold type on the front page,[14] but its leader said 'this is a bold statement, but it will only come as a shock to those who have been cherishing illusions dangerous to themselves'.[15] Within days of the publication of the White Paper in April, however, St Pancras Borough Council decided to follow the example of Coventry in 1954 and renounce civil defence. The row erupted when the Council's General Purposes Committee recommended that civil defence should be stopped because, the Town Clerk informed the Home Office, 'in view of the Government's admission in the recent White Paper that there is no real defence against atomic and hydrogen bomb warfare, we are of the opinion that to continue with civil defence is a complete waste of money'.[16]

An enraged Butler wrote to Sandys the day the St Pancras decision made the evening papers (15 April), informing his colleague that he had been concerned 'at the construction that had been placed on [the crucial 'no defence' sentence] and its possible effect on the public'.[17] He continued: 'I had hoped that the wording we agreed for the paragraphs dealing with civil defence would have been sufficient to safeguard the position, but even in the short time since the publication of the White Paper, it has become increasingly clear that this is not sufficient'. St Pancras was 'the most extreme example of this'. What was more, the Metropolitan Borough called on other local authorities to do the same and impress upon the Government 'the urgency of abolishing all atomic and hydrogen bombs as the only means of abolishing the wholesale slaughter of people in future wars'.[18] Desperate to restrict the malign influence of the 'Communist-controlled' council,[19] Butler implored Sandys to stress the validity of civil defence and quash the 'indefensible' current of argument in the next day's Commons defence debate; but although Sandys added a brief section on civil defence to his speech, he merely echoed the White Paper and failed to adequately expound Butler's views. He did at least stress that 'the nation's available resources should be concentrated not on preparations to wage war so much as on trying to prevent this catastrophe from ever happening',[20] but this hardly suited civil defence's purpose.

Butler himself swiftly moved to crush the St Pancras 'rebellion' in order to stop the 'embarrassment' of other local authorities following suit.[21] But although the issue of St Pancras Council's non-compliance was resolved swiftly, with a Commissioner being appointed to undertake the Council's civil defence functions,[22] it was an embarrassing episode which generated a deal of adverse publicity for the Government's defence policy. Moreover, it seemed to immediately prove the validity of Home Office concerns regarding support for the government's defence policy. Although a look at the press reaction should have placated the Home Secretary, as the *Daily Telegraph* and the *News Chronicle* gave ample space to critics of the St Pancras move,[23] it was a grim warning of the future, as opponents of the Conservative Government's nuclear policy made use of its own published information to launch attacks – especially that single sentence in the Sandys White Paper. It recurred, in mutated form, as a terrible coda damning the Government's policy, reaching its apotheosis early in 1958 when the Campaign for Nuclear Disarmament was formed in London.

Its fingers burnt by the Sandys debacle, the Government retreated from any further public pronouncements on the issue of nuclear war – a policy which it had followed for most of the 1950s. The first official booklet explaining the effects of thermonuclear weapons aimed at the general public was published only in 1957.[24] These deep fears concerning public information reflected a broader culture of secrecy within Whitehall that proved remarkably pervasive. Yet there were also specific fears. The spectre of Coventry loomed large in these thermonuclear years. Gwilym Lloyd-George had been especially quick to suggest that any cut in civil defence provision would have dire consequences among the local authorities.[25] Coventry's actions went to the heart of the government nuclear posture – which argued that some defence could be mounted – and raised the prospect of an unwanted political battle over civil defence and nuclear war. Within Whitehall it seemed imperative to starve such opponents of the ammunition they needed – making the Sandys 'admission' deeply ironic.

An illustrative example of this aversion to publicity was the treatment of a civil defence training manual, 'Radioactive Fallout: Provisional Scheme of Public Control'. This outlined the scheme whereby the Civil Defence Services would control areas affected by fallout and rescue those stranded within them. It was a well thought-out document, which had been first drafted in June 1955, and had been placed on sale for civil defence units, but not the general public. Gwilym Lloyd-George had first attempted to get it published in November 1956 but the Cabinet rejected his plan for two reasons: that if it was published at that point it might be linked with threats of Soviet action during the Suez crisis; and that publication might have the effect of drawing attention to the inadequacy of home defence preparations in general.[26]

In the new Administration four months later, Butler asked Macmillan to reconsider given that the Suez crisis was over, and the Medical Research Council had concurred with the content of the report.[27] Also, as to leading to some sort of pro-civil defence spending clamour, Butler argued that 'past experience suggests that publication is unlikely to occasion any such public response. In fact the less we are able to make large scale physical preparations for home defence the greater becomes the need to show that we are continuing to prepare realistic plans for making the best use of what we can do'. For Butler, there was a great need to publish the document (it had also been foreshadowed in the 1956 White Paper): 'if home defence is to have any meaning a programme of public education of the threat of radioactive fallout is essential. It is a clear duty of the Government to make the facts of nuclear attack known and to give guidance on the kind of plans required to meet the new threat'.[28] Butler was rebuffed, and rebuffed once more when he tried again a month later.[29] He tried a third time in August, and told Macmillan that declassifying the scheme 'would allow us, as opportunity offers, to take credit for a piece of realistic planning, which would provide some answer to the criticisms we constantly face of failing to bring civil defence up to date in relation to the conditions of nuclear warfare'.[30] Yet still Macmillan resisted.[31] When Butler tried for the fourth time, in December 1958, after the local authorities had pressed him to publish it, Macmillan relented.[32]

This was a farcical state of affairs. As Butler pointed out, the memorandum was a rare example of a realistic and effective civil defence plan ready to put into action. Moreover, the Medical Research Council's investigation into *The Hazards to Man of Nuclear and Allied Radiations* had excited little publicity when published in 1956.[33] Macmillan was too scared of the consequences to publish it, an understandable if misguided decision. Publishing it would seem to prove the Government's understanding of the complexities of modern warfare and publicly shown that they were actively planning to save lives. By leaving the public in the dark, it created anxiety over the effects of fallout and showed the Government in the worst possible light, giving the impression that they had no answer to the questions posed by fallout. By the time the pamphlet was published in 1959, the opportunity to shape public opinion on this issue had been lost.[34]

Little changed in terms of civil defence policy in the years following Sandys, with the budget squeezed down to less than £19 million in

1958/59 and staying below £20 million five years running.[35] Policy concentrated on the continued funding of the Civil Defence Corps and other services, and on constructing the alternative system of government. Work on the emergency ports scheme ground to a halt, and the abandonment of the Mobile Defence Corps (MDC) was announced in December 1958, a victim of the end of conscription.[36] The fact that its passing caused not even a ripple in civil defence circles demonstrates how much civil defence thinking had changed. In 1955 the MDC was intended to provide the able-bodied manpower to drive any post-attack rescue effort. It was seen as a central part of the government's plan to cope with thermonuclear war. By 1958, all such plans had gone.

The calm of the post-1956 civil defence world was shaken in 1958 when Macmillan intervened, looking for savings, questioning whether expenditure on civil defence was justified when 'it contributed little towards preparing the country as a whole to withstand nuclear attack'.[37] He thought it 'was illogical to endeavour to increase the numbers who would outlive the immediate effects of a nuclear attack if they and the other survivors were to die thereafter from starvation, thirst or disease'. Personally, Macmillan wanted some degree of recovery measures. He 'doubted... whether it would be politically practicable for the Government publicly to deny all responsibility for the fate of the surviving population in the event of a failure of the deterrent policy'. But providing for both rescue (in the form of the Civil Defence Services) and recovery would be prohibitively expensive, so two options were raised: scrapping the Civil Defence Services and providing some recovery measures with the money saved, or continuing 'the present programme at about the current level of expenditure. This would enable a façade of civil defence preparations to be maintained'.[38]

In the subsequent discussion, the Defence Committee agreed that ideally, something more should be done, but the money could not be found. In the end it was decided that it was safer to do nothing, because 'any change in the existing policy, whether directed to expanding or curtailing the limited preparations already being made, would be liable to attract attention and so to provoke discussion of an issue to which public opinion appeared at present to be remarkably indifferent'. To perpetuate this indifference would be government policy, by continuing the current policy, 'acquiescing in its fundamental illogicality and realising that its main purpose was to maintain the morale of the population rather than to provide them with any effective protection against nuclear attack'. Therefore, the main civil defence effort should be devoted to 'those measures which provided a positive and visible indication of the Government's support for the voluntary civil defence services', such as 'the provision of uniforms and equipment and the holding of civil defence rallies'.[39]

Macmillan's policy was one of privately acknowledged façade. When further attempts to curtail civil defence occurred in 1960, a strategic rationale for their retention was adopted, but for Ministers in 1958 the reason for their existence was clear. To admit they could not save lives would 'undermine morale' which by this time can serve as a euphemism for aiding the disarmament movement. Macmillan's policy really only codified what had been happening since the hydrogen bomb explosions of 1954: providing a public face of nuclear survivability which the government knew to be false. The Civil Defence Corps' role was to convince people that something could be done, denying the likes of Coventry, St Pancras and later the mass-protesters of CND the easy victory of admitting there was no chance of surviving a nuclear war. This meant that much rested on the ability of the Corps to convince the public of this, but it was were never given the wherewithal to do so. Starved of funding, it lacked the equipment and the sophistication to adequately prop up the notion of survivability. With the nuclear disarmers constantly eroding the very idea that nuclear war could be survived, the pillar that was the Corps, already struggling under the weight of its task, would have to come crashing down.

Protesters

Macmillan was talking of public apathy over civil defence at a time when the newly formed Campaign for Nuclear Disarmament was ensuring that nuclear weapons were a major political issue. He was able to do so because in its early years, CND paid little attention to civil defence, concentrating instead on the political aims of securing unilateral nuclear disarmament and mobilising opinion against hydrogen bomb testing. In previous years, the actions of the local authorities in Coventry and St Pancras had shown how opposition to the government's nuclear policy usually expressed itself in antagonism towards civil defence. CND, however, conducted its campaign on a more political and moral plane. In November 1957, J.B. Priestley published his famous article on 'Britain and the Nuclear Bombs' in the *New Statesman* which attacked 'this nuclear madness into which the spirit of Hitler has passed'.[40] It served as a focal point around which the forces which became the Campaign for Nuclear Disarmament coalesced. Yet anti-nuclear sentiment was not created either by Priestley or by those meeting in Canon Collins' rooms in February 1958;[41] it had been building slowly throughout the thermonuclear era. The key historiographical issue concerning the rise of CND is not why it arose in 1958, but why it did not come about sooner.[42]

From 1958 CND based its appeal on the revulsion many felt towards nuclear weapons – linking their destructive powers with an end-of-the-world scenario and contrasting this with the simple moral beliefs of Campaign supporters. Meredith Veldman, in linking CND with other aspects of middle class 'romantic protest' in postwar Britain, has argued that a key 'mission' of CND 'was to convince ordinary individuals that they knew better than the experts, that the almost instinctive emotional revulsion against the idea of nuclear war should be trusted as much as or more so than any strategic calculations'.[43] In an early CND pamphlet, A.J.P. Taylor argued that 'most people agree that the bomb is morally wrong. Most admit that, if used, it would destroy civilised life throughout the world'.[44] This basic 'populist moralism',[45] enshrined by the 'ban the bomb' slogan, was the engine of CND's growth from 1958 onwards. It was when CND, rife with ideological tension, was forced to adopt a more sophisticated policy after 1960 revolving around withdrawal from NATO and neutralism that its message declined in power.[46]

A.J.P. Taylor's argument that war would certainly 'destroy the civilised world'[47] became the orthodox view and demonstrates the massive success of CND in the public sphere. Any argument made to the contrary was opposed as hopelessly optimistic, out-of-date, or deliberately misleading. The Government ceded the initiative on the nuclear debate when, in attempting to link a reduced civil defence programme with the reduced risk of war ushered in by the thermonuclear deterrent, the Sandys White Paper 'admitted' the impossibility of defence against nuclear war.[48] Although it was not until 1963 that CND fully turned to attacking civil defence preparations, the Government's attempts to explain publicly its nuclear defence policy were, from the Sandys White Paper onwards, made in an increasingly hostile and disbelieving context.

Between 1954 and 1957, civil defence had indeed existed in a world of relative public apathy. As we have seen, the threat of further 'Coventrys' led the government to retreat from public discussion of nuclear weapons, instead preserving the existing case for nuclear survival. After the 1957 White Paper's 'admission', the idea that nuclear war could be defended against was open to attack by opponents using Government statements as weapons. These attacks, like those of Taylor above, brought about a change in how nuclear weapons and civil defence were discussed. Armageddon, annihilation and catastrophe were the phrases used: the idiom of complete and utter destruction. Such rhetoric met with little opposition: the government had proved unwilling to share nuclear information with the public, creating a vacuum after 1954 which the powerful language of the disarmers easily filled. What alternative there was often seemed weakly argued or false. CND was contemptuous of what it saw as the bromides prescribed by government agents like the Civil Defence Corps. CND, then, harnessed the growing belief that nuclear weapons were so destructive as to be utterly catastrophic – that the choice over nuclear weapons was binary one between peaceful survival and apocalyptic, world-ending, nuclear destruction.

The importance of this language of annihilation can be seen in the changes in recruitment propaganda for the Civil Defence Services. From the confident, patriotic images of the early 1950s, propaganda had suffered in the years of uncertainty between 1954 and 1956, often relying on the banal. In September 1955 it was possible to begin a recruiting advertisement with 'this is a moment for optimism, and for hope. A suitable moment to thank the men and women of our Civil Defence Service, who by their efforts have helped to proclaim Britain's determination to be free'.[49] Such confidence was absent two years later, when, underneath a cartoon of a civil defence volunteer admonishing those with their heads in the sand, an advert was intent on getting across the 'facts' about civil defence: 'we hear too much of the horrors, not enough of our chances of survival. Some people will tell you that if this country were attacked with H-Bombs, every man jack of the population would be wiped out. *That just isn't true: it isn't anything LIKE the truth.*[50] In three years, the recruitment message had gone from a survival narrative to one emphasising that survival was actually possible. In 1958, this was made explicit with the recruitment campaign bearing the slogan: 'The H-Bomb: What About the Millions of Survivors' (see Figure 6.1). Such propaganda was no match for the intellectual moralism expounded by such supreme communicators as A.J.P. Taylor, J.B. Priestley and other CND advocates. In the early 1960s, civil defence propaganda retreated from the survival message completely, concentrating more on notions of community and self-improvement.

The Campaign increased in popularity in its early years, reaching a peak in 1960 when around 30 per cent of the population indicated in an opinion poll that they supported CND's aim of unilateral nuclear

Figure 6.1 Cover of Civil Defence Pamphlet, 1958.[51]

disarmament.[52] The group had no formal membership until it had already began to decline, so we have no adequate figures for active membership – although tens of thousands participated in its annual marches from Aldermaston to Trafalgar Square, with perhaps as many as 100,000 present in 1960.[53] This was also the year the Campaign saw its policy endorsed by the Labour Party Conference, only for it to be overturned the following year. That 30 per cent of the people appeared to support its aims illustrates the Campaign's failure – most people believed that Britain should keep its nuclear weapons, at least whilst other nations kept theirs. The Macmillan Government maintained the position of being committed to future, multilateral disarmament talks whilst pursuing negotiations on banning nuclear testing in late 1950s and the early 1960s and sought to pour scorn on those who would give up Britain's weapons alone.[54] In this sense, then, we can see that thinking within the Ministry of Defence at the time of the 1956 Policy Review had been borne out: once the issues were discussed – and after 1958 nuclear weapons were rigorously debated – people would support the deterrent. Yet support for the possession of the deterrent did not equate to the belief that civil defence could be restricted for strategic reasons.

The relationship between CND and civil defence was ambiguous, at least in its early years, although it was to turn unrelentingly hostile later. Before around 1961 it did not particularly attack civil defence in itself, but rather what were considered to be the distortions of nuclear reality it encouraged. This, however, left a wide target as civil defence in these years was essentially used as a vehicle for promoting the concept of nuclear survivability without possessing the means of really convincing people. The Civil Defence Corps proved a relatively easy target, suffering from a public image dominated by veterans of the Second World War obsessed by the Blitz.[55] Whereas in the atomic age an image of technical modernity could, just, be presented, this was clearly impossible more than half a decade and a technological revolution later – especially as its equipment stayed largely the same. A Civil Defence Corps exercise in Preston in 1960, for example, was considered by insider journal *Civil Defence* to have 'ended with "thumb's up" all round. The four-hour emergency routine had proved its worth. Weeks of careful planning had gone into Exercise "Prestonian" – it brought the stark reality of nuclear war shapely into focus – but the vital operation closed on a note of quiet satisfaction... and hope'.[56] It was easy to deride such activities. A disastrous piece appeared on BBC Television's *Panorama* in 1960, which portrayed the local Stafford unit as amateur, inefficient and hopelessly divorced from the realities of nuclear war.[57] It was so bad, one newspaper commented, 'that many people thought it was a rag'.[58] Another target was the Women's Voluntary Service's (WVS) series of meetings on nuclear survival. Called 'One-in-Five' talks after the proportion of women they hoped to educate in nuclear first aid and protection, had been launched in 1956 as a relatively informal way of conveying information. Talks were given up and down the land, including in a Barnsley laundrette and, whilst one WVS member was experiencing a rainy holiday, in a caravan park.[59] Opponents of the group's nuclear optimism savagely attacked its scientifically juvenile attempts at promoting survival measures, with one apparently believing WVS volunteers 'would have found it difficult to distinguish between a Geiger counter and a Jaeger counter'.[60]

The outcome of this public debate was that without specifically attacking civil defence, the nuclear disarmament movement had largely succeeded in discrediting it. Thus even those who did not share CND's views on disarmament agreed that civil defence was hopeless. The edition of *Panorama* was a typical example of this. In 1961, the famous revue *Beyond the Fringe* parodied the prospect of nuclear survival in a sketch called 'Civil War', in which Peter Cook's satirical civil defence advocate informed the audience: 'Now, what about radiation, I hear a strangled cry. Well, there is a lot you can do about radiation as soon as the dust has settled – the best thing you can do is to hold your breath and jump into a paper bag. There's nothing like a good old paper bag for protecting you'. Casual references to 'nuclear holocaust' and 'Armageddon' heightened the ridiculousness of civil defence.[61]

In 1962, direct encounters between civil defence supporters and the disarmers became more common. *Peace News* and the Committee of 100 jointly issued a Defence 'Black Paper', which was highly critical of civil defence. In August a group of CND supporters joined their local Corps group to 'find out the facts', to the evident suspicion of the local authorities. The highly critical cultural sphere is illustrated by a hilariously scathing piece by Christopher Booker in the *Guardian*:

> Perhaps some of you have observed the sorry plight of the civil defenders of Bath, Somerset. It seems that they lent twelve handbells, twelve Special Issue Civil Defence Handbells in fact, to the organisers of the local festival for their Venetian evening. And now it transpires that nine of these handbells have mysteriously disappeared. This apparently is little short of tragic for the Civil defenders of Bath, since these

> were the very handbells that they intended to use to warn the citizens of a nuclear attack.[62]

Of course, Booker pointed out, the bells were not really intended for such use: they were the property of the local Civil Defence Campanology Group, which hardly created the impression of efficiency, either.

Christopher Driver, writing in 1964, realised that one of the major effects of CND was to highlight how little effort was expended on civil defence, and how under-prepared the Civil Defence Corps was for meeting any emergency.[63] Despite its manifest political failures, here was one major success for CND – building on deep fears of nuclear war, it exposed the inability of the British state to deal with its consequences. Civil defence volunteers were unable to mobilise support for the government's preferred survival narrative, and opponents of nuclear weapons were able to present civil defence as an outmoded façade (as indeed it was). By the early 1960s, therefore, the life-saving credibility of the Civil Defence Corps – which was essentially all there was of the government's publicly acknowledged civil defence programme – had been fatally undermined. As Driver put it, since 1958 'the sections of the governmental machine entrusted with organising civil defence have had to fight a difficult guerrilla war with public opinion'.[64] The policy consequences of this decline in credibility will be discussed in the next chapter. But the question arises, could the government have handled civil defence better in this period? In keeping money so tight, probably not. Little speaks as powerfully as money in convincing people of government priorities. Without a significant sum, without major physical preparations to provide the evidence, the government could never convince people that civil defence *could* save many lives in a war. Even with such sums, it would have been virtually impossible to persuade people that civil defence had a real role when everyone knew that millions would inevitably die in such a war *however much* the government spent; it was this, and not on whether lives could be saved 'on the periphery' of an attack, by which civil defence was judged.

Bunkers

If one strand of civil defence policy was receiving a buffeting from public debate, then the other was unaffected and unknown, slowly coming to fruition throughout the land. This was the policy to provide an alternative system of government within Britain. Its origins lie back in the Second World War, when Regional Commissioners were assigned to help govern Britain if enemy attacks resulted in the breakdown of communications.[65] The Hall Report in 1953 made it clear that maintaining civilian control of the nation was going to be a major task in the post-attack phase.[66] This conclusion led to the setting up of a sub-committee of the Home Defence Committee under the chairmanship of Sir Thomas Padmore, after whom the committee was named.[67] The Strath Report had also considered action on the machinery of control to be an absolute priority if Britain was to be able to survive a future war[68] and Padmore delivered a report, keenly anticipated by Strath, to HDC and Ministers on 6 July 1955 which outlined an entirely new system. Its first principle was that the nation could not be governed in war from the London citadels, as had been thought possible in the atomic age.[69] Although quitting London in the face of attack would involve risking 'a general exodus' from London and a possible collapse in morale, Padmore outlined a scheme which would involve governing Britain some distance away from London and other target areas.

Padmore recommended two new centres of Government. One 'would be prepared for the reception of the nucleus of central Government at such time as it might be decided to move it from London', and the other would be a 'reserve centre to which a small group of Ministers and officials, capable of taking over direction of the struggle for survival, would be moved before the outbreak of war'.[70] Once in place, 'the central organ of Government would be concerned solely with directing the national struggle for survival' after an attack 'and could not afford to be encumbered with extraneous activities. Large parts of what are normally regarded as the essential functions of the state (and have been regarded as so in past wars) would have to be abandoned temporarily'.[71] As much activity as possible 'should be devolved to the regions', but the necessary work 'to be discharged centrally' would include 'essential overseas relations… control of the military and civil defence authorities, supervision of the central control of essential supplies, shipping and communications, and communication with the civil population by broadcasting and other means'.[72] This could be achieved with a staff of a thousand or less.

The two new centres would have to be built to withstand some degree of heat, blast and radiation, although 'it would be impossible to devise any accommodation for the seat of Government which would be proof against a direct hit, or even a near miss against the hydrogen bomb'.[73] They could, however, be built to withstand an explosion of a 10-megaton bomb if it was at least half a mile away. They would be linked to a Post Office network of vital communications then under construction which would allow Ministers to communicate with overseas governments, the military, and the regional headquarters. The two sites envisaged were codenamed SUBTERFUGE and MACADAM. Only the former was definitely built, at a site near Corsham in the Cotswolds, going through the names STOCKWELL[74] and BURLINGTON[75] (the name under which it became operational) before becoming TURNSTILE.[76] The story of MACADAM is more mysterious, although the project became known as QUADRANGLE[77] and then LINSTOCK.[78]

The alternative system of Government would require 'the maximum degree of devolution', and this was to be achieved along lines similar to those in the Second World War. Ministers, or someone of Ministerial rank, would control one of the 13 civil defence regions (ten in England and one each for Wales, Scotland and Northern Ireland) and be responsible for directing services on the ground. Padmore stressed, however, that unlike the war or atomic age planning, these civilian controls should be located with military controls, and that they would need specially constructed reinforced accommodation to protect against fallout. New sites would be needed for these secret controls, which from 1958 were known as Regional Seats of Government (RSGs).

Prime Ministerial approval for the Padmore report was received on 15 September 1955,[79] establishing a policy of immense importance. The proposed network of war headquarters was seen as the only way that civilian control could be exercised over the whole nation in the event of war, directing civil defence services and the military. All the life-saving civil defence policies we have seen discussed relied on the ability of the government, either centrally or regionally, to control them. Emergency feeding, communications, rescue and medical services would all collapse if there was no organisation to direct them. This alternative system grew in importance throughout the later half of the 1950s to become the most important aspect of civil and home defence planning in response to the threat of nuclear attack: more important even than the efforts to convince the public that many lives could be saved; and whereas that policy was by its essence very public, this one was also, by necessity, incredibly secret.

Secrecy was at the very heart of what we can call the SUBTERFUGE system. The alternative seat of Government was both an integral part of post-nuclear planning, and a vital part in the actual fighting of a nuclear war. It was from this alternative centre that the Prime Minister or one of the deputies pre-selected for the purposes might have to authorise nuclear attack, and the existence of a second centre of command was vital both for the credibility of the deterrent and for ensuring civilian control over the final nuclear decision.[80] Given its importance, the location of the alternative seat of Government was highly secret. As the site could not sustain a direct hit, it was imperative that no potential enemy discovered its location. For this purposes a 'cover story' was constructed to take account of the work undertaken on the site. Before 1959, the story was a simple one as only building work was being completed (because of the budget constraints). From that year, however, more complex scenarios being discussed as more sophisticated work began. In the earlier period, the 'interim' cover story was that the Ministry of Works was tidying it up and 'improving it as war potential in the form of protected accommodation, not for any specific use but because there were clearly many uses to which the Government would be glad to put it in a thermonuclear war'.[81]

By March 1959, as work was progressing, 'a more convincing plan' appeared necessary. The real problem was formulating a cover story which would simultaneously 'satisfy local people and those having access to the site', and not arouse the suspicions of either the press or 'the prospective enemy'.[82] In short, the story needed to be plausible, but not too plausible. In July it was decided that the new cover story 'should describe STOCKWELL primarily as one of a number of Post Office centres for providing internal and overseas communication in war and should indicate that part of the remaining accommodation is being developed as a standby Regional headquarters while any space left over will be used for storage by Government Departments'.[83] This was agreed to by HDC.[84] The press at least were kept away, despite a minor murmur when the *Daily Express* published a story by Chapman Pincher in January 1960 which referred to a deep 'Government headquarters being hollowed out far away from London'.[85] Its secret, however, was presumably not kept well enough to prevent the Soviets ensuring a satellite passed directly above the site from the late 1970s.[86]

The big bunker at Corsham was not so much being hollowed out as refitted (it was an old quarry which had been used as a shadow factory in the Second World War). It must have been what it remains today, an enormously impressive space. The melancholy stone, now redundant but once state-of-the-art communications such as the pneumatic message-tubes, and the abandoned stores of furniture and office supplies give the site a gloom which is ironically enlivened by the jovial Ministry of Defence officials who control the site. The bare, craggy walls are a remnant of its quarry past and a world away from the glossy, modern décor of bunkers depicted by film-makers and others at the height of the cold war. It is huge, and it was a huge secret. For years, Corsham (completed by 1962) and the Regional Seats of Government (only some of which were ever finished, and these only by 1963/64) have exerted an almost magnetic pull for those interested in cold war Britain. The regional system was exposed in 1963, as we shall see in the next chapter, whilst Corsham's existence was announced by Duncan Campbell in his 1982 book, *War Plan UK*, a pioneering investigation into the Britain's cold war preparations.[87] Campbell's studies, along with those of Peter Laurie,[88] ensured that a great deal was known during the cold war about previous plans to govern Britain. Only a decade or so after the end of the cold war was archival secrecy sufficiently relaxed to allow academic historians such as Peter Hennessy to probe the previously dark recesses of the cold war state,[89] and for others, including enthusiastic amateurs, to bring enormous amounts of information to light about various buildings, networks and installations.[90]

This sustained interest in the alternative control system means that more is known about this secret sphere than most of the less controversial aspects of civil defence policy, such as the emergency port scheme.[91] Much of the controversy during the 20 years or so after the mid-1960s was fuelled by a twofold belief in government hypocrisy. Firstly, that it preached peace and disarmament whilst making concrete plans for continuing in power after any attack; for some, these plans seemed brutal confirmation that the government was willing to press on in risking a nuclear war regardless of the cost to others. Secondly, it refused to countenance providing shelters whilst all the time knowing its own safety was secure. Of course, we can see from the documents that this is not how the politicians or officials conceived of the secret government system, but it illustrates the large degree of separation between state and people over measures to defend Britain against nuclear war. For Whitehall, Corsham and RSGs were the *only* way some semblance of control of the nation could be maintained; the only hope that the country would not descend into an anarchy of looting, violence and social decay. For the public, especially the disarmers, the horror of nuclear war was that it would kill everyone. They did not conceptualise nuclear war as something that people would survive. By the early 1960s, as we shall see more clearly next chapter, Whitehall knew all too well that millions would indeed survive, and that many of the horrors would take place *after* an attack, and it was to prevent such horrors that the RSG system and Corsham existed.

From 1957/58 a significant chunk of the rump civil defence budget was being devoted to the control system, from Corsham at the top to the thousands of concrete Royal Observer Corps sites which strewed the landscape from the late 1950s onwards.[92] Whether it would have worked is another matter. Had Corsham become operational, the sheer scale of its operations would have undoubtedly led to its identification by the Soviets very quickly, and the site was never intended to be able to withstand a direct thermonuclear strike. On another level, there was the vexed question of whether it would ever actually be manned? At what point in a crisis did one instigate the precautionary stage which would signal the arrival of Ministerial, though not yet Prime Ministerial, trains and cars? Would visible war preparations be possible, or would they just exacerbate the crisis? All these issues would be discussed in enormous depth from the late 1950s, when the nature of the cold war was such that it was clear that keeping one's nerve and not reacting badly in a crisis were key to avoiding all-out war.

Berlin

The important issues of what could be done and when in any crisis were highlighted during the first stage of the second Berlin crisis, 'the longest and one of the most dangerous of all cold war crises', as John Lewis Gaddis calls.[93] The lack of major and direct East-West antagonism in the few years after 1956 had allowed the civil defence budget to stay low. The renewal of tensions over Berlin prompted Butler in early 1959 – or rather his officials in the Home Office – to begin discussions on the formulation of an emergency 'crash' home defence plan to be put into operation if war came at short notice. Since 1948 civil defence planning had relied on the notion that Britain would know a war was coming six months in advance, enabling the government to implement civil defence policies, yet the crisis appeared out of nowhere. On 17 March 1959 the Home Secretary wrote to colleagues that 'however the international scene develops', the Government needed 'to be sure that the best possible use could be made, if need be, of the resources already available for home defence'.[94] Ministers needed, 'without any considerable expenditure', to maintain public morale should it be tested 'by an increase in international tension', and to be 'able to convince opinion in Parliament that we are not dragging our feet on matters like evacuation which require decisions of policy, and that we have a reasonable and practicable line in mind'.[95] Butler recognised that 'there can be no question of suggesting a modification of existing policy which would improve the home defence position in the next few months', but the poor state of preparations clearly concerned him.[96] He also recognised that home defence preparations had been kept 'necessarily deficient' due to their low priority in the 'last three years' as the possibility of global war was considered remote.

Two issues troubled Butler. The first was that there was no plan to deal with an interim emergency. General Kirkman, Director-General of Civil Defence in the Home Office, called on Departments in February 1959 to draw up plans detailing emergency actions which could be implemented 'without more than seven days' notice'.[97] This was to have been completed by October, but Butler brought the deadline forward to the end of May. Emergency planning was indeed a disaster. It had been agreed in 1957 (after Suez) that Departments should draw up plans to make best use of the resources in a sudden emergency, and even decreed that the Government War Book should set out the action to be taken in the event of an emergency at any time 'irrespective of the current strategic assessment of the likelihood of war'. However, by mid-1958 the pressure for short-term planning had abated and it was decided that 'Departments should prepare realistic interim plans, capable of completion by 1961' (hardly a 'crash' plan).[98] This was obviously a mockery of the original idea of interim planning, and Kirkman believed the 1961 date was 'unacceptable'. It 'would perpetuate for nearly three years the position in which we have no definite plans for making the best use of existing resources should an unexpected emergency occur'.[99] The inability of civil defence planning to deal with an emergency was as marked in early 1959 as it had been after Suez, and it was planned to keep it like that until 1961. Civil defence planners were bending reality to suit their own purposes. As it was more suitable to put off an interim plan, it was argued that one would not be needed until 1961 – when the whole point of the exercise was to plan for unexpected eventualities.

Butler's second concern was the absence of an agreed evacuation policy. Labour MPs had been badgering the Government over the evacuation plan since it was announced that 12 million could be evacuated in early 1957. There had been no further details published as no agreements had been made with the local authorities, and it was clear the scheme was now unworkable. Butler had already stalled in the Commons by admitting that 'we are having a review of the whole scheme in order to bring it thoroughly up to date'.[100] This review by Butler and Henry Brooke, the Minister for Housing and Local Government, began by arguing that current strategic thinking held that the initial Russian attack 'would be aimed in all probability at our nuclear bomber bases and offensive missile sites as a first priority'.[101] This meant that the areas around airfields and Thor missiles sites (essentially the eastern part of England) could no longer be considered safe as reception areas – they would be the first to be bombed. This reduced the amount of reception accommodation available and increased the distances evacuees would need to travel. Now only 5 million evacuees could be accommodated – although accepting greater overcrowding would allow some increase. It was recommended that the transport issue should be reviewed and an emergency interim plan should be pursued, even though it would amount to 'little more than the preparation of instructions to the selected evacuation areas to make improvised arrangements' for the evacuation of the priority classes.[102] The new plan would involve evacuating priority classes from London, Birmingham, Manchester, Merseyside, Tyneside, Leeds/Bradford, Sheffield, Teesside and Hull, but changing the boundaries of these areas back to those of the 1951 evacuation plan rather than 1956. Reducing the size of the evacuation areas allowed the number to be evacuated to be restricted to 5.8 million.

When Ministers met in March, one Committee member disagreed with the Butler/Brooke plan, arguing for a 'stay put' policy: at least individuals in affected areas 'would have food, water and limited protection'.[103] Also, it was considered doubtful whether Ministers would order evacuation 'knowing that this would lead to a defection of the non-priority classes and so, by disrupting essential services and industry, lose in advance the war which it was the object of the deterrent to prevent'. Evacuation therefore should be abandoned and 'the Government should not give a hostage to fortune by announcing a policy which was unrealistic and which would only lead to public pressure for evacuation if tension ever heightened dangerously'. Against a 'staying put' policy was the belief that it 'could well prejudice the deterrent by undermining public morale'. Also, if no official evacuation scheme was in place 'an unofficial exodus of large numbers of the population, including non-priority classes' would take place from the cities in a period of high tension.[104] Order, it was argued, could only be maintained if the Government gave a firm lead and the flight of non-priority classes was likely to be less if priority classes were evacuated under the aegis of the government.

Whether an official evacuation scheme would encourage or deter unofficial evacuation was one of the great imponderables of civil defence. Some considered the emotional pull of 'women and children first' strong enough to keep key workers (usually male) in the cities satisfied in the knowledge that their families were being evacuated and cared for under government auspices. In this view, if no official evacuation scheme existed, it was more likely key workers would travel with the women and children to ensure their safety. But would workers stay in the cities even with official evacuation? Given the widespread knowledge of the destructive powers of thermonuclear weapons, would they really have stayed put as their families rattled off on an evacuation train into the unknown? Would they risk destruction in the cities while allowing their families to fend for themselves in the uncertain post-attack world? Another imponderable question was whether the government would actually order evacuation at a crucial point in an international crisis, knowing the dislocation it would cause and the message it could send the international community. In the end the 5.8 million scheme was agreed in outline,[105] but no firm answers could be found.

Concurrently with the revised look at evacuation, Macmillan and the senior home defence planners were looking again at Corsham, codenamed STOCKWELL at this point, and investigating if it could be made ready on an emergency footing. In an ad hoc meeting chaired by Burke Trend (of the Treasury) it became clear that Corsham could not be made ready at short notice due to the necessary structural and communications work remaining, and could be manned for only around two weeks and with only 1,500 staff (as opposed to its proposed full establishment of 4,000).[106] Harold Macmillan himself was fully apprised of this in May 1959 when the sub-Committee on the Machinery of Government in War sent him a full brief on STOCKWELL,[107] explaining that it would be vulnerable in fallout conditions.[108] Therefore when Macmillan's ad hoc group GEN.684 met to discuss Corsham, it was decided to let STOCKWELL's preparations continue as normal as even increasing expenditure would not drastically speed its completion.[109]

Shortly after this, the new plan outlining what might happen if an emergency occurred after 31 July 1959 was submitted to Ministers.[110] It was grim reading. Although Sir Charles Cunningham, Permanent Secretary of the Home Office, stressed that much more could be done if Departments could discuss the plans with outside bodies (echoes of 1948 here) or could divert staff to planning, it was clear that there would be real value in 'setting down what could be done at short notice'. The envisaged measures would still 'be totally inadequate to prepare the country to meet the devastating effects of a nuclear attack and would not, in any case, add materially to the physical preparations that have so far been made'. In addition to evacuation, the area of most concern was the machinery of government. As we have seen, Corsham was unfinished – as were most of the regional headquarters. Although work could be done in an emergency, 'these headquarters, upon which many home defence plans hinge, will still be only partially effective'.[111]

The key civil defence measures which could be undertaken were paltry – no shelter, local authorities mustering up volunteers to use the 'very limited equipment' in the Civil Defence Corps, and the issue of a leaflet on building a refuge room. Even the attack warning was reliant on the maintenance of the mains electricity supply and fallout warnings were reliant on the various Royal Observer Corps posts surviving the attack.[112] Some attempt at establishing the control system could be mounted, including a half-strength Corsham, the necessary emergency powers could be drafted and enacted by Parliament, and the Civil Defence Corps, such as it was, could at least be put on a war-footing. Such a plan would not have saved many lives and could not have averted the tremendous destruction described in the Strath Report. Three years of inadequate post-Strath civil defence spending had left Britain hopelessly unfit to meet an enemy attack; these were the consequences of the post-1956 civil defence settlement. Perhaps the question should not be why the civil defence position was so poor in 1959 – that much is obvious – but instead why on earth Ministers thought it might be possible to rustle up an emergency plan to save lives given that their whole doctrine had been to starve civil defence of cash on the basis that it was of little use except for pretence.

Worse for those attempting to piece together some life-saving plan, Ministers refused to agree to the 5.8 million evacuation scheme. The initial approval was overturned when it was reconsidered in the Ministerial Committee on Civil Defence on 8 June 1959, with a fundamental split between those who believed in evacuation and those who did not. This indecision led to the issue being taken to the Cabinet,[113] where it was further delayed, the view being expressed that 'it would be desirable to avoid making a statement on evacuation policy for as long as possible'.[114] In December, Henry Brooke submitted another memorandum, suggesting it was time to reach a decision one way or another, either to plan for evacuation on the envisaged scale or to abandon it.[115] He summarised the imponderable questions but when Ministers discussed it for the third time that year, no agreement was reached.[116] Therefore, it was decided that evacuation should form part of the 'general review of home defence policy in 1960'.[117] It had been Butler's main issue of concern when he initiated the review of emergency planning in March 1959, but nine months later the only result had been to tear up the 1956 scheme. Once again a difficult decision on civil defence had been left untaken, just as the decision on an interim home defence plan had lain dormant from January 1957 until June 1959. Only a thorough-going review, a successor to the Strath Report, would be able to cut through the morass of uncertainty and apparent intractability.

Conclusion

Civil and home defence policy-making in 1959 was essentially paralysed by the decisions made in 1956. Ministers had gambled on a global war remaining unlikely, allowing civil defence spending to remain low, believing all along that it could increase in line with cold war tension. International realities meant, however, that shocks to the cold war system were often sharp and unexpected, meaning that the long-lead times envisaged by Monckton and others in 1956 were not possible. As had been decided as far back as 1952, civil defence preparations simply *had* to be in place before an emergency if they were to be effective. There would not be time to achieve anything worthwhile in the run-up to a crisis. The poor returns of the 1959 emergency plan were to be expected: nothing else could be done given the lack of investment in civil defence over the previous years. A big casualty of these spending limits was the government's own policy priority, the control system, starved of funds and unfinished when the emergency came. For Butler and his officials, it looked in early 1959 as though the civil defence gamble might be lost.

It was not lost, but that is not to say it was won. Budget constraints meant more than potential catastrophe in a crisis, they also prejudiced the twin aims of civil defence policy in these years, namely to provide an alternative system of government and to maintain the illusion that the government had genuine life-saving plans. There can be no doubt that such a policy was hindered by the strict control of money: a few million more for equipment, for example, might have gone a long way in convincing some that civil defence was a serious concern. With so few resources, civil defence largely became a laughing stock, increasing the belief that there could be no survival from nuclear attack. But yet CND was never able to capture a majority of public opinion for its aims, although it managed to see unilateralism adopted as official Labour Party policy in 1960 as part of a running, and ultimately unsuccessful, battle with the Labour leadership.[118] Such a policy was the only way CND's aims could be achieved, and its defeat at Labour's 1961 conference can in retrospect be seen as the shattering of its hopes. Given the lack of public support for CND, it could be argued that the disarmers' emphasis on the impossibility of survival actually bolstered support for the deterrent.

It would be dangerously teleological to argue that Ministers were 'right' to cut civil defence so severely on the basis that a) there would not be war; b) the cuts would hardly make much difference if there was; and c) there was still enough substance in civil defence to serve the purposes of the façade policy. But it would also be dangerously ahistorical to argue that they should have invested more, as Home Officials wanted, in the insurance of civil defence. The Government sought to balance provision with economy; it was believed that the returns promised by extra money were not worth the investment. It was also believed that its basic aims of façade and an alternative system of government could be met with minimum investment. The outcome was a split policy, whose public side tottered under the weight of suspicion, dissent and ridicule, whilst the private one stumbled on starved of funds. Refusing to devote money to life-saving was always a gamble; to cut the budget so much that Whitehall could not implement its only real physical commitment might be considered foolish, endangering the prospects of post-attack survival. But despite all this, as the 1960s dawned, the deterrent was still supported, not everyone thought civil defence a joke, and the un-finished fabric of Corsham was still untested by a nuclear weapon.

7
Equipoise, Crisis and Reform

Nineteen-sixty was a key year for Whitehall's civil defence planning. We saw in the previous chapter how the rump civil defence policy of the late 1950s had struggled to convince the public that nuclear war was survivable, in the face of intense opposition from nuclear disarmers and other critics of the government defence policy. By 1960, Whitehall dissatisfaction with the lack of direction in civil defence reached the point at which a new fundamental review had to been undertaken. This review, a successor to the Strath Report of 1955, was designed to settle the issue of civil defence, producing a policy which removed its long-standing flaws. These flaws were deep-seated: there was a very small budget with which to operate; the destructive scale of nuclear war, already virtually unthinkable in 1955, had increased with the vast stockpiles of nuclear weapons available to all sides by 1960; and it was clear that there was little confidence in the government's ability to save lives in any crisis. It would be a successful review indeed which reconciled these problems. These arguments about implementing a coherent, cost-effective scheme which avoided political controversy went to the heart of the reasons for the existence of civil defence.

Of course, the civil defence circle could never be squared in a way the Government might have wished. But the early 1960s did see a fundamental and wide-ranging attempt to reform all aspects of nuclear war planning in order to both meet the new threats in a more realistic way, and to be able to demonstrate to the public that it was were doing so. That is not to say that the planners were under any illusion that these two aims would be met by the same policies: the division of civil defence policy into separate spheres of public and secret remained, but the public side of the policy had to be streamlined and reformed to meet increased public scrutiny. These years saw a combined effort: a full-scale Home Defence Review in 1960, into which new research on the ability of British society to withstand nuclear war fed; and subsequent reviews of evacuation and the Civil Defence Corps. All this was undertaken against a backdrop of high international tension and the intense opposition of CND. The secret outcome was to rationalise further what it was possible for a government to do in a nuclear war; the public outcome was designed to make the façade of civil defence more vigorous, and less easily seen through.

Alongside the work of Home Defence Review were reviews of emergency plans inspired first by the Berlin Wall Crisis of 1961 and then the Cuban Missile Crisis the following year. The original review aimed to ensure that public civil defence policy was credible enough to bolster civilian morale in any crisis; the following crisis reviews resulted in plans to ensure the post-attack British state would be able to function effectively. These were the policy priorities which had been evolved over the previous years. Since 1956, civil defence planning had rested on post-attack governance and the ability of public measures to convince the British people that something could be done to save them. As we have seen, it was policy formulated more by necessity than by design. It pleased few within Whitehall, which partly explains why there was a sense of aimless drift within civil defence during the late 1950s. The work of reform in the early 1960s, based on a new understanding of the nature of the cold war conflict in the age of mutual deterrence, or nuclear 'equipoise', was designed to remove that sense of drift and replace it with a dynamism to ensure that, although limited in scope compared to the plans outlined by Strath, civil defence would be a functional and worthwhile policy in its own right.

The Home Defence Review

When the Home Defence Review (HDR) began, it was part of broader attempts to understand Britain's place in the world and the future nature of nuclear weapons. At the highest level, the Macmillan Government was undertaking a review of 'Future Policy', designed to establish Britain's strategic – in the political and economic as much as the military sense – objectives, capabilities and limitations for the following decade. At a lower level, there was a study of the effects of nuclear war and the nature of deterrence. This latter work was undertaken by the Joint Inter-Services' Group for the Study of All-out War (JIGSAW). Existing within the purview of the Chiefs of Staff structure, as opposed to the Cabinet Office, JIGSAW studied the concept of 'breakdown', the point of attack 'beyond which the cumulative effect of damage to different components will cause a general collapse of national structure'.[1] Or, as Peter Hennessy put it, 'the point at which survivors turn inwards, and cease to be assets to a state which has lost the capacity to govern and the means of waging war, leading both industry and whatever society helplessly continues to slow down of its own accord'.[2] JIGSAW investigated the number of bombs needed to cause breakdown in the United States, the Soviet Union, and the UK, work which stressed the idea of mutual deterrence (the point where both sides could destroy the other with their second-strike capability), and attempted to solve fundamental civil defence problems. The dual nature of JIGSAW's work on deterrence and on the effectiveness of civil defence highlights what can with some usefulness be called the 'civil defence paradox': studies showed that in order to have any hope of 'surviving' nuclear war, extensive civil defence measures would have to be undertaken (the view of Strath and the civil defence establishment); yet those same studies argued that mutual deterrence made war increasingly unlikely, meaning expensive civil defence preparations were unnecessary (a position held in an early form in the late 1940s, firmly adopted as Government policy in the Sandys White Paper, and held with increasing vehemence by the Ministry of Defence from the mid-1950s). JIGSAW's work informed the Ministry of Defence's approach to the Home Defence Review and was part of a wider realisation within Whitehall that the nature of the cold war nuclear confrontation had changed.

HDR was chaired by Freddie Bishop, the acting Cabinet Secretary due to Sir Norman Brook's illness, and included such officials as Burke Trend (Brook's eventual successor), Sir Sidney Kirkman, the Director-General of Civil Defence, and Philip Allen, a survivor from the Strath Group at this point at the Ministry of Housing and Local Government until returning to the Home Office in the autumn. It started its work in February 1960, receiving a series of background studies, including a paper from the JIC on the likelihood and scale of a future war and another on what that war would mean for Britain.[3] The JIC paper radically altered the strategic basis for war planning. Previously it had been assumed that a deterioration of the international situation would allow the government to plan for war around six months before it occurred, meaning vital preparations could be made at this stage. It had been clear for some time, however, that a cold war crisis could arise very quickly, and the adherence to the 'six month' rule as we can call it probably represented wishful thinking on the planners' part. The JIC paper did represent a break with previous thinking, arguing that war

– if it came – was much more likely to arise from such a 'snap' crisis as a result of miscalculation than as a result of a planned long-term build up of tension of the sort which would allow the implementation of last-minute plans.[4] Instead of six months' warning, then, only seven days' warning from actual 'Soviet preparations for global war' could be forecast. Although tension might rise for some weeks beforehand, 'the Government would need to weigh', considering the frantic diplomatic activity that would invariably be taking place, 'the advantages of taking measures which showed their resolution to maintain their position as against the dangers of action which could be regarded as provocative'.[5]

If war did start, it was assumed by the JIC that the Soviets would target the nation's nuclear retaliatory capacity, its centres of population, government and the major ports. These targets, 87 in number, would be attacked with an immense total of 159 three-megaton bombs.[6] The possible effects of such an attack were awesome, unknowable and virtually unthinkable beyond the estimated statistics. In these stark figures the Home Office estimated that 8 million would die and 3 million would be injured from the instant, direct effects of the bombs.[7] Deaths from radiation in 'average' fallout conditions would take the total to 21.5 million dead and 4 million injured, out of a population of 50 million, unless some degree of evacuation and shelter were provided.[8] Even implementation of the unapproved 1959 plan to evacuate 6 million priority-class people from urban centres would save only 5 million lives as fallout would invade the old reception areas even in favourable weather conditions. If unfavourable easterly winds were prevailing, evacuation would save less than 1 million lives as the evacuees would be irradiated in the western half of Britain.[9]

To reduce the fallout casualties to less than 13 million would take some degree of shelter. Shelter had traditionally been a Home Office obsession, and so it was again. It was argued that peacetime shelter provision could save 12.5 million of these casualties. But this would be reliant on a remarkable series of contingencies. These lives could be saved if 'there had been sufficient provisioning of shelters to permit a two weeks stay and if sufficient warning of the approach of fallout had been received to enable the public to reach communal refuge'; and if they remained continuously in their refuge for up to two weeks and then spent not more than 15 hours in getting clear of the fallout area.[10] Moreover, the original figure of 13 million deaths *before* taking into account shelter provision was based on the assumption that 3 million of the 16 million originally pinned down in the highly contaminated 'Z' Zone could be evacuated within 48 hours. But could they be rescued?

Secondly, the 'average weather conditions' for fallout gave the Home Office a figure of 16 million trapped in their homes, but the very worst conditions meant 27 million such people – on top of the 8 million already dead. Only 15 million survivors would be left. The endless list of 'ifs' and other caveats demonstrates the difficulty of planning shelter and evacuation provision in such circumstances. Fallout was so devastating that the direction of wind would make the difference between 16 and 27 million people trapped in their homes. With grim irony, it was noted how, because of the enormously reduced number of people, it would be much easier to ensure that the survivors would have enough food, water, fuel and power to survive.[11] But then the Home Office planners did not investigate the impact on food resources of a successful shelter policy. Had 10 million lives been saved through shelters, many of those would have starved to death as the feeding arrangements collapsed around them, even assuming these facilities survived an attack so devastating it killed or injured half the population of Britain.

A hyper-successful shelter policy would not save the 8 million killed in the initial attack, and the survivors would face a shortage of food which 'might give rise to serious law and order problems'.[12] The Home Office believed, however, that 'in these general conditions, survival appears to be possible, but only if the available resources and the energy of the survivors are properly applied'.[13] What could survival really mean in a nation which had just seen around 21 million of its citizens die? Only the survival of some sort of governing framework which would aid a subsequent, and very slow, recovery of the nation. Although the Home Office paper stressed the vital nature of a control system, its work was too slight and hopeful, too based on assumptions, to convince. Post-attack society, with its fragile, damaged infrastructure of emergency feeding, water supply and fuel and power, would need to be maintained – and would be reliant on continuing imports – if the nation was to 'survive' in any sense.

After understanding what an attack on Britain would entail, the main thrust of HDR's preliminary work was to formulate, in Bishop's words, 'the philosophy of home defence as an addition to the deterrent and its credibility and as a reinforcement of public morale, as well as its purpose for saving life and preserving administration'.[14] The Ministry of Defence paper investigating this was the first time the question of civil defence's deterrent role had been officially examined rather than assumed.[15] It saw 'narrow' Civil defence (excluding measures of government control and communications which had a major military function) as having no influence on the technical element of deterrence, that of inflicting 'damage on the Soviet homeland', but a complex influence on the 'credible' element of deterrence – the Russians' belief that the British Government would authorise a nuclear attack in the final analysis. Although 'no economically feasible scale of civil defence measures in this country could significantly affect the results of a full-scale attack on this country', it was clear that having no civil defence programme in place could, in a period of crisis, lead to an 'overt – and vociferous – element of opposition to any stand taken by the Government of the day which appears to involve a risk of attack on this country'. This might prejudice the Government's ability 'to keep staunchly in line with the declared deterrent policy', and such divided public opinion might be taken by the Soviets as 'a significant rift in an otherwise firm attitude of the Western Powers'.[16]

The MoD believed that such a 'defection' could be avoided by a greater degree of public education on 'the real issues involved in the nuclear equipoise'. This would allow the government to cut back heavily on the more expensive 'tranquillising façade' of civil defence. It argued that public support for the deterrent could be maintained without civil defence, citing the fact that, 'whether through ignorance, indifference or common sense, there has never been any strong reaction in the country at large' to the 'no defence' admission contained in the 1957 White Paper (an interesting assessment of the achievements of CND).[17] However, it was recognised that the most sensible option of scrapping civil defence was impossible because of the political impracticality, so throughout the HDR discussions, MoD officials argued for a minimum programme with no measures to save lives and a drive 'educating the public to accept that the best defence and hope for survival lay in resolute support of the deterrent policy'.[18] This opposition to civil defence became the established Ministry of Defence posture throughout the 1960s, and moved from being the 'minority' view in HDR to becoming the strategic basis for reducing civil defence spending when civil defence was put on a care-and-maintenance basis in 1968.

This largely negative appraisal of the deterrent role of civil defence was contradicted by Kirkman, who was in no doubt about the valuable deterrent role of civil defence.[19] If preparations were abandoned, 'a considerable, and possibly uncontrollable, impetus would inevitably be given to criticism of the deterrent policy'. The Government could not 'reasonably expect a potential enemy to believe that it intended to use nuclear weapons in the last resort if it announced that it was abandoning any serious preparations to succour the survivors of a counter attack', and 'no amount of education of the public in the need to place complete reliance on the deterrent policy could affect this'.[20] Kirkman also stressed the need for genuine life-saving measures to continue in order to maintain 'the support of volunteers, local authorities and others outside the Government service' as 'unless they can be convinced that the organisation is likely to serve a useful purpose, it would not be practicable to keep it alive'.[21]

Given the potentialities of the wartime control network – an operational chain of command from 'central government down through the regions to Sub-Regions and Groups, Areas, Sub-areas and Sectors to warden posts', exercising governmental control whilst also enabling the decentralised control of the civil defence services – Kirkman concluded that it was not necessary to maintain civil defence as a façade 'as there are good grounds for regarding its life-saving activities as of great importance and its contribution to the maintenance of the framework of society as fundamental'. He added 'in any event, while nuclear attack remains a possibility, home defence preparations must be an inescapable responsibility of Government'.[22] When HDR met it affirmed civil defence's central position within the Government's deterrent posture, stressing that 'civil defence preparations lent conviction in the eyes of the Soviet Union to our expressed intention to use our nuclear forces'.[23] If civil defence was abandoned or was 'obviously inadequate', a 'loss of morale and public support for the Government's deterrent policy' might follow, and although 'much could be done to educate the public in the realities of nuclear war, some practicable civil defence measures would be needed if public morale was to be sustained in the face of acute international tension'.[24] This 'majority' view dominated civil defence policy until it was suspended in 1968.[25]

The Home Defence White Paper, then, argued that the 'façade' of civil defence was integral to Britain's deterrent strategy. In doing so, it reflected the awareness that the theory of deterrence was not an abstract truth, but – in John Baylis' words – 'a highly ambiguous and untested concept which involves requirements which are open to a variety of interpretations'.[26] The requirements of deterrence were especially fluid at this time, as the British defence establishment were becoming increasingly concerned about the possibility of war through miscalculation rather than design,[27] and the 'façade' theory was designed to lessen the chances of such a course of events in any crisis.

It is impossible to gauge the extent to which these planners were guided by fear of the political repercussions of a decision to scrap the Civil Defence Corps. The short-term effects of such a decision were not discussed, and the 'public' civil defence measures were maintained on strategic grounds, albeit ones based on a nuanced theory of deterrence.

Given the nature of the Macmillan Government's previous commitment to maintaining the Corps (based on not disturbing the calm waters of perceived apathy), and the criticisms of civil defence that had occurred since, it is hard to believe that fear of immediate adverse reaction did not play at least some small, immeasurable part in the decision. But concluding that public civil defence was necessary was one thing, actually persuading people that civil defence policy was worthwhile was another. HDR argued that the public was beginning 'to dismiss the possibility of taking useful measures to mitigate the effects of nuclear attack';[28] and that unless 'the thesis that sensible plans can and are being made to reduce casualties and to preserve society' in any possible nuclear war was presented vigorously, there was a 'danger of acceptance by the public of a "peace at any costs" policy in a period of tension'. Key to this 'vigorous presentation' would be a demonstration of the 'Government's conviction that home defence preparations are worthwhile'; this could only be done by 'setting out in greater detail than has been accustomed in recent years, the broad lines of what the Government has in mind'.[29] Linking detailed plans to the broad defence policy would raise the profile of civil defence and the morale of the organisation. In some ways, the Home Office clearly believed, the attitude struck by the Government was as important, if not more so, than the actual preparations. Since Strath, the Government had made little direct attempt to influence public opinion. Vitally, there had been no attempt to harness the one obvious source of public information: the annual recruitment campaign for civil defence. The content of the annual drive, its slogans, images and written content, was never discussed within the Cabinet Committee structure, Ministerial or Official: it was solely a Home Office affair. By ignoring civil defence's public face, both before and after 1960, the senior planners neglected a unique apparatus for manipulating perceptions of nuclear war and civil defence.

Some attempt to be more forthcoming and realistic can be seen in Ministerial announcements after HDR. When launching the 1962 recruitment campaign, the Home Secretary, Henry Brooke, gave a message quite different from the main campaign message which concentrated on personal development and skills. Brooke argued that civil defence was 'a human service with a deeply humanitarian purpose. To save lives, to relieve suffering, and to increase the chance of survival',[30] and his broadcast featured a voiceover stating that

> We know that for several square miles where a bomb fell there would be total tragedy and destruction on an unprecedented scale.

> But in the area beyond that, swept by blast and fire, there would be survivors. People shocked and bewildered, and here as soon as it was safe, it would be the job of the Civil Defence Services to be prepared to save life and to salvage everything possible from the chaos.[31]

Of course, the key message stressed survival and succour, but it starkly admitted that there were large areas where nothing could be done, something official statements had been keen to avoid in the previous years. Not for nothing did Christopher Driver note in 1964 that there had been a new openness about civil defence from government in the previous couple of years.[32]

Once the key decision had been taken that civil defence must include a voluntary body designed to save lives, HDR proceeded to fill in the rest of its policy. Obviously, the sort of policy outlined by Strath was out of the question, and the Review spared no one in its anatomy of how poor civil defence preparations were as a result of five years of under-investment.[33] As we have seen, in addition to there being no shelter provision, there was no agreed evacuation scheme after the inconclusive 1959 discussions. Therefore, if an emergency arose in the short-term, the Government would issue advice for everyone to stay put, potentially costing millions of lives. Paper plans existed for the wartime operation of the Civil Defence Corps and other services, but cash, personnel and equipment were all in short supply, especially for fire-fighting. In the Corps, numbers and efficiency were well below operational standard. Moreover, due to the ending of conscription – announced in the Sandys White Paper and in 1960 about to be completed – the military forces available to support civil defence were considerably less than those previously envisaged. Stockpiles of medical supplies and food had been reduced to save money. The lack of preparations for public utilities and industry as a whole was an 'embarrassment'.[34]

On a more positive note, the warning and monitoring infrastructure for fallout had been established. With 48 hours notice sirens would warn of approaching aircraft, and once the Ballistic Missile Early Warning System (BMEWS) was completed in 1963 'some four minutes warning could be given' of incoming missiles. Also, 'good progress' had been made in preparing the country's communications system, but emergency broadcasting plans remained uncompleted. The wartime machinery of control had been agreed, enabling decentralised direction of life-saving operations, 'as the situation demanded... from the Central Government nucleus to Regions, Sub-Regions and Groups, Areas, Sub-Areas and Wardens'. Corsham was virtually finished but little had been completed on constructing special Regional Headquarters, and 'revised plans for using and strengthening existing buildings will not be completed for some time; for sub-regional and lower controls progress is also slow'.[35] Preparations for the ports and shipping emergency organisation were also well advanced. None of those aspects which could be considered a success – Corsham, communications and the emergency ports – were considered civil defence measures in the strict 'narrow' sense, and all had been heavily monitored or initiated by the military.

The final policy proposal concentrated on the by now familiar two themes: ensuring the maintenance of Government control in a future war and ensuring that public morale did not collapse in a period of international tension. Two alternatives were presented: Programme X, costing an average of £19.6 million a year for five years, was 'the most economical programme which could be presented as a reasonably consistent and logical one and would be likely to command confidence among local authorities and home defence workers and through them the general public'. Programme Y would cost less, but whereas 'X' would 'provide a coherent and publicly defendable policy', 'Y' meant shouldering the burden of continued inadequacies.[36] The determination of the planners to secure the greatest return for the scarce funds to be spent on civil defence can be seen from the prioritisation of the different strands of civil defence. For example, there was nothing but a token sum for the water and other industries, and the food stockpile would remain depleted. The fact that the medical stockpile was to be increased demonstrates, however, the desire to fund only the most significant and high profile measures. A further allocation of money was also recommended to complete the national warning system of protected Royal Observer Corps posts by 1964 and the system for government control, with Corsham planned to be finished by 1961/2, and the purpose-built Regional and Sub-Regional Headquarters completed by 1964 (all controls below the Sub-Regional level were to be in place in 1965).[37]

As part of its determination to provide a workable policy, there were two main areas that HDR was determined to get a grip on: evacuation and the Civil Defence Corps. HDR's discussion of evacuation demonstrated the new rigour applied across the board. Decision-making paralysis meant that no agreed plan existed (see Chapter 6 above), and HDR recommended a policy adapted from the aborted 1959 scheme. By excluding adolescents, the aged and the infirm, the boundaries of the 1959 evacuation areas scheme could be extended to include more mothers and children. Of course this would still leave out some major target areas and even those moved would still face great potential danger from fallout. HDR conceded that 'the Government runs the risk of criticism whether it has an evacuation scheme or not. If there is a scheme, it may be criticised for its inadequacy; if there is no scheme, the Government may be accused of imprudence or irresponsibility'. It was pointed out that no scheme could be improvised at short notice, and 'without a scheme the Government would have practically nothing to offer the inhabitants of our largest cities as a means of reducing the number of casualties in a nuclear attack'. It would also 'be likely to lead to demands for an expensive shelter programme'.[38] Whatever the decision, it was vital an early announcement should be made. On shelter itself, no longer one of the major issues in civil defence thinking, two future plans were presented: a survey by local authorities on all premises which could be used in war as communal shelters, and the preparation of guidance for the public on how they could improvise shelter in their own homes which could be issued in an emergency or even in war.

On the Corps, the supporters of a defendable policy believed that its annual budget of £4 million represented an irreducible allocation, and around £1,000,000 in total was envisaged for extra equipment across the services. The big policy initiative was to recast training and recruitment and base the Corps around a newly formed, highly-trained elite membership. This was necessary because although the paper strength of the Corps was 350,000, 'probably not more than 150,000 had done any serious training, and only a small proportion are of high enough quality to be capable of holding posts of responsibility'. The idea was to institute a 'bounty' scheme along the lines of the Territorial Army. Those willing to give full-time service in war and undergo extensive training would receive between £10 and £20 a year. The Home Office hoped numbers taking up the offer would start at 50,000 before rising to a total of 200,000 highly trained people. This would cost £750,000 a year at the beginning, before rising to £2,000,000. The scheme would also probably have to be extended to the Auxiliary Fire Service and the National Hospital Reserve Service.[39]

Arguments in favour of such a scheme were 'that it would be a visible and impressive symbol of the Government's belief in the value of civil defence'. It would boost the morale of the Corps, providing 'a corps d'elite – a nucleus of well-trained men and women who could act as leaders if war came'.[40] Against, it was argued that costs could not be controlled and might exceed forecasts, and that 'tightening up of training requirements and the imposition of an obligation to serve full time in war would probably make little practical difference to the situation if war came', rendering it pointless as well as expensive. No firm recommendation was made, however, and a more thorough review of the issue was suggested for after the report had been discussed.

HDR stressed the need for a fundamental overhaul of civil defence. It had 'reached the point where it needs re-energising, if it is to continue'.[41] It was recommended that Programme X should be adopted, along with plans for a 6 million evacuation scheme, a survey of possible shelter accommodation in buildings, and plans for the emergency manning of the RSGs. The Home Defence Review attempted to save civil defence from both those who believed it had no use and those who were happy to ignore it. Its findings ensured that planning in Britain continued for at least another five years. But the Committee clearly had no real faith in the traditional life-saving capacity of the home defence organisation. Instead, the work of the HDR Committee has to be placed within its economic and cold war context. As the report itself said, the days of a £70 million home defence budget were over; as were the days when an official group could recommend the building of a formidable, wholesale home defence edifice. Indeed, it dealt honestly with the manifest failings of home defence, recognising that without shelters, at least 21 million people would die in an all-out nuclear war. It recognised that home defence could have no real life-saving role, and that its main purpose was to create the image of preparedness; to provide succour for the minds of those questioning the deterrent; and to influence those who, in the final emergency, might see the lack of Government preparations and decide to protest against any possible British participation in a nuclear war. This was reflected in the minuscule budget and the palpable reluctance of all but the most ardent civil defence supporters to increase it. HDR has therefore to be seen not merely in civil or home defence terms, but as a wider part of the deterrent strategy. Civil defence in its traditional sense was dead in 1960, and had been so for some time. It was now a prop in the deterrent strategy, used to bolster the image of British might, resolve, and preparedness: a strategy aimed at influencing the British public as much as the Kremlin.

Home Defence Review: implementation

The real 'philosophy' behind the review can be seen be seen from Bishop's fascinating brief produced for Norman Brook before the Home Defence Committee discussed the final report in December 1960.[42] Bishop praised the positioning of home defence as 'an integral part of the deterrent policy' and rubbished the alternative view held by Ministry of Defence that spending should be curtailed because although home defence had little point (and would not affect public opinion), political expediency alone meant it could not be completely scrapped. It was unrealistic and 'places too much faith in popular support' for the deterrent policy 'in a period of tension'. This was especially so, Bishop's argument runs, given the changing nature of deterrent theory. What he called the 'Sandys attitude' of putting one's faith in inevitable retaliation was outmoded in the new period of 'nuclear equipoise'.[43] The old one-dimensional strategic scenario of massive retaliation to Soviet aggression was gone. The current balance of forces meant that the Soviets could be tempted into 'a test of relative willpower'. In such a crisis, the credibility of the deterrent would be severely tested, and it is at this point public opinion would be at its most vulnerable. Herein lay the case for a worthwhile home defence strategy.

Brook's Home Defence Committee warmly endorsed the report and 'Programme X',[44] although the Cabinet insisted that around £500,000 be shaved off the first part of the programme's budget.[45] Worse, the whole basis of HDR's life-saving strategy was thrown into disarray when Ministers, again, failed to come to an agreement over evacuation policy.[46] In Cabinet, Henry Brooke, Minister for Housing and Local Government, had pushed for an early announcement and argued 'that the choice was simply whether to announce that we were abandoning evacuation or that we were about to start planning for the 6 million scheme'.[47] Other Ministers questioned the advisability of discussing evacuation with local authorities: 'such an announcement might have an adverse effect on support for the defence and foreign policies of the Government'.[48] The matter was referred to a Defence Committee meeting in January 1961, before which Bishop advised Macmillan that the arguments for and against planning an evacuation scheme are evenly balanced'.[49] Although he made it clear that official opinion favoured implementation, Bishop stressed the old imponderables of whether 'any evacuation would be practicable in the precautionary period before global war', and whether 'an official evacuation scheme might serve to inject order or disorder into the movement from large cities that might be expected to occur'. Overall, however, Macmillan was steered towards the HDR argument that if a scheme was adopted then in any crisis the option 'would at least be open', whereas 'if a scheme is not prepared, the Government might have to admit that this was so'.[50] Furthermore, Bishop 'doubted whether an announcement that planning is to start would cause much excitement or lead to any general discussion of defence policy, still less to public alarm'.

If it did, the 'ephemeral' consequences would be nothing compared to the 'considerably more criticism and real embarrassment, in a period of tension, if no planning had been done'.[51]

In the end, the Cabinet's Defence Committee steered a middle course, agreeing to investigate the 6 million scheme with the local authorities but deciding against any early announcement.[52] In fact, Brooke quickly accepted this deferment, recognising that any such statement could only explain the abandonment of the old scheme and the intention to replace it with a more limited scheme. 'People would expect me to make a rather more informative statement than that, after two years of examination of these problems.'[53] Brooke told Butler that he would simply have to stall when answering any questions that came up on the issue, which they did in March.[54] Ministers' difficulties with evacuation are worth probing. On one level it seems baffling that Ministers agreed a policy costing around £19 million per year but refused to plan (at virtually no cost) for the one aspect which would give the policy most credibility. A publicly announced evacuation plan was essential if home defence policy was to have any semblance of credibility, and if the policy was to 'convince' people to support government actions in any crisis – which after all was the strategic basis for pursuing civil defence after 1960. As the planners had always known, evacuation was the cheapest way to save millions of lives in a future war, and if a scheme was agreed beforehand, the government could meet a future crisis secure in the knowledge they had a policy designed to save millions, which, even if its success was far from certain, would surely reduce criticism of the government's policy. This was now the stated point of home defence. Ministers, however, instinctively shrank from any public announcement which might give aid to the nuclear disarmers by appearing to reduce existing provision. Many within Whitehall, both Ministers and officials, feared any public discussion of civil defence and favoured a policy of no or little information aimed at short-term expedience, regardless of the potential long-term cost in terms of credibility, let alone of possible lives lost in a future war.

Overall, however, it must be stressed that the Ministerial and Official discussions following the Home Defence Review, no less than the review itself, represented a real attempt to make progress on civil defence within its new, limited, conceptualisation. For once there was a largely unified purpose within Whitehall to achieve the greatest degree of success within the known boundaries of the budget. The latter point cannot be overstated. The history of Strath was in a way determined by its costly recommendations. Over the next five years Ministers never gave the planners the money the latter thought was necessary. Vitally, they also chopped and changed the budget as the Government lurched from crisis to crisis – there was no unified planning and no civil or home defence programme was secure from one year to the next. The decision of late 1960 to set out a five year budget, although tiny compared to the one desired by Strath, was possible only because the HDR officials produced their detailed report to dovetail with the Government's budgetary requirements, rather than producing a 'shopping list' of cripplingly expensive measures such as universal shelter provision. Once the Cabinet decision had been made, planning could continue – and this included the more detailed studies of evacuation, the Civil Defence Corps, and publicity put in train by R.A. Butler. Although the final preparations had a questionable value in terms of their ability to mitigate the effects of nuclear attack, the result of finally giving the civil defence policy a degree of focus and momentum was intended to be the best possible degree of planning and preparation achievable with limited resources.

Emergency again: the Berlin Wall Crisis, 1961

Post-HDR planning was thrown into confusion by the re-eruption of the Berlin crisis in the summer of 1961, which precipitated the suspension of such long-term planning in favour of mapping out a new 'emergency' scheme to enable Britain to be as prepared as possible to face nuclear war within four months.[55] This is not the place for a detailed analysis of the crisis,[56] but its seriousness should not be underestimated. As Lawrence Freedman put it in relation to those strategists who envisaged how an international crisis might escalate into all-out nuclear war, 'the powder trail from Berlin to a nuclear catastrophe always had a simplicity and credibility that more contrived scenarios lacked'.[57] On 25 June, a worried Macmillan noted in his diary that 'we may drift to disaster over Berlin – a terrible diplomatic defeat or (out of sheer incompetence) a nuclear war'.[58]

The second half of 1961 was a peculiar time for civil defence. In December, the Foreign Secretary, Lord Home, made the front pages by appearing to suggest that the will of the British public to resist Soviet pressure over Berlin was such that 'they are quite ready to be blown to atomic dust' over it.[59] Harold Watkinson, Minister of Defence, also received criticism for telling an audience of Young Conservatives that garden shelters were useless on the same day that a senior figure in the Industrial Civil Defence Service called for a massive shelter programme.[60] Such calls were vociferous in the United States, with that country experiencing what can only be called a 'shelter panic', with a mass building of family shelters, sparking a debate about 'nuclear morality' in American culture.[61] No such phenomenon afflicted Britain. A few builders chanced their arm at offering fallout shelters, only to be attacked for their pains by the *Daily Mirror*'s 'Cassandra' columnist.[62] The odd newspaper article on the utility or otherwise of building shelters really amounted to an overspill of the American panic, and no major British figure called for a shelter programme of the sort being discussed across the Atlantic. It is worth pondering why Britain did not experience a comparable panic. For 'Cassandra', casting a critical eye over America, the answer was simple: there was no point as a nuclear war would be too destructive.[63] A more thoughtful piece in the *Guardian*, though arguing that people outside the main cities should not be mocked for building such shelters, concluded that they were much less useful in the British context.[64] Historians of cold war America have seen the debate about shelters mirroring a wider debate on nuclear survivability.[65] Britain did not share this fate as, by and large, the debate over survival had been settled within the cultural sphere before 1960. It was widely assumed that chances of one's survival in a nuclear war would be very low, probably making it seem futile to pay for a shelter in hard cash. The shelters that were built were almost invariably part of the government structure, although Merton College, Oxford, did announce plans to turn a cellar into protected accommodation.[66]

To return to emergency planning, the Defence Committee discussed on 4 August 1961 the measures which could be taken within four months 'to improve preparedness against the possibility of an emergency in the autumn'.[67] Ministers received advice as to what could be achieved both in secret and with some outside consultation, but they decided any risk of publicity 'would not at present be justified', and so only covert measures could go forward.[68] In secret the Government could prepare all the vital emergency legislation needed before hostilities broke out. In August 1961 nothing was-up-to-date. A draft Emergency Powers (Defence) Bill 'could be completed quickly, but Defence Regulations have not yet been prepared', and producing the 'complete code' of the latter in time 'would be a major undertaking'.[69] Within this time frame, the government's advice to the public could be completed; a pamphlet had been drafted and was ready for distribution at short notice, and a television film and radio announcements could also be prepared. On the warning system, however, the short-term prospect was dire: there was no capacity for warning the public against fallout, apart from improvised arrangements by the police to ring church bells, although this 'might be supplemented by arrangements with the BBC to broadcast warnings'. Had the risk of publicity been acceptable, much more could have been undertaken – such as improving protected accommodation at some Regional Headquarters, and allowing local authorities to do the same. Planners could attempt to bring the Corps 'up to something like its wartime establishment', and organise mobile forces and warden posts, rest centres and the manning of other improvised controls, including a system for warning against fallout. The medical services and water industry could be placed on a war footing, and heavy industry could also be instructed to undertake its own preparations.[70]

The Government control system and its communications were considered of overriding importance. The system could not hope to function as intended. As there would 'have to be considerable improvisation at levels below Region', it was unlikely these sub-Controls could be activated, leaving the government forced to use local authority offices, and police and fire headquarters. The Post Office would have to arrange what communications they could between Regional Headquarters and 'these improvised subordinate controls'.[71] On the vexed issue of just when the government would leave London, there were plans to remove the Prime Minister, twelve Ministers, the Chiefs of Staff and the Cabinet Secretary from London to Corsham by helicopter at the last minute.[72] In the regions, 'eight out of ten regional headquarters could be brought to a higher state of readiness, though some would not be fully protected or large enough to take the full war complement', but two would require makeshift accommodation. It would be impossible for controls below the regional level to be set up before the autumn, and ad hoc arrangements would have to be made for finding accommodation and communication channels for the civil defence forces in the area.

Progress on these issues was swift, demonstrating the new desire to place civil and home defence on a much surer short-term footing, and by September 1961 the eight inadequate regional premises were being improved (with alternative accommodation in the two other areas). Also, the staff earmarked for service had largely been selected, and although these preparations would be even less effective than the standing long-term plan, important preparations had been completed.[73] These included the limited purchase of oil stocks, the redrafting of the public advice booklet, now bearing its final name 'Advice to Householders', and the imminent installation of communications between regions and between regional headquarters and sectors of the warning and monitoring organisation. Also, progress had been made on issues such as public pronouncements in a precautionary phase, the revision of Departmental War Books, and the drafting of the Defence Regulations.[74]

When officials reported this progress to Ministers in October 1961,[75] they again sought to have the consultation ban lifted. Officials wanted the go-ahead to discuss plans with local authorities and the representatives of various industries. This would allow them to consult the principal firms holding food stocks which would be required to implement an emergency rations scheme in war and to make additional peacetime appointments of industry outsiders to emergency wartime control organisations for food distribution and the ports. Ministers did agree that some limited widening of consultation could take place.[76] Overall, the risk of publicity in filling senior control system positions and holding talks with the food and medical supply industries was worth running against the risk of 'prejudicing the establishment of an effective wartime organisation'. Moreover, although consultation would still be severely curtailed, these proposals 'went a good deal further than we had ever gone before and would enable substantial progress in planning to be made'.[77] As in the post-HDR discussions, there was a new sense of purpose permeating the home defence planning machinery in dealing with this wave of emergency planning. In all previous crises, the risk of publicity had overruled public consultations. Planners and Ministers were now determined to be as prepared as possible should the crisis escalate.

Evacuation and the review of the Civil Defence Corps, 1961–2

After the consultations with local authorities had been agreed in February 1961, evacuation policy was back on the Cabinet agenda in February 1962. Interestingly, the term 'evacuation' had been dropped and 'dispersal' adopted.[78] This has importance beyond the merely semantic, as 'dispersal' implies a much more limited moving of population than 'evacuation'. Evacuation, a term so evocative of 1939–40, implied movement from areas of great risk to areas that were safe. Removing the term may be seen as a recognition that in a nuclear attack there would be no 'safe' areas, only potentially 'safer' ones, and that to talk of 'evacuation' in this context would merely court controversy. As Macmillan approvingly noted in the Cabinet discussion, the term 'evacuation' was 'misleading in the context of nuclear war'. Rather than provide safety in rural areas, 'the object of dispersal was to secure better average chances of survival for the population as a whole by spreading them out more evenly through the country'.[79]

The Cabinet paper, produced jointly by Butler, John Maclay (Scottish Secretary) and Charles Hill (Minister of Housing and Local Government), recommended that a dispersal policy be prepared, supplying the caveat that 'its preparation would not commit the Government to the view that dispersal must be ordered in an emergency. No one can foresee whether conditions at the time would permit this to be done'.[80] The actual policy which emerged from discussions with the local authorities, who were strongly in favour of the measure, went further than the one originally envisaged in 1960. It provided for the dispersal of 9.5 million people from England and Wales and another million from Clydeside and Edinburgh. The next steps were a public announcement of the policy, then all local authorities could be informed before detailed planning began. In Cabinet, Butler advocated adopting this strategy because 'it would not be possible for the Government to continue to remain silent on this subject. To announce the abandonment of a policy of dispersal would be unacceptable to public and parliamentary opinion'. Whilst objections to the plan would undoubtedly be raised, 'these could be dealt with by saying that the plan as a whole was still under examination'.[81]

Just two weeks before the Cabinet discussed the new 'dispersal' policy, Butler sent his colleagues the report on the future of the Civil Defence Corps and the Auxiliary Fire Service.[82] Chaired by the ubiquitous Philip Allen, the review committee's report had three main planks extending logically from the HDR concept of civil defence: that the continued existence of the Corps was vital to defence preparation; that the quality, rather than quantity, of the volunteers had to be improved; and that to achieve this, a 'bounty' scheme was needed to encourage the completion of a more rigorous training regime.[83] The complicated wrangling over the financial implications of the bounty delayed Ministerial discussion of the report by some four months.[84] Although the 'nominal strength' of the Corps was 357,000, its trained, 'effective' strength was estimated at less than 170,000.[85] The Corps 'suffered from a tendency to put numbers before quality' and although men aged between 30 and 40 had been eligible to join from 1952, still contained 'an undue number of ageing volunteers who served in civil defence during the last war. Many of them, while retaining their enthusiasm, have found it difficult to adapt themselves to changes of outlook, planning and technique'. Finally, 'it must be accepted that the public conception of the Corps and indeed of the value of civil defence is not as such to encourage the more energetic and capable members of the community to join'.[86] As we saw in the previous chapter, the Corps had a poor public image, and a 1960 study on recruitment commissioned by the Home Office concluded that it was viewed as an 'anachronistic survival which has lingered on from the war'.[87] This image of the Corps helps explain why, despite their numbers, the volunteers were unable to successfully counter the CND message of these years.

To improve the quality of the Corps as a whole and to reach the point where a highly trained caucus could assume positions of responsibility in war, greater training would be needed, and a small financial incentive would be required. These bounty payments, it was hoped, would also boost the morale of the entire Corps, placing it on a similar footing to the Territorial Army and Royal Observer Corps. It was felt that 'no single step could do more to hearten and encourage the Corps... as much for the recognition and status it would confer as for the financial inducement'.[88] It would, additionally, create an impression that the Government was 'serious' about realistic civil and home defence plans. Accepted without the Ministerial Committee meeting,[89] the plan to make changes to the Civil Defence Services as well as the commitment to a dispersal policy was announced in the annual Defence White Paper in February 1962.[90] The bounty scheme, announced in July 1962,[91] was included in the home defence budget for 1963/4.

When the 1962 Defence White Paper was debated in the Commons, the dispersal plan was attacked. William Baxter (Labour, West Stirlingshire) decried its 'hypocrisy' and 'deceitfulness', and wondered whether anyone would really 'believe that civil defence is a reality and a matter of practical politics?'[92] Emrys Hughes criticised the fact that no Minister with responsibility for civil defence was on the Government front bench for the debate.[93] The press, however, were remarkably indifferent to the White Paper's treatment of civil defence,[94] although the *Guardian* noted in July 1962 that CND activity had actually increased interest in the issue and that recruitment might benefit.[95]

After evacuation and the Corps, the main policy left over from the HDR was dealt with by Ministers in spring 1962 – the preparation of advice to the public. In January 1961, Ministers had agreed to the preparation of a new pamphlet to educate the public in civil defence and the nature of a nuclear attack.[96] The intention was to issue 'simple guidance' about measures they could take in an emergency, to be aimed at those 'still confused or ignorant about the probable effects of a nuclear attack'.[97] R.A. Butler had been aware that such a publication 'would require careful preparation to avoid providing ammunition for the critics both of civil defence generally and of the gaps that remain in civil defence preparations'.[98] Ministers approved the draft in May 1962,[99] subject to removing material with 'alarmist' impact.[100] Preparation on the booklet had been suspended because of the Berlin crisis, when priority was given to the drafting 'of more detailed guidance... which could be issued in an emergency'. Since Berlin, the lesson had been learned that 'there must be ready for issue in a period of emergency instructions to the public about what they can do to protect themselves'.[101] This meant that the draft booklet was more informative than that originally envisaged, and that plans were proposed to put it speedily into the public domain in an emergency. As printing and storing 20 million copies would cost £100 million, involve severe problems of distribution in time of crisis (the booklet would need to be sent out very quickly in any period of alert), and might commit the Government to a text possibly 'inappropriate in an emergency some time ahead', it was proposed that 'all national and leading provincial dailies should be consulted at the appropriate time and asked to reproduce the booklet in the pages of every copy of their newspapers in the first or second day of a period of alert'. This would save all the printing and distribution difficulties, using instead the infrastructure which managed to sell 24 million daily newspapers nationwide and ensuring that virtually all households received a copy. In the meantime, copies of the booklet would be printed for all police, civil defence and fire services and some 'might also be put on sale'.[102] The more limited booklet originally conceived in 1961 was shelved, and the controversial final booklet did indeed go on sale in early 1963 as *Civil Defence Handbook No.10: Advising the Householder on Protection against Nuclear Attack*.[103]

FELSTEAD and Cuba

The work completed on evacuation, advice to the public, and the Civil Defence Corps maintained the momentum of the recast civil defence policy from 1960, even though the Berlin crisis had interrupted planning. Successive crises and reviews in 1960–62 meant that civil defence planning had reached a state where it was largely well thought-out and sensible. The eruption of the Cuban Missile Crisis in October 1962,[104] however, raised questions about the flexibility of these plans. The month before the shock crisis, defence planners converged on the Cabinet Office to conduct a transition-to-war exercise codenamed FELSTEAD. Conceived in the same spirit as the concurrent NATO exercise FALLEX 62, FELSTEAD was intended to test the transition-to-war machinery of the government by compiling scenarios of an unfolding international crisis and reactions to this on the home front. It is important not to overstate the importance of these 'war game' exercises, partly because scenarios were created explicitly to test all aspects of the War Book machinery. FELSTEAD, with its attempt to simulate how public and press opinion would react to the crisis and the actions of the 'Government', did highlight important areas for review. The imagined crisis unfolded as the

Soviet Union ('Orangery' in the exercise) stepped up war preparations across Europe; in Britain the 'Precautionary Stage' was declared and the Regional Seats of Government were put on an alert footing.[105] By the fifth day of the crisis, large scale peace demonstrations had occurred in Trafalgar Square and at military bases, there were major population movements away from the cities, and reports of shortages of food and petrol. That morning, the 'Advice' booklet appeared in all newspapers, including pictures of the appointed Regional Commissioners. The Press that day were 'strongly critical of the inadequacy of the steps announced by the Government' – especially its reluctance 'to make a clear statement of its intentions about evacuation... and its failure to make any realistic provision for shelter'.[106] Also at this fifth day point, it was noted that 40 per cent cent of staff detailed for duty in the RSGs had yet to report back to their departments.

The Regional Commissioners were in their regions with some staff on day six, but 'only two of the Regional Seats of Government are ready to receive them... and less than a third of the full complement had arrived at the headquarters'.[107] There was 'unabated' criticism from the press at the lack of evacuation or shelter plans and calls for the Government 'to give a more positive lead'. Regional Commissioners in the 'safer' western areas were seriously concerned about the huge numbers arriving in their regions and the complete lack of plans to deal with them. By day seven, 'normal life is at a standstill', and there were serious public order problems in some rural areas. Two-thirds of the Civil Defence Corps had reported for duty, but a quarter of the staff for Regional Seats of Government had refused to turn up.[108] By the eighth day, when the daily intelligence summary concluded 'that everything points to the fact that the Orange bloc is preparing for war very shortly',[109] national life appeared to be bordering on collapse, with gangs roaming the deserted city centres and public order crises developing in the overcrowded areas in the western half of Britain.[110] Here the exercise ended, with, one can assume, a massive 'Orangery' attack to follow.

FELSTEAD naturally highlighted deficiencies already perceived. For example, the 'dispersal' scheme was still in its planning stage and could not be implemented in an emergency. There was obviously no shelter policy, and aside from the issuing of 'advice', there was little the government could do to assuage the public's fears. FELSTEAD demonstrated the necessity of measures which made the public feel it was being proactively protected by the government. The inability to obtain the recommended stocks of food, it was believed, would fuel massive resentment and anger – including enormous, CND-inspired protests.[111] Most importantly, it suggested that a functioning evacuation scheme, whatever its life-saving merits, would be vital if panic and discontent amongst the public were to be avoided. FELSTEAD's conclusions were unsurprisingly predicted by the HDR deliberations – that the lack of government preparations might endanger morale, and the lack of a clear political lead might endanger public support for a posture of deterrence. Given the decisions of 1961–62, however, Whitehall could hope that in any future exercise, or indeed real emergency, the Government could deliver a more positive response: ordering dispersal and mobilising a well-trained Civil Defence Corps, to give very public examples.

The position in FELSTEAD was also the position during the Cuban Missile Crisis, when Britain came closest to nuclear catastrophe. It is believed that Macmillan was only a few hours away from instituting the secret Precautionary Stage on Sunday 28 October, when the crisis was alleviated.[112] The Precautionary Stage was the signal for the government's transition-to-war plans, including civil defence measures, to be activated. Of course, crisis was averted, and cold war tensions never again reached such a height. Naturally, it was not known at the time that Cuba was to be the closest the cold war came to erupting into all-out thermonuclear war. On the contrary, in November and December 1962 it appeared as merely the latest in an increasingly long line of cold war crises which seemed to be escalating in menace and importance. Thus Cuba led to a speeding up of existing home defence plans and a 'Post-Cuba Review' of transition-to-war planning. When Ministers received a submission on the home defence budget proposing an acceleration of key measures, the report stressed the shortcomings identified in the recent exercises as well as Cuba as justification. Work on the RSGs and the communication and warning systems was to be accelerated at a small additional cost (only around £630,000).[113] This was agreed, as was the proposal to print rationing documents in peacetime, at a cost of £240,000. Even the usually all-conquering consideration of publicity was swept aside.[114] The seriousness of recent crises, and the calamitous results of a lack of rationing in a future emergency flagged in FELSTEAD, must have combined to ensure the proposal was accepted. This acceleration meant that when the civil defence budget was announced in the 1963 Defence White Paper, it had increased by over £3.5 million to £23 million[115] – the first meaningful increase of the thermonuclear era – although in the subsequent Parliamentary debate, civil defence was not raised.[116]

The post-Cuba Review, however, continued into the summer of 1963, focussing on ensuring that the government machinery, in the words of the new Cabinet Secretary, Sir Burke Trend, 'was sufficiently flexible' to react quickly to a 'sudden emergency, in which we might have no more than two or three days warning of the outbreak of war'.[117] This was why three new specially-built RSGs were approved, as their existing accommodation could not be made ready to meet the new two-day target – not to mention why others were extended. Macmillan had already approved the proposal that the Precautionary Stage should be ordered (by the Prime Minister alone, if necessary) earlier in any crisis, to ensure the machinery was up and running.[118] This would include manning Corsham, and the list of Ministers to go to the bunker, to the Regions, and to stay in London with the Prime Minister had been drawn-up in August 1962.[119] Both Macmillan, and later Douglas-Home, identified the two Ministerial Deputies authorised to order nuclear retaliation if a first-strike had made the Prime Minister unable to do so. Macmillan nominated, in his macabre way, R.A. Butler and Selwyn Lloyd as 'First Gravedigger' and 'Second Gravedigger'.[120] Douglas-Home maintained the pair, with Butler designated to remain in London with the Prime Minister, and Lloyd to be posted to H.Q. Bomber Command at High Wycombe.[121]

Other decisions taken in the summer of 1963 included confirmation that no Emergency Powers (Defence) Bill should be introduced in peacetime, due to presumed Parliamentary resistance to its more extreme aspects, but that this bill and all draft Defence Regulations should be completed, submitted to Ministers and after approval printed and stored for emergency use. Also, there should be a Local Government 'War Book' explaining what local authorities would have to do in an emergency rather than leaving it up to individual authorities. And, finally, it was agreed that although the planning assumption would remain that Departments would have 'seven days warning to put their plans into action, they should plan to get as far ahead as possible within two or three days'.[122]

This concentration on the machinery of government and Government War Book measures is explainable as a fine-tuning to ensure the Government was ready to act in any crisis. In the same way that printing ration documents was important, up-to-date war book measures and pre-printed defence regulations would mean that in any future emergency, the Government could state its policy quickly, asserting its authority, establishing its control and implementing its policies immediately, without waiting for essential documentation or legislation to be prepared, printed or distributed. Therefore, one can see this focus as the final push to ensure that British home defence plans, however limited in practical scope, would be on a fully established footing and ready to implement at short notice.

That this is so can be seen in the draft Emergency Powers (Defence) Bill,[123] rightly described as 'ferocious' by Peter Hennessy.[124] After its introduction and enactment during the precautionary stage, the Act would essentially put all powers of law and order, and life and death, in the hands of the Regional Commissioners. If passed it would have amounted to 'a voluntary abdication by Parliament of the whole of their functions during the period of the emergency'.[125] Although such widespread powers seem drastic, there can be no doubt that they would have been vital in the event of nuclear war if the Regional Commissioners were to have any chance of maintaining the control of the population. The whole system of Corsham and Regional Seats of Government, Precautionary Stages, and emergency legislation was designed to give the state the best chance of governing, but there is grave doubt whether it would have worked even with the help of the military. As we have seen Strath envisaged the possibility of some kind of military government. In 1959, in a private lecture to the Home Office, Sir Norman Brook also outlined the prospects of a post-attack military government, making it clear that it was the intention of the government's policy to ensure 'the maintenance for as long as possible of the supremacy of the civil power', and the 'capacity to re-assert civil control, and, as soon as possible, central political control, for the period of recovery after the initial nuclear phase'.[126] F.R. Barratt, a civil servant assigned to the Regional Seat of Government in the North West Region, has written that 'actually I believe that the survivors would have been very lucky if the Armed Forces and the police between them had been able to keep some kind of order with powers over life and death. A collapse into a nasty and brutish nightmare seems more likely in the short term'.[127]

Although the status of the Missile Crisis as the cold war's ultimate crisis is not in doubt, its very danger and the fear it inspired was the harbinger of an enormous downturn in cold war hostilities. It was in response to Cuba, in John Lewis Gaddis' words, that 'a series of Soviet-American agreements began to emerge, at first tacit, later explicit, acknowledging the danger nuclear weapons posed to capitalist and communist worlds alike'.[128] These agreements included the Limited Test Ban Treaty in 1963, the Non-Proliferation Treaty in 1968, and in 1972, both the Anti-Ballistic Missile Treaty and Strategic Arms Limitation Talks, as well as more informal moves towards a cold war *modus operandi*. This represented a real move towards détente and an understanding of the necessity of the nuclear balance: the triumph of the 'idea that the vulnerability that came with the prospect of instant annihilation could become the basis for a stable, long-term Soviet-American relationship'.[129]

Cuba and subsequent détente had profound implications for British civil defence policy. After 1962, the threat of all-out nuclear war annihilating Britain palpably decreased. Certainly, the popularity of CND, already declining from its 1960 peak, seemed to fall away steadily.[130] Richard Taylor argues that 'with the resolution of the crisis, the intense *urgency* which had characterised all movement activism evaporated'.[131] Even worse for CND's continued effectiveness, Cuba seemed to represent in the public mind a vindication of the Government's deterrent argument.[132] Over the course of the 1960s, as we shall see in the next chapter, the decline in the risk of nuclear war, and the concomitant decline in political pressure from the peace movement, allowed the Government to reduce spending on civil defence. Using the increasingly popular metaphor of insurance to discuss civil defence,[133] a marked reduction of the risk of nuclear war enabled a reduction in the premium to be paid.

Conclusion

The Cuban Missile Crisis marked a decisive point in Britain's cold war history, and the downturn in international tensions would be exploited in the following years. For contemporary planners, the review of war planning which followed October's events raised British post-attack preparations to a new level of sophistication. For the first time, the nature as well as the shape of the post-nuclear British state can be seen. It would have been arbitrary and brutal in its use of violence to maintain order, if order would have been possible. For Ministers and planners, the suspension of all civil rights and the use of summary justice would have been a price worth paying for the preservation of some social structure. Better state violence and the execution of food rioters than mob rule, survival of the fittest, and the relentless battle for scarce resources on the part of individuals – better authoritarianism than anarchy. This was the British state attempting to peer into the abyss of what post-attack Britain *might* look like. It was based on an awareness that, contrary to CND arguments, millions would survive a nuclear war. It was also based on the knowledge that for those millions, the real horrors of nuclear catastrophe might only be beginning. There was a hard, undoubtedly unpleasant edge to these plans, but they were the result of deep thinking about the hard, unpleasant picture conjured up of a Britain devastated by nuclear war.

Alongside such planning, of course, went the recasting of the Civil Defence Corps. In these years, there was not even the fiction of the Corps playing a genuine role in the post-attack phase. Sir Sidney Kirkman might argue that the volunteers could make a real impact, but their potential life-saving capabilities played no part in the final justification for retaining the Corps. It was now façade pure and simple; but at least it was attempting to be a convincing one. It also had an established, though still disputed, strategic function: its very existence, its pretence at promoting nuclear survival, would convince people – or at least some of them – not to abandon the government's deterrent policy in any crisis. Within Whitehall, this was articulated in terms of bolstering public morale. Had this secret justification been leaked to CND, it would have been seen as a monstrous falsehood designed to hoodwink the public into blindly stumbling into a nuclear war under the false belief that somehow their lives might be saved. It was a falsehood, and one almost certainly based at least in part on avoiding political controversy. But within the Macmillan Government, it was seen as a necessary aspect of its duty to defend Britain and its people.

8
Gradual Decline and Sudden Fall

The years after the Cuban Missile Crisis were ones of slow decline for civil defence, followed in January 1968 by the swift axing of the policy. The last months of the Conservative Government and the early years of the new Labour Government were hardly characterised by the seismic cold war events that shaped the Macmillan government's attitude to nuclear war between 1959 and 1962. Up until 1967 efforts on civil defence fell away noticeably. There were several reasons for this. Firstly, for practical reasons, the planning effort slackened: much had been achieved in 1961–63 on post-attack planning, such as the defence regulations, government advice, and the alternative system of government; there was, therefore, relatively little still to be done. Secondly, international tension declined markedly from the high point of Cuba. Neither Sir Alec Douglas-Home nor Harold Wilson was forced to spend significant amounts of time managing East-West tensions while in Downing Street. This had obvious ramifications for civil defence. If there was less chance of war, there was less reason to support spending for the contingency of it occurring. Thirdly, the continual economic crises experienced by a Labour Government determined to increase social policy spending put enormous pressure on the entire defence budget; civil defence was always the poor relation in this, and was especially exposed to fluctuations in the financial health of the Government. The impetus for the final act in the civil defence drama was the necessity of heavy cost-cutting in the wake of the 1967 devaluation crisis. Finally, the rapid decline of the nuclear disarmament movement after Cuba meant that the political pressure to maintain public civil defence measures was increasingly absent. The anti-nuclear movement was still important, as we shall see, but the decline in its size and the experience of the early 1960s meant that the government was no longer so fearful that public support for deterrence would collapse in an international crisis unless civil defence services existed.

These reasons existed in symbiosis. Between them they created the paradigm in which civil defence operated. In 1960, the existence of a strong disarmament movement and a high level of international tension ensured that public civil defence measures were continued. The realisation that physical measures had to be implemented to ensure the workability of the alternative system of government even led to an ultra-rare budget increase in 1963/64. After 1964, such pressures were either absent or less marked. When disarmament campaigners exposed the RSG system in 1963 and the government, 18 months later, concluded that the system was unworkable, there was no programme of separate building. The international climate, the relative unlikelihood of all-out global war, meant that civil defence war planning could not demand the sums needed to maintain a level of provision previously deemed vital. In planning public measures, the realisation that few people could criticise the decision allowed the government to first reduce the numbers within the Corps and then – when financial requirements demanded – scrap it all together.

CND and the Spies for Peace

This narrative of declining fortunes for the disarmament movement did not stop it being of importance in the early years of the period, and indeed scoring some spectacular successes. In 1963 CND launched a full-scale campaign to highlight the failings of civil defence, reaching its height with an autumn mock exercise 'FALLEX 63'. This campaign was perhaps inspired by two events occurring earlier in the year: the publication of *Advising the Householder on Protection against Nuclear Attack* and the notorious 'Spies for Peace' episode. The booklet was finally published in January 1963, and although on general sale, was officially a Civil Defence Corps document. (In this it followed other Civil Defence Corps handbooks publicly available such as *Light Rescue*[1] and *Elementary Fire-Fighting*.[2]) It was plainly inadequate in terms of an honest account of the destructive powers of a hydrogen bomb, but it did give simple advice to the layperson about basic warning procedures and how to construct a fallout shelter. Had the booklet been issued to householders during a crisis, in the form of being reprinted in newspapers, a series of seven accompanying *Civil Defence Information Bulletins* would have been broadcast on television. Each five minute long film was presented by a calm uniformed figure giving much the same advice as contained in the booklet.[3]

On the booklet's publication, its shortcomings were seized upon by CND. Its Twickenham branch announced that although the Twickenham area would need up to 5 million sandbags, the local council's Civil Defence Department did not know where to get them and that Handbook No. 10 was not available in any bookshop or library within the borough.[4] Although this was a local case, it illustrated the larger problems of the Government's civil defence policy, and in 1982 Duncan Campbell pointed out that in 1963 sandbagging Hull alone would have exhausted the national supply.[5] The booklet was also attacked by the House of Commons Select Committee on Estimates, who argued that it did not achieve 'any useful purpose', that it did not give the impression that civil defence preparations were 'of any value whatsoever', and that it should be withdrawn.[6] Other MPs slowly followed the Committee's lead. Although it was mentioned in the debate on civil defence in March 1963,[7] no MP attacked the booklet until the debate on 2 December 1963, when it was savaged by Emrys Hughes (Labour, South Ayrshire) on much the same lines as the Estimates Committee.[8] The Government defended the pamphlet arguing that it was for training purposes only, was not designed for the use of ordinary householders and that those who had used the booklet for these purposes had had no complaints.[9]

After *Advising the Householder*, 1963 saw another controversial civil defence policy aired in public, with the sensational blowing of the RSG system during the Aldermaston March in Easter 1963. The people responsible called themselves the 'Spies for Peace', a never-identified group whose members were part of the Committee of 100.[10] The 'Spies' produced a pamphlet, distributed among those on the annual march, entitled 'Danger! Official Secret: RSG-6', which in its own words was 'about a small group of people who have accepted nuclear war as a probability, and are consciously and carefully planning for it' based in 'secret headquarters, each ruled by a Regional Commissioner with absolute power over millions of people... these chosen few are our shadow military government. Their headquarters are called Regional Seats of Government'.[11]

The pamphlet naturally painted the RSG system in an authoritarian light, suggesting Regional Commissioners would be soldiers rather than the Cabinet Ministers we know they were planned to be.[12] Both Christopher Driver and Richard Taylor linked the 'Spies' to anarchist elements of the Committee of 100.[13] The Security Service, despite not being able to shed any light on the individuals involved also investigated 'Spies for Peace' for the Cabinet's Personnel Security Committee a month after the revelations.[14] What seems clear is that the 'Spies' broke into RSG-6 at Warren Row, near Reading, and, they claimed, extracted secret material relating to the RSG system, the government's transition-to-war and civil defence plans, and the results of the previous autumn's NATO exercise FALLEX '62.

Apparently, after their success at Warren Row, the 'Spies' had hoped to 'expose the emergency government system that lay behind the RSG structure... [leading them] to explore an enormous military complex at Corsham: but the group found it impossible to get far enough into the complex to gather sufficient evidence to confirm their suspicions'.[15] The suspicions of the 'Spies for Peace' were correct, for they had of course stumbled on TURNSTILE. There is no evidence to suggest Whitehall knew how close the 'Spies' were to making such a sensational discovery – no mention of their suspicions appeared in the Easter 1963 pamphlet. Given the controversy surrounding the infiltration of Warren Row, had the existence of TURNSTILE become known, it would have been ruinous for the government's civil and home defence plans, as well as being a hugely embarrassing security breach.

The consequences of the revelations of Easter 1963 are illuminating. Newspapers generally condemned the breach of security and the leader in *The Daily Telegraph* declared that 'the pamphlet seems to reflect an amalgam of the worst elements of CND: Communist subversion and pure rebellious irresponsibility'.[16] The *Daily Mail* ran an interview with Henry Brooke in which the Home Secretary called those responsible 'traitors'.[17] This line was also taken by the *Times*, who criticised the increasing anarchist influence within the movement.[18] The *Daily Mirror* called it a 'cheap and harmful stunt' and suggested the 'Spies' deserved the full penalties of the law,[19] although it seemed more much more concerned with the drama of Scotland Yard hunting them down.[20] A week after the revelations were first reported in the press, Harold Macmillan attempted to defuse the crisis, linking in Commons speech the RSG system to the system of Regional Commissioners Britain had put in place during the Second World War:

> It is widely known that our defensive plans for any future war, whether nuclear or conventional, include provision for a similar, essentially civilian organisation. What have been referred to as regional seats of Government are, in fact, the headquarters from which the regional commissioners would operate in a war emergency.... To prepare them... is an obviously essential precaution.[21]

Both in his speech and in his private diary, Macmillan dismissed the importance of the actual revelations. The speech was a masterful exercise in gentle subterfuge, with Macmillan keen to point out the 'essentially civilian' aspects of the RSG system whilst underplaying the military aspects. In fact the existence of control centres had been mentioned on a number of occasions: in Parliament on 5 December 1962,[22] and in the 1963 Defence White Paper.[23]

Macmillan deplored 'the deliberate breach of security', whilst arguing that 'the disclosure of this particular information is not seriously damaging to the national interest'.[24] In his diary, the Prime Minister noted that 'It is not very serious from a practical pt of view, but it's another security failure of the Govt'.[25] For the government, the 'Spies' episode was the latest in a line of security breaches, but in terms of nuclear war planning relatively unimportant. Macmillan thought, and the newspapers agreed, that civilian centres of wartime government were entirely normal and sensible, and few shared the sense of shock felt by 'Spies'. The Security Service was less sanguine about the affair, believing that the pamphlet was merely the start of a wider programme of activities.[26] Aldermaston 1963, however, turned out to be the first and last hurrah of the 'Spies for Peace'. By October 1963 it had been recommended that members of the Committee of 100 who were public servants 'should be excluded, or if already so engaged, removed from work to which security vetting applies', unless Departments wished otherwise.[27] Later, in 1964, it was decided to ensure that no avowed nuclear disarmers would be among those chosen to man the Regional Seats of Government.[28]

CND's autumn FALLEX '63 campaign was based on NATO's own FALLEX '62 exercise, and essentially amounted, on a practical level, to an organised pestering of local civil defence forces for information and a concerted campaign to put across the myriad failings of the government's civil defence policy.[29] It was deliberately timed to coincide with that autumn's civil defence recruitment campaign, and was designed, in the words of the campaign guide, not to 'belittle the efforts of Civil Defence workers who train to help their fellow-citizens in distress', but to exposed the Government's lies, which use civil defence 'to delude people that Britain could survive in an all out nuclear attack'.[30] The effectiveness of the FALLEX '63 campaign is open to debate. A Cabinet Office report on the demonstrations explains that very little was done and little press attention (even locally) given over to CND except for some minor activity in Bristol, Cambridge and Oxford (significantly, university towns). In London, 'no reports of the demonstration have been received; and the inference is that it made little impact'.[31] However, Richard Taylor stresses the educational achievements of FALLEX '63, arguing that 'public consciousness was alerted to the whole issue of civil defence, which had previously been shrouded in mystery. The uncomfortable facts of wholesale human destruction which would inevitably follow a nuclear exchange were made known on a very wide scale, and for the first time'.[32] Although this overstates the importance of FALLEX '63 itself, it neatly encapsulates CND's accumulated impact over the whole 1958–63 period; and although scholarship on CND often gives little space to civil defence, it is one rare example of any real success.[33]

The RSG debate, 1964

The true civil defence impact of the 'Spies' episode took a long time to be felt. For most of 1963 and 1964, civil defence policy-making was largely in abeyance. The five-year plan installed after the Home Defence Review was being implemented, and there were no emergency reviews of the sort which typified the early part of the decade. When the Labour Party won the 1964 General Election, there was little reason to suppose civil defence would feature on its policy agenda. Within two months of its arrival in power, however, the new Government was anxiously attempting to limit civil defence spending.

At issue was the proposed building of six new Regional Seats of Government at an increased cost of £2 million over two years. They were needed as new intelligence assessments concluded that Britain would not now have at least seven days' warning of attack, and therefore bespoke RSG buildings would be needed for immediate use in the six regions which had previously banked on taking over other accommodation in a crisis.[34] The new Chief Secretary to the Treasury, Jack Diamond, suggested to the Home Secretary, Sir Frank Soskice, that the spending be deferred, arguing that the Government was increasing spending enormously on social policy and needed to rein in spending elsewhere. Besides, he argued, a delay would not 'cause any significant difficulty' for home defence preparations.[35] Due to the imminent deadline for the acceptance of the tender for the RSG construction work, a final decision was needed quickly. Soskice, therefore, appealed to the Prime Minister on 18 December.[36] Soskice and his Home Office officials rejected the latest strategic assessment which argued that the RSGs would be on any list of possible Russian targets – obviously a key argument for not building them.[37] 'This assessment', they argued, 'is not based on any direct evidence': a foreign power would not consider extending its attacks beyond nuclear installations and cities because they would be unnecessary, and, in any case, RSGs 'represent no danger... since they have no role in connection with our nuclear strike forces'.[38]

One must wonder why this issue had only just arisen, some 20 months after the 'Spies for Peace' episode. Surely the prospect of the Soviets attacking the RSGs should have been dealt with before December 1964. For example, the *Daily Mail* discussed this issue at the time, telling its readers that 'the bunkers... are sited in areas where H-bomb attack is – or WAS – least likely'.[39] Surely it would have been natural to believe that the enemy's post-attack system of Government was an eminently suitable target for Russian nuclear strategists, but the Home Office felt able to doubt it. Clearly they approved of the advice that suggested that new RSGs needed to be built, but rejected that which argued the opposite. The same day, Diamond sent a countering memo to Wilson,[40] arguing that the 'record peace time increase' in public expenditure was coming 'at a time when the economic and financial situation demands the opposite'. All 'not urgently necessary' expenditure needed to be cut, 'especially on things with low economic or social priority'. It was proposed that the increase should be deferred until the whole civil defence programme was reviewed. Finally, the doubts over whether the RSGs would survive the initial attack strengthened 'an already compelling case both for not incurring this expenditure next year and for reviewing our predecessors' plans for home defence'.[41] After consultation with the Cabinet Secretary,[42] Wilson sided with the Treasury, and the Home Office was defeated.[43]

Usually when a government decision went against the civil defence planners, economic considerations could be blamed. This was partly true in 1964–65, but an important factor was the strategic untenability of the Home Office position. With the Ministry of Defence arguing that measures would be pointless, and the intelligence experts arguing that it was unlikely the RSGs would survive the first hours of a nuclear war, the Home Office was left with a hopeless case. There was no point in building these controls in their existing sites; there would have been a case for building RSGs in different locations, but this would mean starting from scratch and cloaking the measure in the level of security used for the building of Corsham. Both measures would have proved very costly. Of course, the RSG system was the backbone of the government's plans to maintain control in the post-attack period. Abandoning it at the start of 1965, when the next five-yearly civil defence review was due, left the government's plans in turmoil.

Home Defence Review, 1965

The Home Defence Review of 1965 was initiated on 1 February 1965 when Wilson agreed to Soskice's proposal for a fundamental review of policy.[44] It was chaired by Philip Allen, completing a decade of investigating the grim effects of nuclear war. A year and a day later, the results of the review were briefly outlined in Parliament by Soskice's successor, Roy Jenkins.[45] The review, in no way as far-ranging and significant as its predecessors, was based on two principles which demonstrated the trend of civil defence policy. These were the need for economies, and the need to reduce the reliance on ad hoc arrangements due to the new belief that any Precautionary Stage might be as short as two or three days.[46] The main thrust of the report, as Wilson was told, was that 'although the risk of nuclear attack on the United Kingdom is much reduced, it cannot be ignored and home defence cannot be entirely abandoned'.[47] The only controversy, it seems, was over the Civil Defence Corps. The Committee was completely divided as to whether the £11 million spent on the Corps was worth it, although it agreed that the previous argument that it would help shore up morale in a crisis was not reason enough for it to continue.[48] At first, Ministers decided to retain the Corps on the grounds that 'it would not be defensible for the Government to say that no provision at all need be made for the functions now fulfilled by the Corps'; also, although its life-saving capacity was 'marginal', there was a view that 'in such a desperate situation', the Corps' functions 'would be of increased importance and could not be carried out as effectively by other means'; and finally that disbandment 'would be interpreted as meaning that the Government were abandoning all effective measures for civil defence'.[49]

After further studies, however, the life-saving potential of the Civil Defence Corps was seen as inefficient.[50] The Headquarters and Warden sections were seen as an essential part of the control system, and the welfare organisation likewise essential in the survival stage. But the rescue and ambulance sections were 'less easy to justify on operational grounds'.[51] Hence it was decided to scrap them, and this uncertainty over the Corps' future caused the cancelling of the 1965 annual recruitment programme, the first non-election year without one since 1949 – and even local campaigns had occurred in those years.[52] The local-only campaign of 1964 was thus the last attempt to gain members for the Corps (see Figure 8.1), and its focus on the individual a striking counterpoint to the patriotic thrust of 1950 (Figure 3.1) and the communitarian stance of 1954 (Figure 4.1). After negotiations with local authorities, Jenkins was able to announce in the Commons on 14 December 1966 both the axing of the rescue and ambulance sections and the fact that in future the Corps was to 'help the local authorities to man the control system, which is the system of government in emergency; and to provide limited numbers of specialists to help to organise the first aid and welfare resources of the community'.[53] The active strength of the Corps would be reduced from 122,000 to 75,000–80,000, saving £1 million. In reply, Richard Sharples (Conservative, Sutton and Cheam) argued that 'for a comparatively small saving, in the opinion of many civil defence workers he is virtually destroying an organisation which has rendered a great service both in peace and war'.[54] Certainly, the life-saving capacity had been abandoned, and it the Corps's role was reduced to its warden functions: essentially helping to control the public in fallout conditions.

Aside from reviewing the Corps, the Committee spent most of its time attempting to deal with the control system. The restructuring of the control system was heavily influenced by the analysis that the RSGs would be targeted in any future war. Planners made it clear that

Figure 8.1 Civil Defence Corps Advertising, Local Recruitment Campaign, 1964.[55]

some form of flexible, and survivable, system of government must exist to operate at the regional level between central and local government.[56] This led to the conclusion that the RSGs should only be manned after attack, and that a greater burden should be placed on the Sub-Regional Controls (SRCs), of which there were usually two per region. These would be manned pre-attack, usually in previously identified buildings, and they would have some ability to conduct operations for the whole region if the RSG was unavailable for use. The RSG staff would convene in the region away from the premises, which would probably have to be improvised to some extent as the building programme, it was decided, could continue to be deferred. This at least meant that the system was more flexible, but it also meant that it was organised on very tenuous assumptions. It relied on the RSG staff being able to occupy a standing, and previously identified building, and SRCs remaining off the Soviet target list.[57]

Could this new system have worked? On 15 November 1965, the Civil Defence Department of the Home Office sent a letter to all its Regional Civil Defence Directors, asking them to identify premises which would be suitable for the short-term as Sub-Regional Controls.[58] A year later, the Home Office drafted a paper to report on progress.[59] Of the 21 SRCs mentioned, ten were already operational. A few of these were ex-RSGs, such as Kidderminster and Dover. Of the rest, most were in government hands and could be strengthened, but five were in private hands (including the University of Wales at Bangor, and the Craiglands Hotel, Ilkley) and could only be earmarked. The same earmarking process occurred for buildings where the RSG staff could 'gather' pre-attack: the Grand Hotel in Scarborough, University of Wales, Aberystwyth, Arundel Castle, and the less salubrious Durham or Chelmsford Prisons, were all listed as possible premises. In short, there were few premises from which the regions could be governed in a war emergency. Assuming the Soviets would destroy the old RSG sites (and of course, several of those had not been built because of this very assumption), the control system would be in tatters, trying to find buildings with adequate communications in which to operate. Even in the long-term, no money was to be found for new premises. It can only be argued that in the wake of the 'Spies for Peace' revelations and the new assumptions concerning the Soviets' intentions, the government's policy of regional control had collapsed. This had been a central civil and home defence policy in the years following Strath: it was considered of paramount importance, second only to that of the central government headquarters itself. By 1966, all the RSGs should have been completed, and a rare civil defence planning success could have been celebrated. By the middle of 1965, however, the policy which had evolved over the previous eight to ten years was essentially dead.

The 1965 review had little to say about most other measures. It argued that the warning system, public information and dispersal planning should continue on the grounds that they had to the potential to save many lives at a tiny cost.[60] Those 'dispersed' would be the same as those envisaged in 1962, but it was hoped to move them in the two or three days deemed available in the precautionary stage by only dispersing them within 50 miles of the cities, using commuter rail services (for the reason that, post-Beeching review of the railways,[61] only the suburban services had the capacity to move so many people).[62] The Strath Report had been an attempt to get to grips with the thermonuclear era; the 1960 review had tried to outline a home defence 'philosophy' for the age of mutual deterrence; the 1965, review, however, seemed solely concerned with what savings could be justified.

When Jenkins outlined the changes to the Civil Defence Corps in late 1966, he argued that it would allow the Government to cut the home defence budget of £19.7 million in 1966/67 by £1 million the following year.[63] Since Labour assumed power in October 1964, the budget had been cut from £24.1 million in 1964/65, or, more crucially, from the projected cost of £26.9 million in 1965/66 to £18.7 million in 1967/68, a cut of over 30 per cent. The financial problems of the government had exerted a great deal of pressure on the civil defence budget, but it was unable to resist that pressure due to the collapse in the strategic basis of previous policy, and the lack of any international or diplomatic stimulus to spend money. There was no money for the SRCs, and no compelling argument for keeping the rescue functions of the Corps. Moreover, by 1966 it was clear that CND had declined to the extent that the government did not fear admitting that these life-saving measures were being abandoned. Two main results of the review – abandoning the old RSG system and scaling back the Corps – had the effect of stripping away some dead wood from civil defence planning. It was clear that neither would have functioned effectively in wartime. In this sense the review was entirely sensible. It did not, could not, replace them with anything worthwhile; increasing proof that the civil defence cupboard was bare.

The War Game

If CND's decline helped the government curtail provision after the 1965 Home Defence Review, the slide of anti-nuclear feeling in Britain must not be overstated. Nuclear war and civil defence were still capable of creating controversy, as the *War Game* furore proved. In 1965 the BBC produced *The War Game*, a documentary-style drama by Peter Watkins detailing the effects of a nuclear attack on a town in Kent, but decided against broadcasting it, ostensibly due to the violence of the images it contained. The non-transmission of *The War Game* was extremely controversial, with some, Watkins included, believing it was a political decision designed to keep his film, representing the 'truth' about nuclear war, from the screens. The controversy surrounding the non-transmission has been thoroughly investigated in recent years, itself creating some controversy, with the result that this is one of the few aspects of Whitehall's cold war history which has been extensively written about.[64] Whether the Government firmly forced the BBC to 'ban' the programme is not the main point of interest in the civil defence context, although it must be stressed that the key role played in the crisis by Lord Normanbrook (as the ex-Cabinet Secretary, chief planner of much of the British cold war state and now Chairman of the BBC was now called) meant that there was probably very little need for the Government to firmly ban the film; the Chairman himself was very much in tune with what the government might have considered to be in the 'national interest'.

Whatever the reasons for its non-transmission, the decision caused outcry among the nuclear disarmers, who felt that the Government had heavy-handedly intervened to squash debate on civil defence and nuclear war. The BBC, which felt under pressure to assert its independence and to prove its decision had been an honourable one, held closed screenings. Tickets to these screenings, incidentally, were in great demand. The BBC archives detail the attempts of dozens of MPs to get extra seats.[65] The BBC Chairman's attachment to his Whitehall past is illustrated by his stepping in personally to ensure that a much sought-after ticket was sent to a retired civil servant with an interest in the issue: one Sir William Strath.[66] Interestingly, the BBC invited the defence rather than television correspondents of the newspapers. As Tony Shaw put it, 'to most newspapers the production was deemed... gratuitously violent, politically dangerous or monstrously misrepresentative – in short, CND propaganda'.[67]

But despite its reputation and its power, the image of nuclear war and civil defence displayed in *The War Game* is hardly one to which Ministers and planners could have objected. Lord Normanbrook told his successor as Cabinet Secretary, Sir Burke Trend, that 'I have seen the film, and I can say that it has been produced with considerable restraint. But the subject is, necessarily, alarming; and the showing of the film might have a significant effect on public attitudes to the nuclear deterrent'.[68] The power of the film lies in its violence and brutality – key scenes include the execution of food rioters by the police, the social divisions unmasked by evacuation, the results of rationing of medical supplies, and the traumatised survivors. But the reality, as these chapters have shown, would have been undoubtedly worse than that portrayed by Watkins. Key government policies were shown to be a success: evacuation occurs before the attack comes and the government are able to maintain control of food distribution and law and order. For the government, in a genuine post-attack crisis, the execution of looters would be preferable to anarchy resulting from the disintegration of government control. Had a nuclear war broken out on the scale envisaged in the film, the British civil defence planners could only have hoped that their policies worked as well in reality as they did in *The War Game*. The problems over the film were not caused by the difference between it and the government's policy, but between it and the public discourse over that policy. For although many people followed the CND line that nuclear war would be all-destructive, the actual physical damage caused by nuclear war and the post-attack condition of Britain were enormously difficult to conceptualise – as Strath put it, 'beyond the imagination'.[69] Watkins' vision, therefore, could have had an enormous impact on an unprepared public mind caught between two opposing versions of nuclear war – CND's all-encompassing catastrophe, and the government's survivable nuclear war. Officials, meanwhile, understood that the reality would be worse than *The War Game*.

Care-and-maintenance

The factors already outlined in this chapter – long-term decline of the disarmament movement, cold war détente, and regular financial crises – explain why the end of civil defence, when it came, was relatively uncontroversial. In November 1967 the Wilson Government devalued the pound against the dollar, the final wrecking the Government's doomed economic policy. More important for British domestic and overseas policy was the programme of cuts in public expenditure thrashed out in no less than eight Cabinet meetings between 4–15 January 1968.[70] Announced in the House of Commons by Wilson on 16 January, the main measures included the accelerated withdrawal of British troops from the Far East, and also from the Gulf; the scrapping of plans to purchase 50 F-111 aeroplanes from America; the reintroduction of prescription charges; and, perhaps most controversial of all, deferring the raising of the school leaving age from 15 to 16. Wilson himself called this last measure a 'difficult, indeed repugnant' decision to make.[71] In the face of this onslaught of cuts, the transferral of long-moribund civil defence planning to a care-and-maintenance basis received little attention. Wilson announced:

> We have decided to reduce Home Defence – Civil Defence – to a care-and-maintenance basis, with a saving of about £14 million in 1968–9, and £20 million in 1969–70 and in subsequent years. This will involve the disbandment of the Civil Defence Corps, the Auxiliary Fire Service and the Territorial Army Volunteer Reserve Category III.[72]

The proposal had been put to the Cabinet as part of the post-devaluation measures of the new Chancellor, Roy Jenkins.[73] Jenkins outlined the results of a report commissioned by himself and Callaghan (the new Home Secretary), which advised that two options could be pursued: 'a minimum coherent programme' of active home defence preparations, which would cost £19–£20 million per annum, or placing everything on a care-and-maintenance basis, which would cut costs 'to about £13 million in 1968–9, and thereafter to about £7–£8 million per annum'.[74]

The 'minimum' programme meant continuing as before. Civil defence had, after all, been pared to bone in successive expenditure reviews throughout the 1960s. Jenkins was 'quite sure that in present circumstances we must put H.D. on a care-and-maintenance basis'.[75] This meant 'no new physical assets would be created' beyond those already at an advanced stage of planning, 'but existing physical assets would generally be preserved'. The volunteer services 'would be disbanded, and planning and instruction would be limited to what was necessary to enable active preparations to be resumed at some future date'.[76] It was recognised that 'it would not be easy to recruit volunteers again after a lapse of time, or to bring ourselves back to the present state of readiness without intensive effort. But we cannot afford to pay £20 million or more every year as an insurance premium against nuclear attack'.[77] In the Cabinet discussion, Callaghan simply agreed with the proposal, as did Denis Healey, the Defence Secretary, who stated that 'the maintenance of civil defence in this country on the existing scale was not a significant element in the deterrence of nuclear aggression'.[78]

And that was that. A sterling crisis too far, and the whole basis of cold war civil defence was swept away and the Civil Defence Corps consigned to history. As with the 1965–66 Review, the strategic context which allowed civil defence to be so savagely cut was as important as devaluation. Although the need to limit spending post-devaluation was the initial spur, it must be remembered that by 1968 home defence had few supporters left in Whitehall. The Ministry of Defence had been arguing for scrapping it as an irrelevance along these lines since 1960, and by 1968 the case appeared compelling. The strategic and political context had caught up with the MoD argument, making the case against civil defence very strong. With the added economic imperative, it was irresistible. There was, quite simply, little argument for it continuing.

The Government's policy of ending conspicuous civil defence preparations positioned it in-between those implacably opposed to civil defence and those firm supporters of it. This was amply demonstrated in the brief debate on civil defence held on 18 January 1968. No one made any real case for continuing civil defence. David Ennals, Under-Secretary at the Home Office, had to reply both to Hugh Jenkins (Labour, Putney), who called the possibility of civilised life after nuclear attack 'a totally unrealistic fairy tale',[79] and Sir David Renton (Conservative, Huntingdonshire), who argued that both the 'credibility of the deterrent' and 'a most valuable service to humanity' were being 'removed'.[80] Ennals simply stated that 'the extent of civil defence preparations must depend both on the extent of the danger, as represented by the international situation, and on the ability of the country to pay for the cost of civil defence preparations',[81] and that the expense could be justified 'were there to be a situation of mounting international tension; but this, happily is not the present situation'.[82] It was the government's stated policy that once the international position changed, civil defence preparations could be ratcheted up from the level there were suspended at in 1968 (although Roy Jenkins had informed the Cabinet that this would not be possible), which allowed Ennals to side-step the argument that the Government was jeopardising the deterrent. It also allowed him to refute the notion that the Government was ending civil defence preparations because it had come to its senses and realised it was pointless: because it had not, in fact, ended civil defence at all – just suspended it.

The Government, and the local authorities, still had a statutory duty under the Civil Defence Act of 1948 to undertake civil defence plans. The Home Office actually sent a circular to the local authorities outlining that 'the Government's decision must not be construed as implying the abandonment of all civil defence measures'.[83] Future civil defence activity 'should consist primarily of planning how to raise the level of preparations should the circumstances demand it... rather than of making physical preparations against the contingency of an imminent war'.[84] Although the planning obligation remained and official statements stressed that civil defence preparations could be resurrected, 1968 must be seen as the end of postwar civil defence in Britain. When civil defence preparations began again – in a small way in 1972, and more substantially after 1980, both under Conservative Governments, there was no voluntary civil defence organisation, and scant effort was made to protect the population.[85] The Corps, which formed the heart of civil defence policy between 1948/9 and 1968, and had been depleted gradually throughout the 1960s, was finally put out of its misery, and all physical preparations were stopped. The constant battle to update plans and preparations to meet the contingency of nuclear war had been fought and largely lost for more than 20 years, but was now given up.

The decision took place at a time of intense discussion about the future of the nuclear deterrent. Developments in defensive missile technology suggested that Britain's new Polaris fleet might be unable to deter the Soviets from aggression.[86] The validity of this view, and indeed whether it mattered if it was true, was hotly contested in the late 1960s, but had no impact on the care-and-maintenance decision, illustrating the variety of factors which caused civil defence's downfall. In much the same way, the 1969 attempt to reverse the decision demonstrated that civil defence was not purely an issue of defence policy. Sir Burke Trend led the move, citing the 'incalculability of Soviet actions' as illustrated by the invasion of Czechoslovakia.[87] An increase in spending, however, was ruled out by the Home Secretary himself.[88] The continuation of this debate belongs to the history of civil defence's road back to viability in 1972 rather than its decline, but the episode illustrates the state of home defence as the 1960s ended – it was difficult even to muster the enthusiasm of the Minister departmentally most concerned. It is clear that in 1969 there were massive problems in home defence policy which would have detrimentally affected Britain's ability to fight a war, let alone survive it – moreover at a time when Britain's deterrent capability appeared vulnerable. But money and politics had usually trumped defence policy throughout the period. Civil defence ended as it had existed, and it is important to trace this ending back to the formation of the Wilson Government, and even before. Although care-and-maintenance appears as a snap decision in order to save around £20 million a year, we can see that the policy was a logical development of trends discernible from 1960.

Conclusion

These trends can be seen in two strands of the policy: the Civil Defence Corps and what we can call the Control System – the continuation of

Government in and after war. In 1960, the Ministry of Defence had declined to support the continuation of the Civil Defence Corps, believing the 'humanitarian' aspect of civil defence a needlessly expensive charade. The Civil Defence Corps had been reorganised twice in the 1960s to rationalise it and save costs – first to strengthen it by weeding out the inefficient members, then by ending its rescue role – before it was finally axed. It was a justifiable decision, and one which might well have happened sooner. Civil defence in general and the Corps in particular, however, were the Government's shield against accusations of brutality – nuclear war with a human face, if you will. Once it was gone, governments were faced with possessing nuclear weapons but having no policy to save lives in the event of their use – a nightmare scenario for the Conservative Governments and the trumping argument whenever the abolition of the Corps was raised, but an acceptable one in 1968. As mentioned above, the political imperative behind retaining the Corps, so powerful in 1960 (even the MoD admitted that scrapping the Corps would be politically impossible in the short term) was absent in 1968 when the tensions of the cold war had eased enormously and – related to this – the ability of the disarmament movement's polemics to harm governments had lessened.

The second strand, the system of government, is more complex, mostly as a result of the debate around it being conducted in secrecy (except of course, for the 'Spies for Peace' episode). The whole trend of civil and home defence since the Strath Report had been away from the previously dominant Second World War conceptualisation of life-saving and towards a concentration on the preservation of the central, regional and local government and thus the means to maintain authority and the ability to organise a recovery of the nation. When the Wilson Government came to power, the six essential RSGs needed were scrapped partly for economic reasons but there was also a sound strategic rationale for the decision. It was on this level that the care-and-maintenance decision, in the opinion of Trend in 1969, was flawed. By undermining the ability of the Government to maintain law and order, it contravened one of the basic tenets of home defence policy. This was a result of preparations coming to a sudden stop, rather than being allowed to run down, and reach a natural end-point. But then Trend's case was doubtlessly undermined by the fact that there was grave doubt over whether the RSGs or any other government installation could survive an attack.

The abolition of the Civil Defence Corps and the placing of other elements of civil defence into remission provides the historian with a natural break in the history of cold war civil defence, an aspect of Britain's past peculiarly weighed down by its own history. The civil defence triumphs of 1939–45 led partly to the form the Corps took in 1945, and once it was in existence, it could not be abolished. The more its life-saving role in the atomic age and the early thermonuclear era was stressed or exaggerated by politicians, the harder it was then to dismiss it. In other aspects of civil defence policy, however, British planners were far from hidebound by the past, grasping the issues of the atomic, thermonuclear and 'equipoise' ages with vigour and perception. But even the more efficient aspects of the policy appeared outmoded by the developments in nuclear technology. Finally, civil defence's reason for existing seemed to vanish. The decline of cold war tension seemed to many to make the 'insurance policy' dispensable, as the premium seemed excessive compared to the slight risk. Some insurance was still needed – hence care-and-maintenance rather than outright scrapping – but there was disagreement on what level of premium to pay. The politicians wanted the bare minimum, but the planners in 1969 suggested that this minimum was not enough. No one believed a return to the higher level of cover provided by a vast volunteer group was worth paying. Had someone suggested in 1969 Whitehall a policy of the complexity, scope and above all cost of that contained in the Strath Report, there would have been either honest and earnest concerns for their mental health, or a real threat to their future pension. By the end of the 1960s civil defence had few friends left in the corridors of power.

Conclusion

Civil defence was put in cold storage in 1968, 23 years after it had last been stood down. In that time what civil defence meant, cost, and was able to do, had changed dramatically. Indeed, what was understood as civil defence policy in 1945 was simply unrecognisable in 1968. As we have seen, in these years successive governments attempted to wrestle with some intractable problems. There was simply no adequate response to the changing developments of the cold war nuclear threat: providing a coherent life-saving civil defence policy in the age of mutual nuclear deterrence was impossible, and other factors were ever-present to complicate matters. Civil defence was always a delicate balancing of these various inter-locking factors: the threat of war; the scale of any likely attack; the possible responses to such an attack; the government's financial position; and the political climate in which any policies must be announced. Between them, these five factors determined policy, and any evaluation of policy must take them into consideration.

The threat of war was decisive in shaping civil defence. When it looked most likely, in 1950, the government responded with a programme of physical measures designed to complement the wider defence programme. In later years, the threat was seen to decline, negating the need for large-scale measures. Even in 1951, the Attlee government expressly rejected the idea that civil defence expenditure should be tied to that of 'offensive' provision.[1] This highlighted a fundamental tenet of cold war civil defence policy: that even when the threat of war was at its greatest, the duty of government was to concentrate funds on measures which might deter aggression and prevent war. This viewpoint meant that when intermittent crises arose and it looked as if war might occur, civil defence planners were forced into frantic emergency planning, aware that if war came their ad hoc measures would be hopelessly overwhelmed. We can identify, therefore, a basic failure in civil defence provision: when the international climate was tranquil, it could be argued that civil defence was not a pressing concern; but cold war crises were always too sudden to allow a gradual build up of provision, meaning planners were always forced to rely on short-term expedients. No matter how many times it was emphasised, from 1952 onwards, that the nature of the cold war demanded that preparations were made *in advance* of any crisis, policy was always dangerously short-termist, happy to slacken the pace in times of détente and always taken by surprise in any crisis.

The second factor was the envisaged scale and nature of the threatened attack. Obviously, the destructive weight of a prospective attack determined the limits of the possible, and the necessary, in civil defence. It was the sheer power of the hydrogen bomb which meant that life-saving was so difficult, that Britain could not hope to continue to fight a war in continental Europe, and that massive efforts were needed to ensure the survival of British society in the aftermath of attack. It was the scale of attack which determined the cost of the potential measures. Shelters against atomic attack were much more expensive than those of the Second World War; providing shelters across the country to protect against fallout would have been even more so. Reacting to these changes drove change in civil defence thinking. The big reviews of 1945–48, 1953, 1955 and 1960 were all driven by changes in the threatened scale of attack, whether it was the advent of a new type of weapon, or the realisation that such a weapon was held in vast reserves by the enemy. In undertaking these reviews, Whitehall was often tardy: long-term civil defence responses to the atomic bomb should have been completed before 1948. December 1954 war also late in reacting to the hydrogen bomb threat. This, and the often elephantine nature of policy-making in Whitehall, usually meant that when a response had finally been decided on it was meeting a strategic threat which had existed for several years.

The third factor was the possible response to this scale of attack. Obviously, this was the meat-and-drink of civil defence policy-making. Deciding what was possible – and necessary – involved evaluating policy priorities which shaped the nature of civil defence debate. Lengthy debates in the late 1940s on dispersing industry around Britain rested on a belief that such action would be vital to the continuation of British war production after an attack and that it would be possible, physically and economically, to do so.[2] Likewise the decision to build a network of Regional Seats of Government in the late 1950s: they would be necessary to preserve order, and certainly seemed an achievable measure. Both policies ended when it became clear, after all, that they were not possible. It is extremely doubtful whether industrial dispersal was ever a real possibility, but the limited attempts to influence the location of industry were ruined by economic necessity. The RSG system was abandoned when it was decided that the Soviets would blow them up in the initial phase of a future war.[3] Both examples showed civil defence planners having to give up cherished policies only when it became clear that they would not work. This highlights a major issue of civil defence planning: the distance between planners' dreams and strategic and economic realities. The early years of civil defence saw officials, usually from the Home Office, submitting almost fantastical plans costing several hundreds of millions of pounds, only to see them shot down. From 1960 onwards, although civil defence was slight compared to officials' previous hopes, at least plans were drafted with economic and strategic realities firmly in mind: one reason why there was a more settled civil defence policy in the early 1960s.

This gap between planning hopes and planning reality manifested itself in a major split in Whitehall thinking about what was possible and necessary in civil defence. The Home Office firmly believed in the life-saving potential of civil defence and was very reluctant to give it up. In 1960, General Kirkman was strongly arguing that the Civil Defence Corps still had a very real life-saving role to play in a nuclear war. These officials believed that this is what civil defence was for.[4] There were strong advocates of a maximum amount of evacuation, of continuing and strengthening the Civil Defence Corps, of maintaining stockpiles of food and medical supplies, and above all, of some form of shelter provision. The Ministry of Defence, on the other hand, was arguing by 1956 that none of the things were worthwhile.[5] Only the deterrent would stop a war, and even if it did not, then the Home Office plans would not do a great deal to save lives. In the atomic age, it was usually concluded that the money spent on a 'maximum' civil defence policy would be better spent on active measures. In the thermonuclear age, however, it was decided that civil defence of this sort would be wasteful: a heavy insurance premium against a remote contingency which would not, in any case, provide much protection. Civil defence continued, of course, but its limits were more sharply drawn: focussing on governmental (and thus social) survival, and protecting 'public morale' in a crisis by stressing the life-saving role of the Civil Defence Corps. Even the latter was strongly contested by the Ministry of Defence in 1960.[6]

The fourth factor was money. Most of the rejections civil defence policy-formulators received were couched in financial terms, and all the big cuts in provision had their origins in government attempts to cut expenditure. The main example of this occurred in 1956, when the Eden Government's pressing need for savings saw the post-Strath deliberations overturned to be replaced by an entirely new, and bare, conception of civil defence.[7] The other example, of course, was the final decision to place civil defence on a care-and-maintenance basis in 1968, after the previous autumn's devaluation crisis.[8] But money was not all-important. Although often providing the spur, the decisions were always taken on strategic grounds. Government is, after all, essentially a process of managing competing claims for scarce resources. What is key in this context is why, when the axe was about to drop, civil defence bore the cuts. The answer is partly linked to the above discussions of its strategic relevance: in 1956 a significant amount of opinion said that civil defence was too costly, and that as the 'full Strath' had been rejected, it then needed a strategic rethink. In this sense, economic considerations often provided an impetus for the hard strategic decision-making which allowed cuts to happen. Another factor which aided the reduction of expenditure was the short-termism outlined above. In years of relative calm, cuts could be delivered: it was easier to enforce cuts in 1956 or 1964–68, than in 1960 when the international situation was more threatening. In short, civil defence was all too often left exposed to budgetary pressure. These pressures had a negative impact on policy beyond the purely financial, disrupting planning and ensuring that no sustained scheme could be implemented. Remember, the 1956 decision came just months after a five-year scheme had been agreed in principle, and it was followed by yearly budgetary scrambles.

The final factor was the domestic political context. This had little impact during the atomic age, but increased in importance throughout the thermonuclear era. When Coventry challenged the government over the worth of civil defence measures in 1954 it established a worrying precedent.[9] Between then and the rise of CND, the desire to avoid further 'Coventrys' was keen within Whitehall, reinforcing its natural propensity for secrecy, and providing an argument against radically cutting provision.[10] Such arguments were intensified when the Campaign for Nuclear Disarmament became active in 1958. CND and other critics of the government's deterrent policy successfully undermined the already shaky idea of nuclear survival, and their actions had profound implications for civil defence policy. At first the fear of criticism discouraged radical changes in policy in the early days of CND.[11] Then, when civil defence was reviewed in 1960, it was concluded that the danger of people supporting the government's critics in an emergency was so great that the

Civil Defence Corps needed to continue to convince people that some lives might be saved.[12] Lastly, it convinced the government to attempt a more open and realistic policy: the worst flaws in the Corps would be removed and the Government would admit that those in urban centres would not survive.

It is in this sphere where the government's record is perhaps most open to debate. On one level, it is clear that the government failed to maintain its preferred narrative of nuclear survival. CND propaganda was effective and powerful. The limited resources given the Civil Defence Corps meant that it would convince few people that survival was likely. The obsession with secrecy ensured that almost all the public information on nuclear attack was provided by the government's opponents. Had Whitehall taken advantage of the open field presented to it in the years between 1954 and 1958, they may have succeeded in established a discourse of nuclear survival robust enough to deal with the CND alternative. But perhaps it did not need to. CND never commanded the support of so much as a third of the population; and although many non-CND supporters considered the Corps and civil defence in general laughable, they maintained faith in the deterrent. Also, the Corps *was* convincing enough to retain hundreds of thousands of recruits and sign up tens of thousands more. It is tempting to conclude that although the Corps was lambasted in the media, many ordinary people did indeed back its vision of nuclear survivability.

It would be easy to criticise the government for the obvious flaws in civil defence policy. On a basic level, that of its stated aim of alleviating the effects of a nuclear attack, it would have failed. It never received the investment needed to work. The fact that it was not in the end needed hardly amounts to a success. But the purpose of this study is not to praise or criticise, but to understand. Successive governments struggled with the complex factors which shaped civil defence. There was no 'right' civil defence policy waiting to be uncovered. There was never enough money to spend on the measures planners desired; even if there had been, millions would still have died. Civil defence policy was decided as part of a sometimes painful juggling of priorities which ultimately concluded that the policy did not warrant sums of the size desired by planners. On one level, we can argue that this was a 'correct' decision – after all, there was no war. But the cold war was never settled enough to allow Ministers and officials to conclude that a nuclear war, either through calculation or miscalculation, would not come. This is why millions were spent every year on providing the essential elements of the policy. We must conclude that the decision over the likelihood of war was just one of many factors which contributed to the development of policy over the period. Had a war seemed likely or even certain, the British state would have mobilised all its resources to the civil defence cause; but it would have been too late. The fact that a nuclear war usually seemed a very distant or vague prospect, combined with grave doubts about the actual efficacy of civil defence *and* fears about the current economy, meant that the short-term view always prevailed. Current fears were always more important.

Although planners rarely got the sums they asked for, this does not mean civil defence was insignificant – far from it. The scale of the effort, in terms of time discussing it by Ministers, money spent and volunteers recruited, show us that civil defence was a policy of major importance within Whitehall and the country at large. Millions of people absorbed Government recruitment propaganda and hundreds of thousands of people responded to it and signed up: civil defence was a part of the fabric of everyday life for more than 20 years after VE Day. It was a central plank of the state's response to the cold war. Whether it was stockpiling food or building emergency port facilities in the atomic age, founding the Civil Defence Corps or building the Corsham bunker, or indeed keeping the Corps going after 1960, all were rational responses to Britain's cold war strategy as the government envisaged it. Of course, the critics of the government argued that civil defence was nothing more than a sham, a façade – a cruel trick played to dupe the population. This is partially true. In the atomic era, the life-saving role of civil defence was genuinely and strongly felt, but later civil defence was indeed a deliberate façade, but it was also a very real part of Britain's *overall* defence strategy. Also, the protesters understood that the government exploited the patriotic service of the civil defence volunteers to perpetuate the lie behind civil defence. Ironically, however, the service of those volunteers *was* valued by the government – forming as they did a central element in the façade which bolstered the deterrent. So, had they but known it, they played an active part in the defence of Britain. By investigating how civil defence was conceptualised and how it developed over the course of the cold war, then, we can see that although it was a sham and a façade, it was a rational and understandable sham, and in terms of the government's overall defence policy, a necessary façade.

Notes and References

Introduction

1 For their report, see The National Archives, Kew [hereafter TNA], CAB 134/938. HDC(53)7, 'The Initial Phase of a War', Report by the Home Defence Committee Working Party, 24.7.1953.
2 TNA, CAB 134/316. HDC(47)3, 'Appreciation of the Effects of Aerial Bom-bardment in the First Three Months of a Future War on the Central Resources of the Country', Report by Home Defence Committee Working Party, 17.02.1947.
3 See TNA, CAB 134/940. HDC(55)3, 'The Defence Implications of Fall-out from a Hydrogen Bomb'; Report by a Group of Officials, 8.3.1955; TNA, CAB 134/1611. DH(O)(60)5, 'Review of Home Defence Policy', Report by Officials, 8.12.1960.
4 TNA, CAB 134/938. HDC(53)4, 'Distribution of Air Attack on the United Kingdom', Note by the Joint Secretaries, 1.4.1953.
5 Ibid. HDC(53)7, 'The Initial Phase of a War'.
6 Home Office and Air Ministry, *The Effects of the Atomic Bombs at Hiroshima and Nagasaki: Report of the British Mission to Japan* (London, 1946).
7 TNA, CAB 134/1611. DH(O)(60)5, 'Review of Home Defence Policy'.
8 TNA, CAB 134/940. HDC(55)3, 'The Defence Implications of Fall-out from a Hydrogen Bomb'.
9 Ibid.
10 TNA, CAB 134/1611. DH(O)(60)5, 'Review of Home Defence Policy'.
11 See S. Greenwood, *Britain and the Cold War, 1945–91* (Basingstoke, 2000); M. Grant (ed.) *The British Way in Cold Warfare: Intelligence, Diplomacy and the Bomb, 1945–75* (London, 2009).
12 See H. Jones, 'The Impact of the Cold War', in P. Addison and H. Jones (eds) *A Companion to Contemporary British History, 1939–2000* (Oxford, 2005), pp.23–41.
13 T. Geiger, *Britain and the Economic Problem of the Cold War* (Aldershot, 2004).
14 P. Hennessy and G. Brownfeld, 'Britain's Cold War Security Purge: The Origins of Positive Vetting', *Historical Journal*, 25:4 (1982), pp.965–74.
15 'Recruits Over 300,000', *Civil Defence*, 6:3 (April 1954), p.2.
16 J. Baylis, *Ambiguity and Deterrence: British Nuclear Strategy, 1945–1964* (Oxford, 1995).
17 The word nuclear, which is often used to describe both atomic and thermo-nuclear weapons, is used as such a catch-all term in this book. It is important, however, not to elide the two very different types of weapons and so *atomic* and *thermonuclear* are used extensively.
18 The detailed history of the three phases is, of course, provided in the individual chapters of the book.
19 See the official history, T. O'Brien, *Civil Defence* (London, 1955).

20 TNA, CAB 134/82. CDC(48)10 (Revise), 'Background and Policy for Civil Defence Planning', Report by the Civil Defence Joint Planning Staff, 7.7.1948.
21 TNA, CAB 131/1. DO(46)31st Meeting, 1.11.1946.
22 TNA, CAB 131/10. DO(51)1st Meeting, 23.1.1951.
23 TNA, CAB 134/938. HDC(53)7, 'The Initial Phase of a War'.
24 TNA, CAB 134/940. HDC(55)3, 'The Defence Implications of Fallout from a Hydrogen Bomb'.
25 TNA, CAB 134/1245. HD(M)(55)2nd Meeting, 27.10.1955.
26 TNA, CAB 134/1315. PR(56)3rd Meeting, 9.6.1956.
27 As Penny Summerfield and Corinna Peniston-Bird show, they were discreet terms which implied very different forms of service for those performing them: civil defence being passive, and home defence being militarily aggressive: P. Summerfield and C. Peniston-Bird, *Contesting Home Defence: Men, Women and the Home Guard in the Second World War* (Manchester, 2007), pp.84–5.
28 A similarly structured anatomy of usage has been suggested for the cold war as existed between 1939–45, with civil defence being 'concerned with the British people during and after an attack on the UK' and included measures such as 'evacuation, shelter, food provision and emergency hospitals', whereas 'home defence covered a much wider area of both civil and military preparation which aimed to ensure national survival during and after air attack', and included policies such as 'the machinery of government in war, strategic location of the industry, town planning and stockpiling': N. Bliss, 'The Role of Sir Norman Brook in the Construction of the Cold War State, 1945–51'. Unpublished MA in Contemporary British History thesis, Department of History, Queen Mary, University of London, 2000; this view is endorsed by Peter Hennessy in his *The Secret State: Whitehall and the Cold War* (Penguin, 2003), p.126. Any division between the two, however, does not take account of the essentially fluid nature of the uses of terms throughout Whitehall, let alone among the wider public. Harold Wilson conflated the two terms when announcing the care-and-maintenance policy in 1968 (House of Commons, *Official Report*, 16.1.1968, col.1589), and in 1967 Home Office officials argued that civil defence was 'the organisation by means of which, if nuclear war seemed imminent, all the resources of the nation – central, local, industrial and voluntary, could quickly be co-ordinated in pursuit of one single aim – to ensure our survival as a nation', embracing all the measures usually called 'home defence' (TNA, HO 322/44. General Cyril Horton to Air Vice Marshall Sir Walter Merton, 3.1.1967).
29 Over the course of 23 years from 1945 to 1968 civil and home defence were largely interchangeable terms. For example, a bewildering array of cabinet committees existed in this period, usually conflating the term. In general, however, we can see a trend of 'civil defence' gradually being supplanted by 'home defence' in official usage as the traditional life-saving role of the policy becomes less important. This terminological shift is undoubtedly due to an official desire to avoid uncomplimentary comparisons between cold war provision and the 'classic' civil defence policies of the Second World War: one example of this being renaming evacuation 'dispersal' in 1962. Throughout the book, civil defence is the term mostly preferred, but there

is no hard and fast rule and 'home defence' is used when the context demands it.

30 TNA, CAB 131/19. D(58)18th Meeting, 10.9.1958.
31 TNA, CAB 134/1476. CD(59)3, 'Home Defence Preparations', Report by the Chairman of the Official Committee on Civil Defence, 3.6.1959.
32 TNA, CAB 134/2039. HDR(60)12, 'The Influence of Civil Defence Measures in the United Kingdom on the Effectiveness of the Deterrent', Note by the Secretaries, 26.4.1960.
33 TNA, CAB 134/2039. HDR(60)11, 'Civil Defence in Relation to United Kingdom Defence Policy', Note by Director-General of Civil Defence, 24.4.1960.
34 TNA, CAB 134/1611. DH(O)(60)5, 'Review of Home Defence Policy'.
35 TNA, PREM 13/23. John Diamond to the Prime Minister, 18.12.1964.
36 TNA, CAB 128/43. C(68)1st Meeting, 4.1.1968; C(68)8th Meeting, 15.1.1968.
37 This section owes a debt to an impressive series of works on civil defence and nuclear culture in America: especially, P.S. Boyer, *By the Bomb's Early Light* (New York, 1985); G. Oakes, *The Imaginary War* (Oxford, 1994); L. McEnaney, *Civil Defense Begins at Home* (Princeton, 2000); D. Garrison, *Bracing for Armageddon* (Oxford, 2006); A.D. Grossman, *Neither Dead nor Red: Civilian Defence and American Political Development during the Early Cold War* (London, 2001); and K.D. Rose, *One Nation Underground: The Fallout Shelter in American Culture* (New York, 2001).
38 Bodleian Library, Department of Western Manuscripts, University of Oxford. Harold Macmillan Diary, 4.11.1962.
39 Garrison, *Bracing for Armageddon*, pp.35–42.
40 D.L. Snead, *The Gaither Committee, Eisenhower and the Cold War* (Columbus, 1999).
41 See M.A. Henriksen, *Dr Strangelove's America: Society and Culture in the Atomic Age* (Berkley, 1997), pp.192–239 for an interesting discussion of 'survivalism' and its problems.
42 See Rose, *One Nation Underground*.
43 The literature on the Campaign for Nuclear Disarmament is large. The most useful material is Christopher Driver, *The Disarmers: A Study in Protest* (London, 1964); P. Byrne, *The Campaign for Nuclear Disarmament* (London, 1988); R. Taylor, *Against the Bomb: The British Peace Movement, 1958–65* (Oxford, 1988); and H. Nehring, 'The British and West German Protests against Nuclear Weapons and the Cultures of the Cold War', *Contemporary British History*, 19:2 (2005), pp.223–41.
44 Garrison, *Bracing for Armageddon*, pp.3–18.
45 For an intimation of the secrecy still surrounding these issues in twenty-first century Britain, see P. Hennessy, *The Secret State*, pp.224–5.
46 TNA, CAB 121/272. TWC(46)1, 'Likely Morale Effect of Atomic Bombs', 12.1.1946.
47 Murray S. Levine cited in Henriksen, *Dr Strangelove's America*, p.98.
48 For example, R. Lapp, *Voyage of the Lucky Dragon* (Penguin, 1958); R. Lapp, *Kill or Overkill* (London, 1963).
49 See Taylor, *Against the Bomb*.
50 L.S. Wittner, *Resisting the Bomb: A History of the World Nuclear Disarmament Movement, 1954–70* (Stanford, 1997).
51 Rose, *One Nation Underground*, p.240n.

Chapter 1 The Cold War and the New Civil Defence

1 Mass-Observation Archive [M-OA], University of Sussex. FR 2272, 'The Atomic Bomb', p.2.
2 Editorial, *The Times*, 7.8.1945.
3 Editorial, *The Times*, 8.8.1945.
4 Letter to *The Manchester Guardian*, 15.8.1945.
5 Letter to *The Times*, 15.8.1945.
6 M. Davie (ed.) *The Diaries of Evelyn Waugh* (London, 1976), p.631, entry for 9.8.1945.
7 Editorial, *The Manchester Guardian*, 15.8.1945.
8 G. Orwell, 'London Letter to *Partisan Review*', in Sonia Orwell and Ian Angus (eds) *The Collected Essays, Journalism and Letters of George Orwell. Volume III: As I Please, 1943–1945* (London, 1968), p.400.
9 'Use of Atomic Bomb: Dean of Ely's Comment on Church Views', *The Times*, 21.8.1945.
10 M-OA. FR 2272, 'Public Reactions to the Atomic Bomb', p.1.
11 R. Knox, *God and the Atom* (London, 1945); see M. Grant, 'Clouds of Uncertainty', *The Tablet*, 30.7.2005.
12 M. Gowing, *Independence and Deterrence: Britain and Atomic Energy, 1945–52. Volume I: Policy Making* (Basingstoke, 1974), pp.52–3.
13 G. Orwell, 'You and the Atom Bomb', in Sonia Orwell and Ian Angus (eds) *The Collected Essays, Journalism and Letters of George Orwell. Volume IV: In Front of Your Nose, 1945–1950* (London, 1968), p.6.
14 L. Woolf, 'Britain and the Atomic Bomb', *Political Quarterly*, 17:1 (1946), p.14.
15 Ibid.
16 M-OA. FR 2485, 'Atomic Weather', 1947.
17 TNA, RG 23/157. 'Enquiry into Opinions and Attitudes of People Eligible to Join the New Civil Defence Services, for the Home and Scottish Offices'.
18 M-OA. FR 2272 , 'The Atomic Bomb'.
19 House of Commons, *Parliamentary Debates*, Vol. 413, cols.95–113, 16.8.1945.
20 TNA, CAB 130/3. GEN 75/1, 'The Atomic Bomb', Memorandum by the Prime Minister, 28.8.1945.
21 Ibid.
22 See B. Cathcart, *Test of Greatness: Britain's Struggle for the Atomic Bomb* (London, 1994), p.9.
23 Published in M. Gowing, *Independence and Deterrence. Volume 1*, pp.78–81.
24 S. Schrafstetter, '"Loquacious ... and Pointless as Ever"? Britain, the United States and the United Nations Negotiations on International Control of Nuclear Energy, 1945–48', *Contemporary British History*, 16:4 (2002), p.91; R. Smith and J. Zametica, 'The Cold Warrior: Clement Attlee Reconsidered, 1945–1947', *International Affairs*, 61:2 (1985), 237–63.
25 Cathcart, *Test of Greatness*, p.24; P. Hennessy, *The Secret State: Whitehall and the Cold War* (London, 2003), p.47.
26 Gowing, *Independence and Deterrence. Volume I*, p.19.
27 TNA, CAB 80/97. COS(45)548(O), 'Examination of Effects of the Bombing of Japan', Note by the Air Ministry, 22.8.1945.
28 See TNA, PREM 8/194. 'Report on the Effects of the Atomic Bombs at Hiroshima and Nagasaki'.

29 Home Office and Air Ministry, *The Effects of the Atomic Bombs at Hiroshima and Nagasaki: Report of the British Mission to Japan* (London, 1946).
30 Ibid., p.5.
31 Ibid., pp.8, 19.
32 Ministry of Reconstruction, *Housing*, Cmd 6609 (London, 1945).
33 *The Effects of the Atomic Bombs*, pp.15–16.
34 Ibid., p.16.
35 Ibid.
36 Ibid., p.4.
37 Ibid., p.3.
38 Ibid., p.4.
39 See TNA, CAB 134/316. HDC(46)2, 'Future Developments in Weapons and Methods of War', 31.7.1946; See TNA, HO 322/99. 'Memorandum on the Organisation of Post War Civil Defence', by Sir John Hodsoll.
40 TNA, CAB 134/316. HDC(46)2, 'Future Developments in Weapons and Methods of War', 31.7.1946.
41 TNA, CAB 121/272. TWC(46)8, 'Scale of Attack on Certain Cities', 16.2.1946.
42 TNA, CAB 134/316. HDC(46)2, 'Future Developments in Weapons and Methods of War', 31.7.1946.
43 Ibid.
44 Ibid.
45 Ibid.
46 TNA, CAB 121/272. TWC(46)8, 'Scale of Attack on Certain Cities', 16.2.1946.
47 See G. Oakes, *The Imaginary War* (Oxford, 1994); A.D. Grossman, *Neither Dead nor Red: Civilian Defence and American Political Development during the Early Cold War* (London, 2001); and L. McEnaney, *Civil Defense Begins at Home* (Princeton, 2000).
48 TNA, CAB 134/316. HDC(46)18, 'Future Scale of Air Attack on the United Kingdom', Memorandum by the Chiefs of Staff Committee, 12.12.1946; HDC(47)3, 'Appreciation of the Effects of Aerial Bombardment in the First Three Months of a Future War on the Central Resources of the Country', Report by Home Defence Committee Working Party, 17.02.1947.
49 J. Baylis, *Ambiguity and Deterrence: British Nuclear Strategy, 1945–1964* (Oxford, 1995), pp.50–2.
50 See TNA, HO 322/99. 'Civil Defence Planning: Progress Report' for Secretary of State, by Oswald Allen, 16.1.1946.
51 TNA, CAB 134/316. HDC(47)10 (revise), 'Civil Defence Policy: Report', Memorandum by the Home Defence Committee, 7.10.1947.
52 TNA, HO 322/99. 'Memorandum on the Organisation of Post War Civil Defence', by Sir John Hodsoll, 7.2.1946.
53 House of Commons, *Official Report*, 22.3.1948, cols.2696–9.
54 'Exercise Britannia', *The Economist*, 5.6.1948.
55 'Old Answers on Civil Defence', *The Economist*, 3.7.1948.
56 M. Smith, 'Architects of Armageddon: Scientific Advice and the State in Cold War Britain, 1945–68', British Society for the History of Science Annual Conference, Keble College, Oxford, 4–6 July 2008.
57 TNA, CAB 134/80. CD(M)(48)1, 'Composition and Terms of Reference', Note by the Secretary, 30.8.48.

58 A. Bullock, *Ernest Bevin: Foreign Secretary* (Oxford UP, 1984), p.513; the papers were TNA, CAB 129/23. CP(48)5, 'Policy in Germany', Memorandum by the Secretary of State for Foreign Affairs, 5.1.1948; CP(48)6, 'The First Aim of British Foreign Policy', Memorandum by the Secretary of State for Foreign Affairs, 4.1.1948; CP(48)7, 'Review of Soviet Policy', Memorandum by the Secretary of State for Foreign Affairs, 5.1.1948; CP(48)8, 'Future Foreign Publicity', Memorandum by the Secretary of State for Foreign Affairs, 4.1.1948.
59 TNA, CAB 134/316. HDC(47)2nd Meeting, 1.7.1947.
60 TNA, CAB 129/12. CP(46)307, 'Location of Power Stations', Memorandum by the Under-Secretary of State for Air, 29.7.1946.
61 TNA, CAB 129/11. CP(46)297, 'Location of Power Stations', Memorandum by the Minister for Fuel and Power, 25.7.1946; TNA, CAB 131/1. DO(46)31st Meeting, 1.11.1946.
62 TNA, CAB 131/5. DO(47)3rd Meeting, 24.1.1947.
63 The main issues were summarised for the Cabinet by TNA, CAB 129/18. CP(47)110, 'Power Station at Bankside', Memorandum by the Chancellor of the Exchequer, 26.3.1947; the decision was taken by TNA, CAB 128/9. CM(47)34th Meeting, 1.4.1947.
64 TNA, CAB 134/316. HDC(47)10 (revise), 'Civil Defence Policy: Report', Memorandum by the Joint Secretaries, 7.10.1947.
65 TNA, CAB 131/5. DO(47)24th Meeting, 14.11.1947.
66 'Mr Churchill's Warning: Nation in Peril Under Socialism', *The Sunday Times*, 7.12.47.
67 TNA, PREM 8/750. Henley to Graham-Harrison, 11.12.47.
68 TNA, CAB 134/316. HDC(47)3rd Meeting, 31.7.1947.
69 TNA, CAB 134/82. CDC(48)10 (Revise), 'Background and Policy for Civil Defence Planning', Report by the Civil Defence Joint Planning Staff, 7.7.1948.
70 J.L. Gaddis, *We Now Know: Rethinking Cold War History* (Oxford, 1993), p.48.
71 A. Deighton, *The Impossible Peace: Britain, the German Problem and the Origins of the Cold War* (Oxford, 1990), p.7.
72 A. Shlaim, 'Britain, the Berlin Blockade and the Cold War', *International Affairs*, 60:1 (1984), p.1.
73 A. Bullock, *Ernest Bevin: Foreign Secretary*, p.583.
74 See TNA, DEFE 4/14. COS(48)97th Meeting, 12.7.1948.
75 TNA, CAB 130/38. GEN 241/4th Meeting, 22.7.1948.
76 TNA, CAB 131/5. DO(48)12th Meeting, 21.7.1948.
77 Ibid.
78 TNA, CAB 131/6. DO(48)47, 'The Defence Position', Note by the Prime Minister, 26.7.48.
79 TNA, CAB 134/82.CDC(48)1st Meeting, 12.3.48.
80 TNA, CAB 131/6. DO(48)47, 'The Defence Position'.
81 Ibid.
82 TNA, CAB 131/5. DO(48)18th Meeting, 27.7.1950.
83 'Chairman' is a gendered phrase which has been retained on the grounds that it was the phrase used at the time, and that not a single meeting or committee discussed in this book was chaired by a women, an unsurpris-

ing fact given the make-up of the higher reaches of the civil service at the time.

84 TNA, CAB 134/82. CDC(48)3rd Meeting, 28.7.1948.

85 Ibid. CDC(48)14, 'Preparation for Civil Defence', Note by General Irwin, 14.8.48.

86 Ibid. CDC(48)16, 'Preparation for Civil Defence', Report to the Defence Committee, 19.8.1948.

87 Ibid.

88 Ibid.

89 Ibid.

90 Ibid.

91 TNA, CAB 131/6. DO(46)47, 'The Defence Position'.

92 TNA, CAB 134/82. CDC(48)16, 'Preparation for Civil Defence'.

93 Ibid.

94 TNA, PREM 8/1355. Brief for Attlee on GEN 253.

95 TNA, CAB 134/80. CD(M)(48)3, 'Preparation for Civil Defence', Note by the Home Secretary, 10.9.48.

96 Ibid.

97 See 'Demob Delayed 3 Months', *Daily Express*, 15.9.1948.

98 'Civil Defence Plans Approved', *Daily Telegraph*, 16.9.1948; Geoffrey Cox, 'Our Civil Defence Plan is Ready', *News Chronicle*, 16.9.1948; 'Civil Defence', *Daily Telegraph*, 17.9.1948; 'Civil Defence', *The Economist*, 25.9.1948.

99 TNA, CAB 130/41. GEN 253/1st Meeting, 1.10.1948.

100 Ibid.

101 TNA, PREM 8/1355. Brief for Attlee on GEN 253, by W.S. Murrie, 1.10.1948.

102 Ibid.

103 Hennessy, *The Secret State*, p.125.

104 TNA, CAB 134/80. CD(M)(48)2nd Meeting, 18.11.1948.

105 Ibid.

106 House of Commons, *Official Report*, 23.11.1948, col.1119.

107 Ibid., col.1090.

108 Ibid., cols.1090–1.

109 TNA, HO 322/1. Draft instructions from Mr Brass to Sir Alan Ellis (Parliamentary Counsel), 19.6.1948.

110 Sir John Anderson had been Home Secretary and Minister of Home Security between the outbreak of war and October 1940; before this he was responsible for drafting civil defence preparations as Lord Privy Seal. He left the government after Labour's victory but was appointed as the chairman of Attlee's Atomic Energy Advisory Committee due to his knowledge of 'Tube Alloys'.

111 House of Commons, *Official Report*, 23.11.1948, cols.1102–16.

112 Ibid., cols.1102–4.

113 *Statutory Instruments 1949*. 'No.1432: Civil Defence: The Civil Defence (General) Regulations, 1949'.

114 'No. 1433: Civil Defence: The Civil Defence Corps Regulations, 1949'.

115 Ibid.

116 These included Civil Defence Circular 6/1949: 'Civil Defence Act, 1948: Functions of Local Authorities', 9.6.1949; 16/1949: 'First Aid Training for

Members of the Civil Defence Corps', 31.8.1949; 21/1949: 'Civil Defence Corps: Recruitment Procedure', 3.10.1949.

117 Baylis, *Ambiguity and Deterrence*, pp.56, 83–4.

118 'Civil Defence in the Future', *The Economist*, 29.11.1947.

Chapter 2 Preparing for a Third World War

1 See A. Shonfield, *British Economic Policy since the War* (Harmondsworth, 1958); for a discussion of these views see J. Park, 'Wasted Opportunities? The 1950s Rearmament Programme and the Failure of British Economic Policy', *Journal of Contemporary History*, 32:3 (1997), 357–79.

2 For example, see 'War Cloud over Korea, *Daily Telegraph*, 26.6.1950.

3 'Attlee: No Need for Call to Britain Yet', *Daily Mirror*, 14.7.1950.

4 TNA, CAB 131/8. DO(50)12th Meeting, 6.7.1950.

5 TNA, CAB 128/18. CM(50)43rd Meeting, 6.7.1950.

6 S. Dockrill, 'Britain's Strategy for Europe: Must West Germany be Rearmed? 1948–51, in R.J. Aldrich (ed.) *British Intelligence, Strategy and the Cold War, 1945–51* (London, 1992), pp.193–214.

7 P. Hennessy, *Never Again: Britain, 1945–51* (London, 1992), p.415; for a deeper and broadly revisionist approach to the subject, see T. Geiger, *Britain and the Economic Problem of the Cold War: The Political Economy and the Economic Impact of the British Defence Effort, 1945–55* (Aldershot, 2004).

8 TNA, PREM 8/1355. Home Secretary to Prime Minister, 4.7.1950.

9 Ibid. 'Civil Defence', Note by the Home Office, 3.7.1950.

10 Ibid.

11 TNA, HO 357/3. CDJPS(50)26, 'Report on Civil Defence Planning, 1950', Report by the CDJPS, 7.9.1950. The CDJPS was housed in the Home Office and headed by General S.F. Irwin; it was largely made up of Home Office officials and scientists.

12 TNA, PREM 8/1355 'Civil Defence', Note by the Home Office, 3.7.1950.

13 TNA, CAB 134/81. CD(M)(50)12, 'Expenditure over the Next Four Years', Report by the Chairman of the Official Committee, 18.7.1950.

14 Ibid.

15 Ibid.

16 TNA, CAB 131/8. DO(50)15th Meeting, 24.7.1950.

17 TNA, CAB 128/18. CM(50)50th Meeting, 25.7.1950.

18 Ibid. CM(50)87th Meeting, 18.12.1950.

19 TNA, DEFE 5/25. COS(50)534, 'Hypothesis for Defence Preparations', Note by the Secretary 21.12.1950.

20 Ibid.

21 TNA, CAB 129/44. CP(51)18, 'Defence Preparations by Civil Departments', Report to the Cabinet, 18.1.1951.

22 TNA, CAB 131/10. DO(51)1st Meeting, 23.1.1951.

23 TNA, CAB 129/44. CP(51)18, 'Defence Preparations by Civil Departments'.

24 TNA, CAB 131/10. DO(51)1st Meeting, 23.1.1951.

25 TNA, CAB 134/812. DTC(52)8, 'Third Annual Report', 25.4.1952.

26 TNA, PREM 8/1355. Home Secretary to Prime Minister, 11.8.1950, covering 'Ability of Civil Defence to Meet an Emergency in July 1951', Report by the Chairman Civil Defence Joint Planning Staff.

27 TNA, CAB 134/789. DTC(51)1st Meeting, 1.1.1951.
28 Ibid.
29 TNA, CAB 129/44. CP(51)18, 'Defence Preparations by Civil Departments', Report to the Cabinet, 18.1.1951.
30 Ibid. CP(51)19, 'Civil Defence Preparations', Memorandum by the Home Secretary, 18.1.1951.
31 Ibid.
32 Ibid.
33 TNA, CAB 131/10. DO(51)1st Meeting, 23.1.1951.
34 Ibid.
35 Ibid.
36 Ibid.
37 House of Commons, *Official Report*, 29.1.1951, col.583.
38 Ibid.
39 See W.D. Crocoft and R.J.C. Thomas, *Cold War: Building for Nuclear Confrontation* (Swindon, 2003), chapter 5.
40 TNA, CAB 131/12. D(52)10, 'Civil Defence Preparations', Note by the Home Secretary, 4.4.1952; D(52)18, 'Civil Defence Preparedness – Financial Considerations', Memorandum by the Home Secretary, 6.5.1952.
41 Ibid. D(52)10, 'Civil Defence Preparations'.
42 Ibid. D(52)18, 'Civil Defence Preparedness – Financial Considerations'.
43 Ibid. D(52)10, 'Civil Defence Preparations'.
44 TNA, CAB 131/12. D(52)5th Meeting, 14.5.1952.
45 Ibid. D(52)5th Meeting, 14.5.1952.
46 See J. Baylis and A. Macmillan, 'The British Global Strategy Paper of 1952', *Journal of Strategic Studies*, 16:2 (1993), pp.200–26; J. Baylis, *Ambiguity and Deterrence: British Nuclear Strategy, 1945–1964* (Oxford, 1995), pp.126–51; S. Greenwood, *Britain and the Cold War, 1945–91* (Basingstoke, 2000), pp.107–10.
47 TNA, DEFE 5/40. COS(52)361, 'Defence Policy and Global Strategy', 15.7.1952.
48 Ibid.
49 TNA, CAB 134/812. DTC(52)14, 'War Plans and Preparations', Memorandum by the Chairman, 19.8.52.
50 Ibid.
51 Ibid.
52 Ibid. DTC(52)25, 'Review of the Civil Defence Programme', Memorandum by the Chairman of the Official Committee on Civil Defence, 15.10.1952.
53 Ibid. DTC(52)32, 'Defence Preparations by Civil Departments', Note by the Joint Secretaries, 23.12.1952.
54 Ibid. DTC(52)25, 'Review of the Civil Defence Programme'.
55 Ibid.
56 TNA, CAB 134/938. HDC(53)1, 'Terms of Reference and Composition', Note by the Secretary of the Cabinet, 26.2.53.
57 TNA, CAB 134/139. DTC(51)11, 'Revised Composition and Terms of Reference', Note by the Secretary of the Cabinet, 3.4.1951; DTC(51)20, 'Responsibility for War Planning', Memorandum by the Secretary of the Cabinet, 22.5.1951.
58 TNA, CAB 134/938. HDC(53)2, 'Form of Work', Memorandum by the Chairman, 26.2.1953.
59 Ibid. HDC(53)4, 'Distribution of Air Attack on the United Kingdom', Note by the Joint Secretaries, 1.4.1953.

60 Ibid. HDC(53)7, 'The Initial Phase of a War', Report by the Home Defence Committee Working Party, 24.7.1953.
61 TNA, CAB 134/316. HDC(47)3, 'Appreciation of the Effects of Aerial Bombardment in the First Three Months of a Future War on the Central Resources of the Country', Report by Home Defence Committee Working Party, 17.02.1947.
62 TNA, CAB 134/938. HDC(53)7, 'The Initial Phase of a War'.
63 Ibid.
64 Ibid.
65 Ibid.
66 Ibid.
67 Ibid.
68 Ibid.
69 Ibid.
70 Ibid. HDC(53)3rd Meeting, 29.7.1953.
71 Ibid.
72 Ibid.
73 TNA, CAB 134/942. HDC(54)7, 'Second Stage of a War', Report by the Home Defence Working Party, 22.3.1954.
74 TNA, CAB 134/813. DTC(53)4th Meeting, 30.12.1953.
75 'From the Select Committee on Estimates, Session 1953–54: Civil Defence', *Reports from Committees. Session 3 November 1953–25 November 1954* (HMSO, 1953).
76 Ibid.
77 Ibid.
78 Ibid.
79 'The C.D. Muddlers Shock M.P.s', *Daily Mirror*, 23.12.1953; see also, 'Severe Criticisms of Civil Defence Organisation', *Manchester Guardian*, 23.12.1953.
80 'Civilians Defenceless', *The Economist*, 9.1.1954.
81 TNA, PREM 11/606. Sir Norman Brook to the Prime Minister, 23.12.1953.
82 Ibid.
83 TNA, CAB 134/792. CD(O)(54)1st Meeting, 13.1.1954.
84 House of Commons, *Official Report*, 28.1.1954, written answer cols.272–8.
85 'A Wrong Approach', *The Times*, 29.1.1954.
86 'Defenceless Undefended', *The Economist*, 6.2.1954.
87 'From the Select Committee on Estimates, Session 1953–54: Civil Defence', *Reports from Committees. Session 3 November 1953–25 November 1954*.
88 TNA, CAB 134/812. DTC(52)8, 'Third Annual Report: The State of War Plans and Preparations', 25.4.1952.
89 TNA, CAB 21/2375. Robert Hall to Sir Norman Brook, 7.11.1951.
90 TNA, HO 357/3. CDJPS(50)26, 'Report on Civil Defence Planning, 1950', Report by the CDJPS, 7.9.1950.
91 TNA, HO 357/7. CDJPS(54)6, 'Report on Civil Defence Planning, 1953', Report by the CDJPS, 20.2.1954.
92 Ibid.; See D. Campbell, *War Plan UK: The Truth about Civil Defence in Britain* (London, 1982) for an illuminating discussion of these plans.
93 'From the Select Committee on Estimates, Session 1953–54: Civil Defence', *Reports from Committees. Session 3 November 1953–25 November 1954*.
94 TNA, CAB 134/80. CD(M)(49)3rd Meeting, 25.7.1949.
95 See TNA, HO 357/4. CDJPS(51)49, 'Report on Civil Defence Planning, 1951', Report by the CDJPS 2.10.51.

96 TNA, HO 357/7. CDJPS(54)6, 'Report on Civil Defence Planning, 1953'.
97 L.V. Scott *Conscription and the Attlee Governments: The Politics and Policy of National Service 1945–51* (Oxford, 1993).

Chapter 3 Protecting the Public

1 The best account of home front morale is R. Mackay, *Half the Battle: Civilian Morale in Britain during the Second World War* (Manchester, 2002); other problems with shelters are discussed in the late Angus Calder's classic, *The People's War* (London, 1969).
2 House of Commons, *Official Report*, 19.11.1947, cols.1135–8.
3 See TNA, HO 197/33. 'The Safety-Cost Relationship of Various Types of Shelters against Atomic and High Explosive Bombs', Note by Sir Reginald Stradling, undated [c.1946]; TNA, HO 205/361. '2nd December, Shelter Policy Working Party', Note of a meeting, 2.12.1948.
4 TNA, CAB 134/316. HDC(46)13, 'Shelter Policy', Memorandum by the Home Office, 16.10.1946.
5 K.O. Morgan, *Labour in Power* (Oxford, 1985), p.161.
6 Ibid. HDC(46)2nd Meeting, 24.10.1946.
7 TNA, CAB 134/80. CD(M)(48)1st Meeting, 16.9.1948.
8 Ibid.
9 Ibid. CD(M)(49)1, 'Shelter Policy', Report by the Official Committee on Civil Defence, 14.3.49.
10 Ibid.
11 Ibid.
12 See Ibid. CD(M)(49)4, 'Shelter Policy', Note by the secretaries, 16.5.1949.
13 TNA, CAB 134/81. CD(M)(50)15, 'Shelter Policy', Report by the Official Committee, 17.10.1950.
14 Ibid.
15 Ibid. CD(M)(50)6th Meeting, 23.10.1950.
16 House of Commons, *Official Report*, 9.11.1950, cols.1124–5.
17 See TNA CAB 134/81. CD(M)(51)5, 'Provision of Shelter in Construction Work', Note by Sir Frank Newsam, 28.7.51.
18 The literature on evacuation is extensive, but little has bettered the official history: R.M. Titmuss, *Problems of Social Policy* (London, 1950); see also J. Welshman, 'Evacuation and Social Policy during the Second World War: Myth and Reality', *Twentieth Century British History*, 9 (1998), pp.28–53.
19 Titmuss, *Problems of Social Policy*, chapter 3.
20 See TNA, HO 357/14. 'Working Party on Evacuation and Care of the Homeless'.
21 TNA, CAB 134/80. CD(M)(49)8, 'Outline Plan for Evacuation and Care of the Homeless', Report by the Official Committee on Civil Defence, 19.7.49.
22 Ministry of Health, *Civil Defence Act, 1948: Memorandum on Evacuation* (London, 1950).
23 Ibid.
24 Ibid., pp.2–3.
25 TNA, HO 357/7. CDJPS(54)6, 'Report on Civil Defence Planning, 1953', Report by the CDJPS, 20.2.1954.

26 TNA, CAB 134/80. CD(M)(49)8, 'Outline Plan for Evacuation and Care of the Homeless', Report by the Official Committee on Civil Defence, 19.7.49.
27 TNA, CAB 131/12. D(52)10, 'Civil Defence Preparations', Note by the Home Secretary, 4.4.1952.
28 See S. Guy, '"Someone Presses a Button and its Goodbye Sally", *Seven Days to Noon* and the Threat of the Atomic Bomb', in A. Burton et al (eds) *The Family Way: The Boulting Brothers and Postwar British Film Culture* (Trowbridge, 2001), pp.143–54.
29 TNA, CAB 134/81. CD(M)(50)7, 'Evacuation and Dispersal Policy in Phase III', Memorandum by the Chairman of the Official Committee, 3.5.50.
30 Ibid.
31 Ibid. CD(M)(50)3rd Meeting, 18.5.1950.
32 TNA, HO 357/7. CDJPS(54)6, 'Report on Civil Defence Planning, 1953'.
33 Ibid.
34 TNA, CAB 134/938. HDC(53)7, 'The Initial Phase of a War', Report by the Home Defence Committee Working Party, 24.7.1953.
35 TNA, CAB 134/316. HDC(47)5, 'Organisation of Post-War Civil Defence', Note by the Home Office Representative, 19.6.1947.
36 House of Commons, *Official Report*, 19.11.1947, cols.1135–8.
37 'Home Secretary Opens Depot for C.D. Mobile Column', *Manchester Guardian*, 5.1.1953.
38 'Experimental Mobile Column', *Civil Defence*, 4:3 (Jan–Mar 1953), p.5.
39 See 'Over 213,000 Recruits to the Civil Defence Corps', *Civil Defence*, 4:2 (Oct–Dec 1952), p.4.
40 See, for example, the lengthy correspondence on this issue in TNA, HO 322/110, 'Recruitment of Women'.
41 TNA, HO 322/158. CDC(P)(49)5, 'Working Party on Publicity for the Recruitment for the Civil Defence Corps', Note by the Secretary, 5.7.1949.
42 'Who's Fault?', *Civil Defence*, 1:4 (April–June 1950), p.10.
43 'Mr Ede Disappointed', *Civil Defence*, 1:4 (April–June 1950), p.4.
44 Ibid.
45 'Who's Fault?', *Civil Defence*, 1:4 (April–June 1950), p.10.
46 TNA, INF 2/118. 'Civil Defence Recruitment Campaigns, 1950–57'.
47 Ibid.
48 TNA, RG 23/157. 'Enquiry into Opinions and Attitudes of People Eligible to Join the New Civil Defence Services, for the Home and Scottish Offices'.
49 'Recruitment as of 30 June 1950', *Civil Defence*, 2:1 (July–Sept 1950), p.1.
50 TNA, INF 2/118. 'Civil Defence Recruitment Campaigns, 1950–57'.
51 See 'Attlee: We Fight a World Conspiracy', *Daily Mirror*, 31.7.1950; 'A World-wide Conspiracy: Premier's Warning', *Manchester Guardian*, 31.7.1950.
52 Ibid.
53 TNA, INF 2/118. 'Civil Defence Recruitment Campaigns, 1950–57'.
54 Home Office, *Civil Defence Manual for Basic Training, Volume II: Atomic Warfare* (London, 1950).
55 'Mr Ede on the Progress of Civil Defence', *Civil Defence*, 2:2 (Oct–Dec 1950), pp.1–2.
56 'Civil Defence and the Bomb, *The Economist*, 29.7.1950.
57 'Atomic Warfare', *Manchester Guardian*, 26.7.1950.
58 'Civil Defence Recruitment in England and Wales', *Civil Defence*, 2:4 (April–June 1951), p.2.

59 TNA, RG 23/167. 'Second Enquiry to Estimate the Effect of the 1950 Recruitment Campaign, to Discover Useful Themes for the 1951 Campaign and the Characteristics of those Likely to Join the Civil Defence Services'.
60 TNA, INF 2/118. 'Civil Defence Recruitment Campaigns, 1950–57'.
61 'Half Way to Civil Defence Recruitment', *Civil Defence*, 4:3 (Jan–March 1953), p.2.
62 TNA, INF 2/118. 'Civil Defence Recruitment Campaigns, 1950–57'.
63 'Over 200,000 Recruits', *Civil Defence*, 4:1 (July–Sept 1952), p.1.
64 Home Office, *First Report of the Advisory Committee on Publicity and Recruitment for the Civil Defence and Allied Services*, Cmd.8708 (London, 1952).
65 Ibid.
66 See, for example, 'News from the Divisions', *Civil Defence*, 4:3 (Jan–Mar 1953), p.12.
67 'The Night of Terror', *Daily Mirror*, 2.2.1953; 'Civil Defence in Action: Harrow Railway Disaster', *Civil Defence*, 4:2 (Oct–Dec 1952), p.4.
68 TNA, INF 2/118. 'Civil Defence Recruitment Campaigns, 1950–57'.
69 See 'New Conditions of Eligibility: Home Secretary Announces New Committee on Recruiting', *Civil Defence*, 4:1 (July–Sept 1952), p.3; 'Experimental Mobile Column', *Civil Defence*, 4:3 (Jan–March 1953), p.1; 'Home Secretary at Crawley', *Civil Defence*, 5:1 (July–Sept 1953), p.4.
70 'Experimental Mobile Column', *Civil Defence*, 4:3 (Jan–March 1953), p.1.
71 House of Commons, *Official Report*, 18.7.1952, col.2512.
72 'Recruits Over 300,000', *Civil Defence*, 6:3 (April 1954), p.2.
73 'From the Select Committee on Estimates, Session 1953–54: Civil Defence', *Reports from Committees. Session 3 November 1953–25 November 1954* (HMSO, 1953).
74 Home Office, *Second Report of the Advisory Committee on Publicity and Recruitment for the Civil Defence and Allied Services*, Cmd.9131 (London, 1954).
75 House of Commons, *Official Report*, 28.1.1954, cols.273–8W.
76 'Mixed Reception for Report', *Civil Defence* , 6:2 (March 1954), p.3.
77 Ibid.
78 TNA, HO 322/158. CDC(P)(49)5, 'Working Party on Publicity for the Recruitment for the Civil Defence Corps', Note by the Secretary, 5.7.1949.
79 'Over 200,000 Recruits', *Civil Defence*, 4:1 (July–Sept 1952), p.1.
80 'Recruits Over 300,000', *Civil Defence*, 6:3 (April 1954), p.2.
81 TNA, INF 2/118. 'Civil Defence Recruitment Campaigns, 1950–57'.
82 'Over 200,000 Recruits', *Civil Defence*, 4:1 (July–Sept 1952), p.1.
83 'Coventry', *Civil Defence*, 6:1 (Jan–Feb 1954), p.12.
84 TNA, INF 13/281. 'Civil Defence Recruitment'.
85 See Attlee's statement: House of Commons, *Official Report*, 29.1.1951, col.583; also, Fyfe's response to the Estimates Committee: House of Commons, *Official Report*, 28.1.1954, cols.272–8W.

Chapter 4 The Hydrogen Bomb Revolution

1 The British discussion of these tests is discussed in Lorna Arnold, *Britain and the H-Bomb* (Basingstoke, 2001).
2 See P. Hennessy, *The Secret State: Whitehall and the Cold War* (London, 2003), p.50; I. Clark and N.J. Wheeler, *The British Origins of Nuclear Strategy, 1945–55* (Oxford, 1989), p.210.

3 'The Monster', *Daily Mirror*, 2.4.1954; 'The Horror Bomb', *Daily Mirror*, 2.4.1954.
4 P. Catterall (ed.) *The Macmillan Diaries: The Cabinet Years, 1950–57* (London, 2003), p.302, entry for 28.3.1954.
5 'Radioactive Fish Alarm in Japan', *The Times*, 20.3.1954; the story of the boat was graphically told in the best-selling Ralph E. Lapp, *The Voyage of the Lucky Dragon* (Harmondsworth, 1958).
6 'H-Bomb can Wipe Out Any City, Strauss Reports after Tests', *New York Times*, 1.4.1954; Lorna Arnold, *Britain and the H-Bomb* (Basingstoke, 2001), p.20.
7 BBC Written Archives Centre, Caversham, Berks [Hereafter BBCWAC], R19/1486, 'Hydrogen Bomb', Nesta Pain to Lawrence Gilliam, 31.8.1954.
8 Ibid.
9 TNA, HO 322/136. Letter from the Town Clark, Coventry, to the Home Secretary, 7.4.1954.
10 'A Bomb and a Town', *Daily Mail*, 8.4.1954.
11 Denis Holmes, '3,000 to March Against CD Ban: Blitz Hero Leads Protests to Stop Coventry Shutdown', *Daily Mail*, 8.4.1954.
12 'Coventry', *Civil Defence*, 6:1 (Jan–Feb 1954), p.12.
13 See 'Coventry Debacle', *Civil Defence*, 6:6 (July 1954), p.2.
14 TNA, CAB 134/915. HA(54)17th Meeting, 16.7.1954; TNA, HO 322/136. 'Civil Defence: City of Coventry', Order by David Maxwell Fyfe, 24 July 1954.
15 'Civil Defence is Being Deliberately Attacked', *Civil Defence*, 6:7 (August 1954), p.1.
16 'C.D. and the H-Bomb: Home Secretary's Pronouncement', *Civil Defence*, 6:5 (June 1954), pp.1–2.
17 B. Wood, 'Urbanisation and Local Government', in A.H. Halsey (ed.) *Trends in British Society since 1900* (London, 1972), p.277.
18 House of Commons, *Official Report*, 27.5.1954, cols.41–44W; see also, 'Self Protection under Atomic Attack', *Civil Defence*, 6:3 (April 1954), pp.14–16.
19 TNA, INF 2/118. 'Civil Defence Recruitment Campaigns, 1950–57'.
20 Ibid.
21 See B. Cathcart, 'Penney, William George, Baron Penney (1909–1991)', *Oxford Dictionary of National Biography* (Oxford, 2004). [http://www.oxforddnb.com/view/article/49920, accessed 25 Feb 2005]
22 TNA, CAB 130/101. GEN 461/1st Meeting.
23 Ibid.
24 TNA, CAB 134/808. DP(54)6, 'United Kingdom Defence Policy', Memorandum by the Chiefs of Staff, 1.6.1954.
25 For the full story of the Hydrogen bomb decision see Arnold, *Britain and the H-Bomb*; Hennessy, *The Secret State*, pp.49–60; Katherine Pyne, 'Art or Article? The Need for and Nature of the British Hydrogen Bomb, 1954–58', *Contemporary British History*, 13:3 (1999), pp.562–85.
26 TNA, CAB 134/808. DP(54)6, 'United Kingdom Defence Policy'.
27 Ibid. DP(54)3rd Meeting, 16.6.1954.
28 TNA, CAB 134/792. CD(O)(54)13, 'First Review of Civil Defence Plans', Note by the Chairman of the Civil Defence Joint Planning Staff, 4.5.1954.
29 House of Commons, *Official Report*, 27.5.1954, cols.41–44W.
30 TNA, CAB 134/792. CD(O)(54)3rd Meeting, 11.5.1954.

31 TNA, CAB 134/808. DP(54)5th Meeting, 6.7.1954.
32 Ibid. DP(54)11, 'Defence Preparations by Civil Departments', Report by the Chairman of the Home Defence Committee 3.7.1954.
33 Ibid. DP(54)9, 'Civil Defence Plans', Memorandum by the Home Secretary, 22.6.1954.
34 Ibid. DP(54)11, 'Defence Preparations by Civil Departments'.
35 See TNA, CAB 134/792. CD(O)(54)13, 'First Review of Civil Defence Plans', Note by the Chairman of the Civil Defence Joint Planning Staff, 4.5.1954; CD(O)(54)15, 'Evacuation and Shelter Policy', Memorandum by General Irwin, 12.7.1954; CD(O)(54)21, 'Interim Reports on Certain Civil Defence Plans', Note by General Irwin, 20.10.1954.
36 Ibid. CD(O)(54)15, 'Evacuation and Shelter Policy'.
37 Ibid.
38 Ibid.
39 Ibid.
40 TNA, CAB 134/789. CD(M)(54)7th Meeting, 27.7.1954.
41 TNA, T 227/1129. R.W.B. Clarke to Sir Alexander Johnston, 10.9.1954.
42 Ibid.
43 Ibid.
44 H.G. Wells, *The War of the Worlds* (London, 2005), pp.92–104.
45 This was 'Project East River'; see G. Oakes, *The Imaginary War* (Oxford, 1994); A.D. Grossman, *Neither Dead nor Red: Civilian Defence and American Political Development during the Early Cold War* (London, 2001); and L. McEnaney, *Civil Defense Begins at Home* (Princeton, 2000).
46 See TNA, HO 322/8. 'Appointment of Director-General of Civil Defence'; such an appointment had been an aim of the Home Office for some years. For Churchill and Butler's rejection of it in 1952 see PREM 11/42. William Armstrong to J.R. Colville, 5.11.1952.
47 TNA, T 227/1129. R.W.B. Clarke to Sir Alexander Johnston, 10.9.1954.
48 Ibid.
49 TNA, CAB 134/792. CD(O)(54)21, 'Interim Reports on Certain Civil Defence Plans'.
50 John Baylis argues that nuclear strategy was in a state if flux in late-1954 as the Government attempted to reconcile various strategies with each other and the desire to save cash: J. Baylis, *Ambiguity and Deterrence: British Nuclear Strategy, 1945–1964* (Oxford, 1995), p.195.
51 Ibid. CD(O)(54)24, 'Emergency Feeding', Note by the Ministry of Food, 25.11.1954; Ibid. CD(O)(54)5th Meeting, 27.10.1954.
52 TNA, CAB 21/4054. 'Fall Out', Note by Norman Brook, 9.11.54.
53 Ibid.
54 For the history of such exchanges, see S.J. Ball, 'Military Nuclear Relations between the United States and Great Britain under the Terms of the McMahon Act, 1946–58', *Historical Journal*, 38:2 (1995), pp.439–54.
55 TNA, CAB 21/4350. 'Inter-Departmental Organisation for War Planning', Note by Sir Norman Brook, 12.11.1954; TNA, CAB 134/939. HDC(54)19, 'Inter-Departmental Organisation for War Planning', 1.12.1954.
56 Ibid. 'Fallout', undated draft by Sir Fredrick Brundrett.
57 TNA, CAB 129/72. C(54)289, 'Fallout', Memorandum by the Minister of Defence, 9.12.1954.

58 Ibid.
59 Ibid.
60 Ibid.
61 Ibid.
62 TNA, DEFE 13/45. Notes on 'Fallout', by William Strath, undated.
63 TNA, CAB 21/4054. 'Note of a Meeting in the Foreign Secretary's Room, 9 December 1954'.
64 See TNA, DEFE 13/45. Macmillan to PM, 10.12.1954, PM's scrawled note dated 12.12.1954.
65 TNA, CAB 21/4054. 'Note of a Meeting in the Foreign Secretary's Room, 9 December 1954'.
66 TNA, CAB 129/72. C(54)289, 'Fallout', Memorandum by the Minister of Defence, 9.12.1954.
67 TNA, CAB 21/4054. Sir Norman Brook to the Prime Minister, 10.12.1954.
68 Ibid. Sir Norman Brook to the Prime Minister, 13.12.1954.
69 TNA, CAB 21/3595. Sir Norman Brook to Permanent Under-Secretaries of State, 17.12.1954.
70 TNA, CAB 134/792. CD(O)(54)21, 'Interim Reports on Certain Civil Defence Plans', Note by General Irwin, 20.10.1954.
71 TNA, CAB 21/4350. K.L. Stock to Sir Kenneth Strong, 3.2.1955. Stock was writing to Strong, head of the Joint Intelligence Bureau: 'you will, I hope, not be unduly disquieted that this Secretariat continues to keep more or less silent! It is the quiescence of a monstrous gestation, not of lethargy'.
72 TNA, CAB 21/4054. 'Note of a Meeting in the Foreign Secretary's Room, 9 December 1954'.
73 Ministry of Defence, *Statement on Defence, 1955*, Cmd.9391 (London, 1955), p.3.
74 Ibid., pp.3–4
75 Ibid., p.3.
76 Ibid., pp.7–8.
77 Ibid., p.22.
78 Ibid., p.23.
79 Ibid., p.30.
80 Ibid., p.26.
81 'Without Delay', *The Times*, 1.3.1955.
82 'From Defence to Deterrence: A New Order of Priorities', *The Economist*, 26.2.1955.
83 'Britain v. the H-Bomb: Churchill's Six Failures', *Daily Mirror*, 18.2.1955.
84 TNA, DEFE 13/30. D(55)1st Meeting, 13.1.1955.
85 Catterall (ed.) *The Macmillan Diaries*, p.398, entry for 2.3.1955.
86 House of Commons, *Official Report*, 2.3.1955, col.1895.
87 Ibid., cols.1910–11.
88 Ibid., col.1942.
89 Ibid., cols.1937–46.
90 Maurice Edelman (Labour, Coventry, North). Ibid., col.1946.
91 TNA, CAB 158/20. JIC(55)12, 'The "H" Bomb Threat to the UK in the Event of a General War', 13.1.1955.
92 Hennessy, *The Secret State*, p.113.
93 TNA, CAB 158/20. JIC(55)12, 'The "H" Bomb Threat to the UK in the Event of a General War'.

94 Ibid.
95 TNA, CAB 21/3595. Notes on SG(55)5, 4.1.1955.
96 Ibid.
97 TNA, CAB 134/940. HDC(55)3, 'The Defence Implications of Fall-out from a Hydrogen Bomb'; Report by a Group of Officials, 8.3.1955.
98 Ibid.
99 Ibid.
100 Ibid.
101 Ibid.
102 Ibid.
103 Ibid.
104 Ibid.
105 Ibid.
106 Ibid.
107 Ibid.
108 Ibid.
109 Ibid.
110 Ibid.
111 Ibid.
112 Ibid.
113 Ibid.
114 J. Hughes, 'The Strath Report: Britain Confronts the H-Bomb, 1954–5', *History and Technology*, 19:3 (2003), p.258. Original emphasis.
115 Hennessy, *The Secret State*, p.138.

Chapter 5 Years of Decision

1 TNA, DEFE 13/45. 'The Defence Implications of Fall-out from a Hydrogen Bomb (D(55)17 and 18)', 21.4.1955; TNA, CAB 21/4350. 'Central War Plans Secretariat', Note from Strath to Chilvers, 13.5.1955.
2 TNA, DEFE 13/45. 'The Defence Implications of Fall-out from a Hydrogen Bomb (D(55)17 and 18)'.
3 Ibid.
4 TNA, CAB 134/940. HDC(55)4, 'Minutes of an Informal Meeting Held on 16 March 1955', 17.3.1955; HDC(55)1st Meeting, 17.3.1955; TNA, CAB 130/109. GEN 491/1st Meeting, 24.3.1955.
5 TNA, CAB 130/109. GEN 491/1st Meeting, 24.3.1955.
6 Ibid.
7 Ibid.
8 TNA, CAB 134/940. HDC(55)4, 'Minutes of an Informal Meeting Held on 16 March 1955'.
9 See J. Baylis, *Ambiguity and Deterrence: British Nuclear Strategy, 1945–1964* (Oxford, 1995), p.207.
10 TNA, CAB 134/793. CD(O)(55)2, 'Revision of War Plans', Note by the Secretary of the Cabinet, 23.5.1955.
11 Ibid. CD(O)(55)14 (Final), 'Research Programme for Civil Defence', Note by the Home Office, 3.10.1955; CD(O)(55)26, 'Scale of Fire-fighting Preparations', Note by the Home Departments, 7.10.1955; CD(O)(55)8, 'War Plans of the Health Departments', Note by the Joint Secretaries, 3.8.1955; CD(O)(55)23, 'Water Supply', Note by the Ministry of Housing

and Local Government, 20.9.1955; CD(O)(55)15, 'Gas Industry Due Functioning Programme', Memorandum by the Ministry of Fuel and Power', 12.9.1955.

12 TNA, CAB 134/1245. HD(M)(55)4, 'Defence Expenditure by Civil Departments', Report by the Home Defence Committee, 11.10.1955.

13 Ibid.

14 Ibid.

15 Ibid.

16 Ibid.

17 Ibid. HD(M)(56)1, 'Defence Expenditure by Civil Departments', Memorandum by the Chairman of the Home Defence (Ministerial) Committee, 3.1.1956.

18 For an interesting although hardly sympathetic analysis of the 'Climacteric of 1955', see A. Shonfield, *British Economic Policy Since the War* (Harmondsworth, 1958), pp.196–227; also, E. Dell, *The Chancellors* (London, 1997), pp.199–202.

19 TNA, CAB 134/1245. HD(M)(56)1, 'Defence Expenditure by Civil Departments'.

20 Ibid. For the White Paper itself: Ministry of Defence, *Statement on Defence*, Cmd.9691 (London, 1956).

21 TNA, CAB 134/940. HDC(55)3, 'The Defence Implications of Fall-out from a Hydrogen Bomb', Report by a Group of Officials, 8.3.1955.

22 TNA, DEFE 13/45. 'The Defence Implications of Fall-out from a Hydrogen Bomb (D(55)17 and 18)'.

23 TNA, CAB 134/1245. HD(M)(55)10, 'Shelter Policy', Note by the Home Secretary, 25.10.1955.

24 TNA, CAB 134/793. CD(O)(55)11, 'The Implications of Shelter Policy', 20.8.1955; TNA, CAB 134/940. HDC(55)3rd Meeting, 10.10.1955; TNA, CAB 134/1245. HD(M)5, 'Shelter', Note by the Chairman of the Home Defence Committee, 11.10.1955.

25 TNA, CAB 134/1245. HD(M)(55)10, 'Shelter Policy', Note by the Home Secretary, 25.10.1955.

26 Ibid. HD(M)(55)1st Meeting, 13.10.1955.

27 Ibid. HD(M)(55)10, 'Shelter Policy', Note by the Home Secretary, 25.10.1955.

28 Ibid.

29 Ibid.

30 Ibid.

31 Ibid. HD(M)(55)2nd Meeting, 27.10.1955.

32 Ibid.

33 TNA, AIR 8/1836. 'Brief for Under Secretary of State for Air and the Chief of the Air Staff on Shelter Policy', 6.12.1955.

34 Ibid.

35 TNA, CAB 131/16. DC(55)17th Meeting, 7.12.1955.

36 Ibid.

37 TNA, CAB 134/793. CD(O)(55)22, 'Evacuation and Peripheral Dispersal', Memorandum by the Home Office, the Ministry of Housing and Local Government and the Scottish Office, 17.11.1955.

38 Ibid.

39 TNA, CAB 134/940. HDC(55)4th Meeting, 16.12.1955.

40 Ibid.

41 TNA, T 227/1130. 'Evacuation and Peripheral Dispersal', Note by Sir Alexander Johnston, 6.1.1956.

42 Ibid.
43 Ibid.
44 Ibid.
45 TNA, CAB 134/1206. CDC(56)1st Meeting, 11.1.1956.
46 Ibid.
47 Ibid.
48 Ibid.
49 Ibid. CDC(55)2, 'Evacuation Policy', Note by the Secretaries, 25.1.1956.
50 Ibid.
51 Ibid. CDC(55)3, 'Evacuation Policy', Note by the Chairman, 31.1.1956.
52 Ibid. CDC(56)2nd Meeting, 6.2.1956.
53 Ibid.
54 Ibid.
55 Ministry of Defence, *Statement on Defence, 1956*, p.25.
56 TNA, CAB 134/1245. HD(M)(56)1st Meeting, 22.2.1956.
57 Ibid.
58 House of Commons, *Official Report*, 26.2.1956, cols.1032–4.
59 'Defence Plan for Nuclear War', *Manchester Guardian*, 29.2.1956; '"12,000,000 will be Evacuated" – If Britain is in Danger of H-War', *Daily Mirror*, 29.2.1959.
60 Ministry of Defence, *Statement on Defence, 1956*, p.22.
61 'Answers!', *Daily Mirror*, 1.3.1956.
62 'Missing the Point', *Observer*, 4.3.1956.
63 P. Catterall (ed.) *The Macmillan Diaries: The Cabinet Years, 1950–57* (London, 2003), p.528, entry for 19.1.1956.
64 Ibid., p.523, entry for 3.1.1956.
65 Ibid., p.530, entry for 26.1.1956.
66 TNA, CAB 21/3203. Home Secretary to Minister of Defence, 15.5.1956.
67 Ibid.
68 Ibid.
69 TNA, CAB 134/1315. PR(56)3, 'The Future of the United Kingdom in World Affairs', 1.6.1956.
70 K. Ruane and J. Ellison, 'Managing the Americans: Anthony Eden, Harold Macmillan and the Pursuit of "Power-by-Proxy" in the 1950s', *Contemporary British History*, 18:3 (2004), p.157.
71 T.C.G. James, in 'The Move towards the Sandys White Paper of 1957', seminar held July 1988 (Institute of Contemporary History, 2002, http://www.icbh.ac.uk/icbh/witness/sandys/), pp.22–3.
72 Catterall (ed.) *The Macmillan Diaries*, p.564, diary entry for 9.6.1956.
73 M. Grant, 'Home Defence and the Sandys White Paper, 1957', *Journal of Strategic Studies*, 31:6 (2008), pp.925–49.
74 TNA, CAB 134./1315. PR(56)8, 'Home Defence Policy Review', Memorandum by the Minister of Defence, 7.6.1956.
75 Ibid.
76 Ibid.
77 Ibid.
78 Ibid. PR(56)3rd Meeting, 9.6.1956.
79 TNA, CAB 21/3203. 'Record of a Meeting Held in the Minister of Defence's Room', 13.6.1956.
80 Ibid.

81 Ibid.
82 TNA, CAB 134./1315. PR(56)3rd Meeting, 9.6.1956.
83 TNA, CAB 21/3203. 'Record of a Meeting Held in the Minister of Defence's Room', n.d.
84 TNA, CAB 134/1245. HD(M)(56)2, 'Home Defence Policy', Memorandum by the Minister of Defence, 18.6.1956.
85 TNA, CAB 21/3203. Lloyd-George to Monckton, 18.6.1956.
86 Ibid.
87 Ibid.
88 TNA, CAB 134/1245. HD(M)(56)2nd Meeting, 20.6.1956.
89 Ibid. HD(M)(56)4, 'Defence Expenditure by Civil Departments', Report by the Home Defence Committee, 29.6.1956.
90 Ibid.
91 TNA, CAB 21/3346. Prime Minister to Minister of Defence, 3.7.56.
92 TNA, CAB 134/1315. PR(56)19, 'Home Defence', Memorandum by the Chancellor of the Exchequer, 12.7.1956.
93 Ibid.
94 TNA, CAB 21/3508. 'Prime Minister's Brief on PR(56)19, Home Defence', Note by Sir Norman Brook, 13.7.1956.
95 Ibid.
96 TNA, CAB 134/1315. PR(56)6th Meeting, 13.7.1956.
97 Ibid.
98 Ibid.
99 Ibid.
100 TNA, CAB 134/1207. C(O)D(56)23 (Final), 'Defence Expenditure by Civil Departments, 1957/58–1959/60', Report by the Official Committee on Civil Defence, 30.10.1956.
101 Ibid.
102 TNA, CAB 134/1315. PR(56)40, 'Defence Expenditure by Civil Departments', Note by the Chairman of the Home Defence Committee, 20.12.1956.
103 M. Grant, 'Home Defence and the Sandys Defence White Paper, 1957', pp.946–7.
104 See W. Loth, *Overcoming the Cold War: A History of Détente* (Basingstoke, 2003), pp.36–8.
105 TNA, CAB 134/1315. PR(56)40, 'Defence Expenditure by Civil Departments', Note by the Chairman of the Home Defence Committee, 20.12.1956.
106 TNA, CAB 129/84. CP(57)7, 'Home Defence', Memorandum by the Secretary of State for the Home Department, 7.1.1957.
107 Ibid.

Chapter 6 Separate Spheres of Civil Defence

1 TNA, CAB 134/1245. HD(M)(56)2, 'Home Defence Policy', Memorandum by the Minister of Defence, 18.6.1956.
2 TNA, CAB 134/1246. HDC(56)2nd Meeting, 3.12.1956.
3 Ibid.
4 See 'Russian Warning to Britain and France', *The Times*, 6.11.1956.
5 NA, HO 322/206. 'War Planning', Note by A.J.E. Brennan and D.J. Trevelyan, 16.11.1956.

6 Ministry of Defence, *Defence: Outline of Future Policy*, Cmnd.124 (London, 1957).
7 TNA, CAB 129/86. C(57)69, 'Statement on Defence, 1957', 15.3.1957.
8 For an in-depth analysis of the drafting of the white Paper and its civil defence significance see M. Grant, 'Home Defence and the Sandys Defence White Paper, 1957', *Journal of Strategic Studies*, 31:6 (2008), pp.925–49.
9 Ministry of Defence, *Defence: Outline of Future Policy*, p.2.
10 Grant, 'Home Defence and the Sandys Defence White Paper, 1957', p.941.
11 Ministry of Defence, *Defence: Outline of Future Policy*, p.12.
12 Grant, 'Home Defence and the Sandys Defence White Paper, 1957', pp.941–2.
13 'Comment: 80 Days', *Daily Mail*, 5.4.1957.
14 'Britain Pins Faith to Missiles', *Manchester Guardian*, 5.4.1957.
15 'New Model', *Manchester Guardian*, 5.4.1957.
16 TNA, HO 322/135. Town Clerk, Metropolitan Borough of Saint Pancras to the Under Secretary of State, Home Office, 11.4.1957.
17 TNA, PREM 11/4155. Butler to Sandys, 15.4.1957.
18 Ibid.
19 Ibid., Butler to Macmillan, 10.12.1957.
20 House of Commons, *Official Report*, Vol.568, cols.1760–5.
21 TNA, PREM 11/4155. Butler to Sandys, 15.4.1957.
22 TNA, HO 322/135. F.A. Newsam to the Town Clerk, St Pancras Borough Council, 27.5.1957.
23 'St Pancras may Drop Civil Defence', *Daily Telegraph*, 16.4.1957; 'Row Brews on Civil Defence', *News Chronicle*, 16.4.1957.
24 Home Office, *The Hydrogen Bomb* (London, 1957).
25 TNA, CAB 21/3203. Lloyd-George to Monckton, 18.6.1956.
26 TNA, PREM 11/2222. R.A. Butler to Harold Macmillan, 15.3.1957.
27 Ibid.
28 Ibid.
29 Ibid. R.A. Butler to Harold Macmillan, 26.4.1957.
30 Ibid. R.A. Butler to Harold Macmillan, 13.8.1957.
31 Handwritten note on Ibid.
32 Ibid. R.A. Butler to Harold Macmillan, 3.12.1958
33 Medical Research Council, *The Hazards to Man of Nuclear and Allied Radiations*, Cmd.9780 (London, 1956).
34 Home Office, *Radioactive Fall-Out: Provisional Scheme of Public Control* (HMSO, 1959).
35 See M. Grant, 'Civil Defence Policy in Cold War Britain, 1945–68'. Unpublished PhD Thesis, Department of History, Queen Mary, University of London (2006), Appendix B.
36 House of Commons, *Official Report*, 3.12.1958, cols.141–2W.
37 TNA, CAB 131/19. D(58)18th Meeting, 10.9.1958.
38 Ibid.
39 Ibid.
40 J.B. Priestley, 'Britain and the Nuclear Bombs', *New Statesman*, 2.11.1957.
41 For the early history of CND, see R. Taylor, *Against the Bomb: The British Peace Movement, 1958–65* (Oxford, 1988).
42 P. Hennessy, *The Secret State: Whitehall and the Cold War* (London, 2003), p.101.

43 M. Veldman, *Fantasy, the Bomb, and the Greening of Britain: Romantic Protest, 1945–80* (Cambridge, 1994), p.202.
44 A.J.P. Taylor, *The Deterrent Myth* (London, 1958), p.1.
45 R. Taylor, *Against the Bomb*, p.43.
46 Ibid. pp.55–6.
47 A.J.P. Taylor, *The Deterrent Myth*, p.1.
48 Ministry of Defence, *Defence: Outline of Future Policy*, p.2.
49 TNA, INF 2/118. 'Civil Defence Recruitment Campaigns, 1950–57'.
50 Civil Defence Recruitment Advertising, *The Times*, 26.9.1957. Original emphasis.
51 TNA, HO 303/3. 'Recruiting Publicity, Recruitment Statistics 1950–53'.
52 C. Driver, *The Disarmers: A Study in Protest* (London, 1964).
53 R. Taylor, *Against the Bomb*, p.57.
54 See S. Twigge, 'Disarmament and Non-Proliferation', in M. Grant (ed.) *The British Way in Cold Warfare: Intelligence, Diplomacy and the Bomb, 1945–75* (London, forthcoming 2009).
55 TNA, CAB 21/4762. 'Motivational Factors and Recruitment to the Civil Defence Corps', Report by Market Research Department, F.C. Pritchard, Wood & Partners Ltd, October 1960.
56 'Preston's Biggest C.D.Exercise', *Civil Defence*, 12:12 (December 1960), p.13.
57 TNA, HO 303/4. Transcript of 'Panorama' programme, tx 10.10.1960.
58 Ibid. 'They Thought Civil Defence Programme was TV Rag', *Western Daily News*, 12.10.1960.
59 '"One-in-Five" – A Talking Point', *Civil Defence*, 9:12 (December 1957), p.5.
60 Driver, *The Disarmers*, p.186.
61 R. Wilmut (ed.) *The Complete Beyond the Fringe* (London, 1987), p.82.
62 C. Booker, 'Miscellany', *Guardian*, 18.7.1962.
63 Driver, *The Disarmers*.
64 Ibid., p.183.
65 R.M. Titmuss, *Problems of Social Policy* (London, 1950), pp.16–17.
66 TNA, CAB 134/938. HDC(53)7, 'The Initial Phase of a War', Report by the Home Defence Committee Working Party, 24.7.1953.
67 See CAB 134/941. Home Defence Committee Machinery of Government in War Sub-Committee.
68 TNA, CAB 134/940. HDC(55)3, 'The Defence Implications of Fallout from a Hydrogen Bomb', Report by a Group of Officials, 8.3.1955.
69 Ibid. HDC(55)7(Revise), 'Submission to Ministers on the Machinery of Government in War', Report by a Working Party of Officials, 6.7.1955.
70 Ibid.
71 Ibid.
72 Ibid.
73 Ibid.
74 TNA, CAB 134/1611. DH(O)(59)5, 'Security: Code Words', Note by the Secretaries, 21.4.1959.
75 TNA, CAB 134/1619. DH(O)(MG)(61)14, 'Security: Code Words', Note by the Secretaries, 19.7.1961.
76 TNA, CAB 134/2022. HDC(63)3, 'TURNSTILE', Note by the Secretaries, 25.1.1963.

77 TNA, CAB 134/1618. DH(O)(MG)(60)14, 'QUADRANGLE', Note by the Secretaries, 28.4.1960.
78 TNA, CAB 134/2024. HDC(MG)(62)20, 'LINSTOCK', Note by the Secretaries, 19.11.1962.
79 TNA, CAB 134/941. HDC(MG)(55)8, 'Machinery of Government in War', Note by the Secretary, 15.9.1955.
80 On the issue of nuclear command and control, see S. Twigge and L. Scott, *Planning Armageddon: Britain, the United States and the Command of Western Nuclear Forces, 1945–1964* (Amsterdam, 2000).
81 TNA, CAB 134/1617. DH(O)(MG)(59)2, 'Security of SUBTERFUGE', Note by the Secretaries, 10.3.1959.
82 Ibid.
83 Ibid. DH(O)(MG)(59)17(Final), 'Security of STOCKWELL: Report to the Chairman of the Home Defence Committee', Report by the Sub-Committee on Machinery of Government in War, 21.7.1959.
84 TNA, CAB 134/1611. DH(O)(59)2nd Meeting, Confidential Annex, 12.8.1959.
85 Chapman Pincher, 'The Strange Case of the Whitehall Moles', *Daily Express*, 21.1.1960.
86 P. Hennessy, *The Secret State*, p.187.
87 D. Campbell, *War Plan UK: The Truth about Civil Defence in Britain* (London, 1982).
88 P. Laurie, *Beneath the City Streets: A Private Inquiry into the Nuclear Preoccupations of Government* (Harmondsworth, 1972).
89 Hennessy, *The Secret State*.
90 B. Clarke, *Four Minute Warning: Britain's Cold War* (Stroud, 2005); for details about a wide-range of British cold war sites, see the website Subterranean Britannica: www.subbrit.org.uk.
91 A good place to start is BBC Wiltshire website on the bunker: http://www.bbc.co.uk/wiltshire/underground_city
92 W.D. Crocoft and R.J.C. Thomas, *Cold War: Building for Nuclear Confrontation* (Swindon, 2003), chapter 5.
93 J.L. Gaddis, *We Now Know: Rethinking Cold War History* (Oxford, 1993), p.139.
94 TNA, CAB 134/1476. CD(59)1, 'Home Defence Preparations', Memorandum by the Home Secretary, 17.3.59.
95 Ibid.
96 Ibid.
97 Ibid.
98 TNA, CAB 134/1437. C(O)(59)1, 'Interim Planning', Memorandum by the Director-General of Civil Defence, 11.2.1959.
99 Ibid.
100 House of Commons, *Official Report*, 26.2.1959, cols.1267–8.
101 TNA, CAB 134/1476. CD(59)2, 'Interim Report on Evacuation'.
102 Ibid.
103 Ibid. CD(59)1st Meeting, 25.3.1959.
104 Ibid.
105 Ibid.
106 TNA, CAB 134/1617. DH(O)(MG)(59)3, 'Central Government and Regional Headquarters: Interim Planning', Note of an ad hoc meeting, 17.4.1959.

107 Ibid. DH(O)(MG)(59)8, 'STOCKWELL: Report to the Prime Minister', Note by the Secretaries, 14.5.1959.
108 Ibid.
109 Ibid. DH(O)(MG)(59)10, 'STOCKWELL: Report to the Prime Minister', Note by the Secretaries, 8.6.1959; covering GEN 684/1st Meeting, 5.6.1959.
110 TNA, CAB 134/1476. CD(59)3, 'Home Defence Preparations', Report by the Chairman of the Official Committee on Civil Defence, 3.6.1959.
111 Ibid.
112 Ibid.
113 TNA, CAB 128/33. CC(59)38th Conclusions, 30.6.1959.
114 TNA, CAB 134/1476. CD(59)7, 'Evacuation', Memorandum by the Minister of Housing and Local Government, 4.12.1959.
115 Ibid.
116 Ibid. CD(59)3rd Meeting, 8.12.1959.
117 Ibid.
118 This story is lucidly told in P. Williamson, *Hugh Gaitskell: A Political Biography* (London: Cape, 1979), Chapter 22.

Chapter 7 Equipoise, Crisis and Reform

1 TNA, DEFE 10/402. SG(60)35, 'Note on the Concept and Definitions of Breakdown', Edgar Anstey, 10.6.1960; for the group's work see especially Richard Moore, 'A JIGSAW Puzzle for Operational Researchers: British Global War Studies, 1954–62', *Journal of Strategic Studies*, 20:2 (1997), pp.75–91.
2 P. Hennessy, *The Secret State: Whitehall and the Cold War* (London, 2003), p.152.
3 TNA, CAB 134/2039. HDR(60)3 (Revise), 'Nature of Threat to the United Kingdom', Note by the Secretaries, 4.3.1960; HDR(60)8, 'Assessment of the Effects of Attack on the United Kingdom', Note by the Home Office, 5.8.1960.
4 Ibid. HDR(60)3 (Revise), 'Nature of Threat to the United Kingdom'.
5 Ibid.
6 Ibid.
7 Ibid. HDR(60)8, 'Assessment of the Effects of Attack on the United Kingdom', Note by the Home Office, 5.4.1960.
8 Ibid.
9 Ibid.
10 Ibid.
11 Ibid. HDR(60)3rd Meeting, 11.4.1960.
12 Ibid. HDR(60)8, 'Assessment of the Effects of Attack on the United Kingdom', Note by the Home Office, 5.4.1960.
13 Ibid.
14 Ibid. HDR(60)2, 'Business of the Committee', Note by the Chairman, 9.2.1960.
15 Ibid. HDR(60)12, 'The Influence of Civil Defence Measures in the United Kingdom on the Effectiveness of the Deterrent', Note by the Secretaries, 26.4.1960.
16 Ibid.

17 Ibid.
18 TNA, CAB 134/2040. HDR(60)40, 'The Public Presentation of Home Defence Plans', Note by the Secretaries, 21.9.1960.
19 TNA, CAB 134/2039. HDR(60)11. 'Civil Defence in Relation to United Kingdom Defence Policy', Note by Director-General of Civil Defence, 24.4.1960.
20 Ibid.
21 Ibid.
22 Ibid.; this idea of 'inescapable responsibility' had been dismissed by the MoD, see Ibid. HDR(60)12. 'The Influence of Civil Defence Measures in the United Kingdom on the Effectiveness of the Deterrent'.
23 Ibid. HDR(60)4th Meeting (confidential annex), 2.5.1960.
24 Ibid.
25 TNA, CAB 134/1611. DH(O)(60)5. 'Review of Home Defence Policy', Report by Officials, 8.12.1960.
26 J. Baylis, *Ambiguity and Deterrence: British Nuclear Strategy, 1945–1964* (Oxford, 1995), p.6.
27 P. Cradock, *Know Your Enemy: How the Joint Intelligence Committee Saw the World* (London, 2002).
28 TNA, CAB 2040. HDR(60)40, 'The Public Presentation of Home Defence Plans', Note by the Secretaries, 21.9.1960.
29 Ibid.
30 'Civil Defence 1962: Ministerial Broadcast', *Civil Defence*, 19.9.1962.
31 Ibid.
32 C. Driver, *The Disarmers: A Study in Protest* (London, 1964), p.185.
33 TNA, CAB 134/2040. HDR(60)9, 'Current Home Defence Policy and Preparations', Note by the Home Office, 6.4.1960.
34 Ibid.
35 Ibid.
36 TNA, CAB 134/1611. DH(O)(60)5, 'Review of Home Defence Policy', Report by Officials, 8.12.1960.
37 Ibid.
38 Ibid.
39 Ibid.
40 Ibid.
41 Ibid.
42 TNA, CAB 21/5182. F.A. Bishop to Sir Norman Brook, 12.12.1960.
43 Ibid.
44 Ibid. Sir Norman Brook to the Prime Minister, 14.12.1960.
45 Ibid. Ronald Harris to F.A. Bishop, 30.12.1960.
46 Ibid. Freddie Bishop to the Prime Minister, 16.1.1961.
47 Ibid.
48 Ibid.
49 Ibid.
50 Ibid.
51 Ibid.
52 Ibid. Henry Brooke to R.A. Butler, 6.2.1961.
53 Ibid.
54 Ibid. Also, see House of Commons, *Official Report*, 30.3.1961, cols.1529–30.

55 TNA, CAB 134/1437. C(O)D(61)2, 'Home Defence', Note by the Chairman, 4.8.1961.
56 The best analysis of the crisis from the British perspective is J.P.S. Gearson, *Harold Macmillan and the Berlin Wall Crisis* (Basingstoke, 1998).
57 L. Freedman, 'Berlin and the Cold War', in J.P.S. Gearson and K. Schake (eds) *The Berlin Wall Crisis: Perspectives on Cold War Alliances* (Basingstoke, 2002), p.1.
58 Bodleian Library, Department of Western Manuscripts, University of Oxford. Harold Macmillan Diary, 25.6.1961.
59 Michael King, 'Home – "We Would Face the A-blast"', *Daily Mirror*, 14.12.1961.
60 'Survival and Shelters', *Civil Defence*, 13:11 (November 1961), p.3.
61 See K.D. Rose, *One Nation Underground: The Fallout Shelter in American Culture* (New York, 2001).
62 'Cassandra', 'The Thorns', *Daily Mirror*, 24.1.1962.
63 'Cassandra', 'No Place to Hide', *Daily Mirror*, 6.2.1962.
64 John Madox, 'Shelter from Fall-out', *Guardian*, 28.11.1961.
65 M.A. Henriksen, *Dr Strangelove's America: Society and Culture in the Atomic Age* (Berkley, 1997), pp.203–10.
66 'College Cellar Converted into Nuclear Shelter', *Guardian*, 27.1.1962.
67 TNA, CAB 134/1437. C(O)D(61)2, 'Home Defence', Note by the Chairman, 4.8.1961.
68 Ibid.
69 Ibid.
70 Ibid.
71 Ibid.
72 TNA, CAB 21/6083. Note on 'Prime Minister's Helicopter Party', by R.W. Stephenson, 4.10.1961.
73 TNA, CAB 134/1437. C(O)D(61)6, 'Progress in Home Defence Preparations'.
74 Ibid.
75 TNA, CAB 134/1477. CD(61)4, 'Home Defence – Short-Term Planning', Report by the Official Committee on Civil Defence, 13.10.1961.
76 Ibid. CD(61)2nd Meeting, 18.10.1961.
77 Ibid.
78 TNA, CAB 129/108. C(62)26, 'Home Defence: Dispersal Policy', Memorandum by the Home Secretary, the Secretary of State for Scotland and the Minister of Housing and Local Government, 9.2.1962.
79 TNA, CAB 128/36. C(62)13th Meeting, 13.2.1962.
80 TNA, CAB 129/108. C(62)26, 'Home Defence: Dispersal Policy'.
81 TNA, CAB 128/36. C(62)13th Meeting, 13.2.1962.
82 TNA, CAB 134/1477. CD(62)1, 'Civil Defence Corps and Auxiliary Fire Service', Memorandum by the Home Secretary, 18.1.1962.
83 Ibid.
84 TNA, CAB 134/1437. C(O)D(61)2nd Meeting, 12.9.1961.
85 Ibid.
86 Ibid.
87 TNA, CAB 21/4762. 'Motivational Factors and Recruitment to the Civil Defence Corps', report by Market Research Department, F.C. Pritchard, Wood & Partners Ltd, October 1960.

88 TNA, CAB 134/1477. CD(62)1, 'Civil Defence Corps and Auxiliary Fire Service'.
89 Ibid. CD(62)2, 'Civil Defence Corps and Auxiliary Fire Service', Note by the Chairman, 26.1.1962.
90 Ministry of Defence, *Statement on Defence, 1962: The Next Five Years*, Cmnd.1639 (London, 1962), pp.16–17.
91 'Bounties for C.D. Officers', *Guardian*, 18.7.1962.
92 House of Commons, *Official Report*, 5.3.1962, col.120.
93 Ibid., col.210.
94 L. Beaton, 'Defence: As You Were', *Guardian*, 23.2.1962.
95 'Bounties for C.D. Officers', *Guardian*, 18.7.1962.
96 TNA, CAB 134/1477. CD(61)2, 'Education of the Public', Memorandum by the Home Secretary, 27.1.1961.
97 Ibid.
98 Ibid.
99 Ibid. CD(62)5, 'Advice to the Public – Booklet', Note by the Chairman, 18.5.1962.
100 Ibid. CD(62)1st Meeting, 18.7.1962.
101 Ibid. CD(62)5, 'Advice to the Public – Booklet'.
102 Ibid.
103 Home Office, *Civil Defence Handbook No. 10: Advising the Householder on Protection against Nuclear Attack* (HMSO, 1963).
104 See L.V. Scott, *The Cuban Missile Crisis and the Threat of Nuclear War: Lessons from History* (London, 2007).
105 TNA, CAB 175/2. GEN 772/1st Meeting, 12.9.1962.
106 Ibid. GEN 772/15, 'United Kingdom Background Situation at 1000 Hours, 18th September 1962'.
107 Ibid. GEN 772/19, 'United Kingdom Background Situation at 1000 Hours, 19th September 1962'.
108 Ibid. GEN 772/22, 'United Kingdom Background Situation at 1000 Hours, 20th September 1962'.
109 Ibid. GEN 772/15, 'Intelligence Summary for the Morning of 21st September, 1962 (Day PS8)'.
110 Ibid. GEN 772/25, 'United Kingdom Background Situation at 1000 Hours, 21st September 1962'.
111 Ibid. GEN 772/15, 'United Kingdom Background Situation at 1000 Hours, 18th September 1962'.
112 Hennessy, *The Secret State*, pp.165–6.
113 TNA, CAB 134/1477. CD(62)8, 'Home Defence Budget 1963/4', Report by the Chairman of the Official Committee, 18.12.1962.
114 Ibid. CD(62)2nd Meeting, 20.12.1962.
115 Ministry of Defence, *Statement on Defence*, Cmnd.1936 (HMSO, 1963).
116 House of Commons, *Official Report*, 4.3.1963, cols.31–164; 5.3.1963, cols.221–350.
117 TNA, DEFE 13/321. Sir Burke Trend to Minister of Defence, 21.5.1963; see Hennessy, *The Secret State*, pp.165–8 on the Post-Cuba Review.
118 Ibid. 'Copy of a Minute to the Prime Minister from the Secretary of the Cabinet dated 1st August 1963'.
119 TNA, CAB 21/6083. Michael Cary to Mr Bligh, 15.11.1962.

120 TNA, CAB 21/6081. Note to Prime Minister from Norman Brook, 5.10.1961, with Macmillan's handwritten notes.
121 TNA, CAB 21/6083. 'Machinery of Government in an Emergency', n.d. For more on the delicate balancing of such command and control matters see Twigge and Scott, *Planning Armageddon*.
122 TNA, DEFE 13/321. Sir Burke Trend to Minister of Defence, 21.5.1963.
123 Ibid. Review of Government War Book Planning In the Light of the Cuba Crisis, 20.05.1963.
124 Hennessy, *The Secret State*, p.166.
125 Ibid.
126 TNA, CAB 21/4959. 'Cabinet Government', Lecture by Sir Norman Brook, 26.6.1959.
127 Letter from F.R. Barratt to Peter Hennessy, 25.06.2002.
128 J.L. Gaddis, *The Cold War* (London, 2006), p.81.
129 Ibid.
130 See Driver, *The Disarmer*, pp.140–8.
131 R. Taylor, *Against the Bomb: The British Peace Movement, 1958–65* (Oxford, 1988), p.90. Original emphasis.
132 Ibid.; see also P. Byrne, *The Campaign for Nuclear Disarmament* (London, 1988), p.51; See L.V. Scott, *The Cuban Missile Crisis and the Threat of Nuclear War: Lessons from History* (London, 2007), p.144.
133 See L.J. Vale, *The Limits of Civil Defence in the USA, Switzerland, Britain and the Soviet Union* (Basingstoke: Macmillan, 1987), pp.135–6.

Chapter 8 Gradual Decline and Sudden Fall

1 Home Office, *Civil Defence Handbook No. 5: Light Rescue* (HMSO, 1961).
2 Home Office, *Civil Defence Handbook No. 4: Elementary Fire-Fighting* (HMSO, 1960).
3 IWM, HOY 66, 'Advice to Householders: Civil Defence Information Bulletin Nos 1–7'.
4 C. Driver, *The Disarmers: A Study in Protest* (London, 1964), pp.189–90.
5 D. Campbell, *War Plan UK: The Truth about Civil Defence in Britain* (London, 1982), p.274.
6 House of Commons, *Eleventh Report from the Estimates Committee, Session 1962–63: Home Office* (HMSO, 1963), p.28.
7 See House of Commons, *Official Report*, 1.3.1963, cols.1661–85.
8 Ibid., 2.12.1963, cols.939–44.
9 Ibid., cols.944–50.
10 R. Taylor, *Against the Bomb: The British Peace Movement, 1958–65* (Oxford, 1988), p.184; however, a pair of obituaries from 2000 apparently identified two of the 'Spies': Donald Rooum, 'Nicolas Walter', *The Guardian*, 13.3.2000; Richard Hillesley, 'Tom Kinsey', *The Guardian*, 25.11.2000.
11 TNA, CAB 21/6027. 'Spies for Peace, 'Danger! Official Secret: RSG-6'.
12 Ibid. S(O)(PS)(64)4, 'Staff Appointed to Regional Seats of Government', Note by the Home Office, 19.05.1964.
13 Driver, *The Disarmers*, p.183; Richard Taylor, *Against the Bomb*, p.257.
14 TNA, CAB 21/6027. S(PS)(63)7, Personnel Security Committee, 'Spies for Peace', Note by the Security Service, 09.05.1963.

15 Taylor, *Against the Bomb*, pp.262–3. This information comes from an interview with an anonymous source.
16 *Daily Telegraph*, 16.04.1963.
17 'Brooke Talks to the *Mail*', *Daily Mail*, 15.4.1963.
18 'CND Undercurrents', *The Times*, 16.4.1963.
19 'Cheap Stunt', *Daily Mirror*, 15.4.1963.
20 See front page story, 'Yard Hunt for "Ban Bomb" Spy', *Daily Mirror*, 13.4.1963.
21 House of Commons, *Official Report*, 23.4.1963, col.24.
22 House of Commons, *Official Report*, 5.12.1962, col.1463.
23 Ministry of Defence, *Statement on Defence*, Cmnd.1936 (London, 1963).
24 House of Commons, *Official Report*, 23.4.1963, col.24.
25 Bodleian, Macmillan Diary, 16.4.1963.
26 TNA, CAB 21/6027. S(PS)(63)7, Personnel Security Committee, 'Spies for Peace', Note by the Security Service, 09.05.1963.
27 Ibid. SC(63)7, 'Spies for Peace', Note by Chairman of the Official Committee on Security', 14.10.1963.
28 Ibid. S(O)(PS)(64)4, 'Staff Appointed to Regional Seats of Government', Note by the Home Office, 19.05.1964.
29 See British Library of Political and Economic Science Archives, London School of Economics. Campaign for Nuclear Disarmament Archive, CND/1/38, 'Fall X '63'.
30 Ibid., 'Civil Defence and Fallex 63 Campaigns', n.d.
31 TNA, CAB 21/6027. 'Summary of Regional Reports on CND Demonstration FALLEX 63', Note by J.T. Paget to N.T. Ross, 31.12.1963.
32 Richard Taylor, *Against the Bomb*, p.99.
33 Driver, *The Disarmers*, p.191.
34 Ibid. Sir Frank Soskice to the Prime Minister, 18.12.1964.
35 TNA, PREM 13/23. J. Diamond to Sir Frank Soskice, 17.12.1964.
36 Ibid. Sir Frank Soskice to the Prime Minister, 18.12.1964.
37 Ibid.
38 Ibid.
39 'Survival: Twelve Secret Bunkers Built for H-war "Governments"', *Daily Mail*, 15.4.1963.
40 TNA, PREM 13/23. John Diamond to the Prime Minister, 18.12.1964.
41 Ibid.
42 Ibid. Handwritten note on margin.
43 Ibid. Prime Minister to Sir Frank Soskice, 23.12.1964.
44 TNA, PREM 13/797. Sir Frank Soskice to Prime Minister, 1.2.1965.
45 House of Commons, *Official Report*, 2.2.1966, cols.1089–91.
46 TNA, PREM 13/797. Sir Burke Trend to the Prime Minister, 21.9.1965.
47 Ibid.
48 TNA, CAB 134/2023. HDC(65)3, 'Home Defence Policy: First Report by the Home Defence Review Committee', 23.4.1965.
49 TNA, PREM 13/797. Sir Burke Trend to the Prime Minister, 21.9.1965.
50 See, for example, TNA, CAB 134/2883. HDR(66)2, 'Future of Home Defence', Note by the Secretaries, 12.1.1966.
51 TNA, CAB 134/2634. CD(O)(PC)(66)7, 'The Home Defence Review: Presentation of Government Policy'.
52 TNA, CAB 21/5185. J.E. Fraser to Mr Rogers, 3.8.1965.
53 House of Commons, *Official Report*, 14.12.1966, cols.458–9.

54 Ibid., cols.459–60.
55 TNA, HO 303/25. '1964–65 Civil Defence Recruitment Campaign: Local Press Advertising'.
56 TNA, HO 322/353. UKLP/HDR(CS)(65)6, 'Home Defence Committee: A Precis of the Report of the Sub-Committee of the Control System', undated.
57 Ibid.
58 Ibid. Letter from the Civil Defence Department of the Home Office to all Regional Civil Defence Directors, 15.11.1965.
59 TNA, HO 322/354. 'Home Defence Committee: Civil Defence Planning Sub-Committee. The Wartime Control System in England and Wales: The Location of Controls', Draft note by the Home Office, October 1966.
60 TNA, CAB 134/2023. HDC(65)3, 'Home Defence Policy: First Report by the Home Defence Review Committee'.
61 See C. Loft, 'Reappraisal and Reshaping: Government and the Railway Problem, 1951–64', *Contemporary British History*, 15:4 (2001), pp.71–92.
62 TNA, CAB 134/2634. CD(O)(PC)(66)7, 'The Home Defence Review: Presentation of Government Policy'.
63 House of Commons, *Official Report*, 14.12.1966, cols.458–9.
64 See T. Shaw, *British Cinema and the Cold War: The State, Propaganda and Consensus* (London, 2000); J.R. Cook and P. Murphy, 'After the Bomb Dropped: The Cinema Half-Life of *The War* Game (1965)', *Journal of Popular British Cinema*, 3 (2000), pp.129–32; T. Shaw, 'The BBC, the State and Cold War Culture: The Case of Television's *The War Game* (1965)', *English Historical Review*, 121:494 (2006), pp.1351–84; J. Chapman, 'The BBC and the Censorship of *The War Game* (1965)', *Journal of Contemporary History*, 41:1 (2006), pp.75–94; M. Wayne, 'Failing the Public: The BBC, *The War Game*, and Revisionist History: A Reply to James Chapman', *Journal of Contemporary History*, 42:4 (2007), pp.627–37; J. Chapman, 'The War Game Controversy – Again', *Journal of Contemporary History*, 43:1 (2008), pp.105–12.
65 BBCWAC. R101/436/1, '"War Game" Showing: General Correspondence'.
66 BBCWAC. R101/437/1, '"War Game, The": Showing: General Correspondence'. Note to Chairman from A.L. Hutchinson, 16.12.1965.
67 Shaw, *British Cinema and the Cold War*, p.139.
68 TNA, CAB 21/5808. 'HMG Censorship of BBC Film "The War Game"'. Lord Normanbrook to Sir Burke Trend, 7/9/1965.
69 TNA, CAB 134/940. HDC(55)3, 'The Defence Implications of Fall-out from a Hydrogen Bomb', Report by a Group of Officials, 8.3.1955.
70 See TNA, CAB 128/43. C(68)1st Meeting, 4.1.1968; C(68)8th Meeting, 15.1.1968.
71 House of Commons, *Official Report*, 16.1.1968, col.1586.
72 Ibid., col.1589.
73 TNA, CAB 129/135. C(68)5, 'Public Expenditure: Post-Devaluation Measures', Memorandum by the Chancellor of the Exchequer, 3.1.1967.
74 TNA, CAB 134/2892. HDR(67)9(Final), 'Home Defence Expenditure', Report, 1.1.1968.
75 TNA, CAB 129/135. C(68)5, 'Public Expenditure: Post-Devaluation Measures'.
76 Ibid.
77 Ibid.
78 TNA, CAB 128/43 Part one. CC(68)3rd Conclusions, 9.1.1968.

79 House of Commons, *Official Report*, 18.1.1968, col.2093.
80 Ibid., cols.2097–8.
81 Ibid., col.2099.
82 Ibid., col.2100.
83 Civil Defence Circular 2/1969, 11.3.1969.
84 Ibid.
85 See Duncan Campbell, *War Plan UK*, pp.137–77.
86 The literature on this issue is reasonably large. See P. Hennessy (ed.) *Cabinets and the Bomb* (Oxford, 2007); J. Baylis, 'British Nuclear Doctrine: The "Moscow Criteria" and the Polaris Improvement Programme', *Contemporary British History*, 19:1 (2005), 53–65; K. Stoddart, 'The Wilson Government and Responses to Anti-Ballistic Missiles, 1964–1970', *Contemporary British History*, 23:1 (2009), 1–33; C. Haddon, 'British Intelligence, Soviet Missile Defence, and the British Nuclear Deterrent, 1964–1970', in M. Grant (ed.) *The British Way in Cold Warfare: Intelligence, Diplomacy and the Bomb, 1945–75* (London, 2009), pp.159–75.
87 TNA, CAB 196/28. 'Home Defence', Note to the Prime Minister from Sir Burke Trend, 9.7.1969; for the full review of the consequences of the care-and-maintenance decision one year on, see TNA, CAB 134/2871. HDC(69)5. 'Review of the Effect of the Care and Maintenance Decision on Arrangements for Government in War', Note by R.W.J. Hooper, 17.6.1969.
88 TNA, CAB 196/28. Callaghan to the Prime Minister, 29.7.1969.

Conclusion

1 TNA, CAB 131/10. DO(51)1st Meeting, 23.1.1951.
2 See TNA, CAB 131/1. DO(46)31st Meeting, 1.11.1946.
3 TNA, PREM 13/23. John Diamond to the Prime Minister, 18.12.1964.
4 TNA, CAB 134/2039. HDR(60)11, 'Civil Defence in Relation to United Kingdom Defence Policy', Note by Director-General of Civil Defence, 24.4.1960.
5 TNA, CAB 134/1315. PR(56)8, 'Home Defence Policy Review', Memorandum by the Minister of Defence, 7.6.1956.
6 TNA, CAB 134/2039. HDR(60)12, 'The Influence of Civil Defence Measures in the United Kingdom on the Effectiveness of the Deterrent', Note by the Secretaries, 26.4.1960.
7 TNA, CAB 134/1315. PR(56)3rd Meeting, 9.6.1956.
8 TNA, CAB 128/43. C(68)1st Meeting, 4.1.1968; C(68)8th Meeting, 15.1.1968.
9 TNA, HO 322/136. Letter from the Town Clark, Coventry, to the Home Secretary, 7.4.1954.
10 TNA, CAB 21/3203. Lloyd-George to Monckton, 18.6.1956.
11 TNA, CAB 131/19. D(58)18th Meeting, 10.9.1958.
12 TNA, CAB 134/1611. DH(O)(60)5, 'Review of Home Defence Policy', Report by Officials, 8.12.1960.

Bibliography

Primary sources

Unpublished sources

The National Archives, Kew, Surrey

AIR 8 Air Ministry and Ministry of Defence: Department of the Chief of the Air Staff: Registered Files.
AIR 20 Air Ministry, and Ministry of Defence: Papers accumulated by the Air Historical Branch.
CAB 21 Cabinet Office and predecessors: Registered Files (1916 to 1965).
CAB 80 War Cabinet and Cabinet: Chiefs of Staff Committee: Memoranda.
CAB 81 War Cabinet and Cabinet: Committees and Sub-committees of the Chiefs of Staff Committee: Minutes and Papers.
CAB 121 Cabinet Office: Special Secret Information Centre: Files.
CAB 128 Cabinet: Minutes (CM and CC Series).
CAB 129 Cabinet: Memoranda (CP and C Series).
CAB 130 Cabinet: Miscellaneous Committees: Minutes and Papers (GEN, MISC and REF Series).
CAB 131 Cabinet: Defence Committee: Minutes and Papers (DO, D and DC Series).
CAB 134 Cabinet: Miscellaneous Committees: Minutes and Papers (General Series).
CAB 158 Ministry of Defence and Cabinet Office: Central Intelligence Machinery: Joint Intelligence Sub-Committee later Committee: Memoranda (JIC Series).
CAB 159 Ministry of Defence and Cabinet Office: Central Intelligence Machinery: Joint Intelligence Sub-Committee later Committee: Minutes (JIC Series).
CAB 175 Cabinet Office: War Books.
DEFE 4 Ministry of Defence: Chiefs of Staff Committee: Minutes.
DEFE 5 Ministry of Defence: Chiefs of Staff Committee: Memoranda.
DEFE 10 Ministry of Defence: Major Committees and Working Parties: Minutes and Papers.
DEFE 13 Ministry of Defence: Private Office: Registered Files (all Ministers).
HO 197 Ministry of Home Security: Chief Engineer's Department, Registered Files.
HO 205 Ministry of Home Security: 'O' Division: Correspondence and Papers.
HO 225 Home Office: Scientific Adviser's Branch: Reports (CD/SA Series).
HO 303 Home Office: Publicity and Public Relations (PTY Symbol Series) Files.
HO 322 Home Office: Civil Defence (Various Symbol Series) Files.
HO 357 Home Office: Civil Defence Joint Planning Staff: Papers.
INF 2 Ministry of Information and Central Office of Information: Guard Books and Related Unregistered Paper.

INF 13 Ministry of Information and Central Office of Information: Posters and Publications.
PREM 8 Prime Minister's Office: Correspondence and Papers, 1945–1951.
PREM 11 Prime Minister's Office: Correspondence and Papers, 1951–1964.
PREM 13 Prime Minister's Office: Correspondence and Papers, 1964–1970.
RG 23 Government Social Survey Department: Social Survey: Reports and Papers.
T 227 Treasury: Social Services Division (SS and 2SS series) Files.

Mass-Observation Archive, University of Sussex

File Report 2272, 'The Atomic Bomb'.
File Report 2485, 'Atomic Weather'.

Imperial War Museum Film and Video Archive, London, SE1

COI 801, 'A Fable of Today'.
HOY 58, 'The H-Bomb'.
HOY 66, 'Advice to Householders: Civil Defence Information Bulletin Nos 1–7'.

BBC Written Archives Centre, Caversham, Berkshire

R19/1486, 'Hydrogen Bomb'.
R101/436/1, '"War Game" Showing: General Correspondence.
R101/437/1, '"War Game, The"': Showing: General Correspondence.
T32/1241/2, 'Panorama, tx 59.06'.

Bodleian Library, Department of Western Manuscripts, University of Oxford

Harold Macmillan Diary. Unpublished transcript very kindly provided by Dr Peter Catterall.

British Library of Political and Economic Science, London School of Economics

Campaign for Nuclear Disarmament Archive.

Newspapers and Periodicals

Alert, Civil Defence, Daily Express, Daily Mail, Daily Mirror, Daily Telegraph, The Guardian, Home Guard and Civil Defence Review, Manchester Guardian, News Chronicle, The New Statesman and Society, Sunday Times, The Times.

Official publications

J.E. Fothergill and D.L. Lambeth, *Recruitment to the Civil Defence Forces* (Central Office of Information Social Survey, 1950).
Home Office, *Manual of Basic Training* (HSMO, 1949–1953).
Home Office, *Civil Defence Manual for Basic Training, Volume II: Atomic Warfare* (London, 1950).
Home Office, *Civil Defence Circulars* (HSMO, 1952–1966).
Home Office, *First Report of the Advisory Committee on Publicity and Recruitment for the Civil Defence and Allied Services*, Cmd.8708 (London, 1952).

Home Office, *Second Report of the Advisory Committee on Publicity and Recruitment for the Civil Defence and Allied Services*, Cmd.9131 (London, 1954).
Home Office, *The Hydrogen Bomb* (London: 1957).
Home Office, *Radioactive Fall-Out: Provisional Scheme of Public Control* (HMSO, 1959).
Home Office, *Civil Defence Handbook No. 4: Elementary Fire-Fighting* (London, 1960).
Home Office, *Civil Defence Handbook No. 5: Light Rescue* (London, 1961).
Home Office, *Civil Defence Handbook No. 10: Advising the Householder on Protection against Nuclear Attack* (London, 1963).
Home Office and Air Ministry, *The Effects of the Atomic Bombs at Hiroshima and Nagasaki: Report of the British Mission to Japan* (London, 1946).
House of Commons, *Official Report* (London: 1945–1968).
House of Commons, 'From the Select Committee on Estimates, Session 1953–54: Civil Defence', *Reports from Committees. Session 3 November 1953–25 November 1954* (London, 1953).
House of Commons, *Eleventh Report from the Estimates Committee, Session 1962–63: Home Office* (London, 1963).
D.L. Lambeth, *Recruitment to the Civil Defence Services – II* (Central Office of Information Social Survey, 1950).
Medical Research Council, *The Hazards to Man of Nuclear and Allied Radiation*, Cmd.9780 (London, 1957).
Medical Research Council, *The Hazards to Man of Nuclear and Allied Radiation: A Second Report*, Cmnd.1225 (London, 1960).
Ministry of Defence, *Statement on Defence, 1954*, Cmd.9075 (London, 1954).
Ministry of Defence, *Statement on Defence, 1955*, Cmd.9391 (London, 1955).
Ministry of Defence, *Statement on Defence*, Cmd.9691 (London, 1956).
Ministry of Defence, *Defence: Outline of Future Policy*, Cmnd.124 (London, 1957).
Ministry of Defence, *Report on Defence: Britain's Contribution to Peace and Security*, Cmnd.363 (London, 1958).
Ministry of Defence, *Report on Defence: Progress of the Five-Year Defence Plan*, Cmnd.662 (London, 1959).
Ministry of Defence, *Report on Defence, 1960*, Cmnd.952 (London, 1960).
Ministry of Defence, *Report on Defence, 1961*, Cmnd.1288 (London, 1961).
Ministry of Defence, *Statement on Defence, 1962: The Next Five Years*, Cmnd.1639 (London, 1962).
Ministry of Defence, *Statement on Defence, 1963*, Cmnd.1936 (London, 1963).
Ministry of Defence, *Statement on Defence, 1964*, Cmnd.2270 (London, 1964).
Ministry of Defence, *Statement on Defence, 1965*, Cmnd.2592 (London, 1965).
Ministry of Health, *Civil Defence Act 1948: Short Term Plan for Evacuation* (London, 1950).
Ministry of Health, *Civil Defence Act 1948: Memorandum on Evacuation* (London, 1950).
Ministry of Reconstruction, *Housing*, Cmd.6609 (London, 1945).
Statutory Instruments 1949, No.1432. 'Civil Defence: The Civil Defence (General) Regulations, 1949'.
Statutory Instruments 1949, No.1433. 'Civil Defence: The Civil Defence Corps Regulations, 1949'.
Treasury, *Statements Relating to the Atomic Bomb* (London, 1945).

Secondary sources

Published

A. Adamthwaite, 'Britain and the World, 1945–9: The View from the Foreign Office', *International Affairs*, 61:2 (1985), pp.223–35.

A. Adamthwaite, '"Nation Shall Speak unto Nation": The BBC's Response to Peace and Defence Issues, 1945–58', *Contemporary Record*, 7:4 (1993), pp.557–77.

R. Aldrich (ed.), *British Intelligence, Strategy and the Cold War, 1945–51* (London, 1992).

L. Arnold, *Britain and the Hydrogen Bomb* (Basingstoke, 2001).

S.J. Ball, 'Military Nuclear Relations between the United States and Great Britain under the Terms of the McMahon Act, 1946–58', *Historical Journal*, 38:2 (1995), pp.439–54.

S.J. Ball (ed.), *Parliament and Politics in the Age of Churchill and Attlee: The Hedlam Diaries, 1935–51* (Cambridge, 1999).

E. Barker, *The British Between the Superpowers* (London, 1983).

J. Baylis, *Ambiguity and Deterrence: British Nuclear Strategy, 1945–1964* (Oxford, 1995).

J. Baylis, 'British Nuclear Doctrine: The "Moscow Criteria" and the Polaris Improvement Programme', *Contemporary British History*, 19:1 (2005), pp.53–65.

J. Baylis and J. Garnett (eds), *The Makers of Modern Nuclear Strategy* (London, 1991).

J. Baylis and A. Macmillan, 'The British Global Strategy Paper of 1952', *Journal of Strategic Studies*, 16:2 (1993), pp.200–26.

P.M.S. Blackett, *Fear, War and the Bomb: Military and Political Consequences of Atomic Energy* (New York, 1949).

P. Bolsover, *Civil Defence: The Cruellest Confidence Trick* (London, 1982).

T.J. Botti, *The Long Wait: The Forging of the Anglo-American Nuclear Alliance, 1945–58* (New York and London, 1987).

P.S. Boyer, *By the Bomb's Early Light* (New York, 1985).

P.G. Boyle, 'Oliver Franks and the Washington Embassy, 1948–52', in J. Zametica (ed.), *British Officials and British Foreign Policy, 1945–50* (Leicester, 1990), pp.189–211.

P.G. Boyle, 'Review Article: The Cold War Revisited', *Journal of Contemporary History*, 35:3 (2000), pp.479–89.

R. Brandon, *The Burning Question: The Anti-Nuclear Movement since 1945* (London, 1987).

J. Brown, '"A is for Atom, B is for Bomb": Civil Defense in American Public Education, 1948–1963', *Journal of American History*, 75:1 (1988), pp.68–90.

N. Brown, *Nuclear War: The Impending Strategic Deadlock* (New York, 1964).

A. Buchan, 'Britain and the Nuclear Deterrent, *Political Quarterly*, 31:1 (1960), pp.36–45.

A. Bullock, *Ernest Bevin: Foreign Secretary* (Oxford, 1985).

D. Butler and A. King, *The British General Election of 1964* (London, 1965).

P. Byrne, *The Campaign for Nuclear Disarmament* (New York, 1988).

A. Calder, *The People's War* (London, 1969).

D. Campbell, *War Plan UK: The Truth about Civil Defence in Britain* (London, 1982).

B. Cathcart, *Test of Greatness: Britain's Struggle for the Hydrogen Bomb* (London, 1996).
B. Cathcart, 'Penney, William George, Baron Penney (1909–1991)', *Oxford Dictionary of National Biography* (Oxford, 2004) [http://www.oxforddnb.com/view/article/49920, accessed 25 Feb 2005].
P. Catterall (ed.), *The Macmillan Diaries: The Cabinet Years, 1950–57* (London, 2003).
J. Chapman, 'The BBC and the Censorship of *The War Game* (1965)', *Journal of Contemporary History*, 41:1 (2006), pp.75–94.
J. Chapman, 'The War Game Controversy – Again', *Journal of Contemporary History*, 43:1 (2008), pp.105–12.
I. Clark, *Nuclear Diplomacy and the Special Relationship* (Oxford, 1994).
I. Clark and N.J. Wheeler, *The British Origins of Nuclear Strategy, 1945–1955* (Oxford, 1989).
B. Clarke, *Four Minute Warning: Britain's Cold War* (Stroud, 2005).
B. Collier, *The Defence of the United Kingdom* (London, 1957).
J.R. Cook and P. Murphy, 'After the Bomb Dropped: the Cinema Half-Life of *The War* Game (1965)', *Journal of Popular British Cinema*, 3 (2000), pp.129–32.
J. Cox, *Overkill: The Story of Modern Weapons* (Harmondsworth, 1981).
P. Cradock, *Know Your Enemy: How the Joint Intelligence Committee saw the World* (London, 2002).
D. Craig and M. Egan, *Extreme Situations: Literature and Crisis from the Great War to the Atom Bomb* (London, 1979).
N. Crowson, 'Citizen Defence: the Conservative Party and its attitude to national service, 1937–57', in R. Weight and A. Beach (eds), *The Right to Belong: Citizenship and National Identity in Britain, 1930–60* (London, 1998), pp.205–22.
M. Davie (ed.), *The Diaries of Evelyn Waugh* (London, 1976).
T.C. Davies, *Stages of Emergency: Cold War Nuclear Civil Defense* (Durham, NC, 2007).
G. DeGroot, *The Bomb: A History of Hell on Earth* (London: Pimlico, 2005).
A. Deighton, *The Impossible Peace: Britain, the German Problem and the Origins of the Cold War* (Oxford, 1990).
A. Deighton (ed.), *Britain and the First Cold War* (London, 1990).
E. Dell, *The Chancellors* (London, 1997).
E. Dell, *A Strange Eventful History: Democratic Socialism in Britain* (London, 2000)
M. Dockrill, *British Defence since 1945* (Oxford, 1988).
S. Dockrill, 'Britain's Strategy for Europe: must West Germany be rearmed? 1948–51', in R.J. Aldrich (ed.), *British Intelligence, Strategy and the Cold War, 1945–51* (London, 1992), pp.193–214.
C. Driver, *The Disarmers: A Study in Protest* (London, 1964).
J. Edwards, 'Roger Makins: "Mr Atom"', in J. Zametica (ed.), *British Officials and British Foreign Policy, 1945–50* (Leicester, 1990), pp.8–38.
M. Foot, *Aneurin Bevan. Volume II: 1945–1960* (London, 1973).
A. Foster, 'The British Press and the Coming of the Cold War', in A. Deighton (ed.), *Britain and the First Cold War* (London, 1990), pp.11–31.
L. Freedman, *Britain and Nuclear Weapons* (London, 1980).
L. Freedman, *The Evolution of Nuclear Strategy* (Basingstoke, 1983).
L. Freedman, 'Berlin and the Cold War', in J.P.S. Gearson and K. Schake (eds), *The Berlin Wall Crisis: Perspectives on Cold War Alliances* (Basingstoke, 2002), pp.1–9.

J.P.G. Freeman, *Britain's Nuclear Arms Control Policy in the Context of Anglo-American Relations, 1957–68* (Basingstoke, 1986).
J.L. Gaddis, *We Now Know: Rethinking Cold War History* (Oxford, 1993).
J.L. Gaddis, *The Cold War* (London, 2006).
D. Garrison, *Bracing for Armageddon* (Oxford, 2006).
J.P.S. Gearson, *Harold Macmillan and the Berlin Wall Crisis* (Basingstoke, 1998).
T. Geiger, *Britain and the Economic Problem of the Cold War* (Aldershot, 2004).
A. Gorst, 'British Military Planning for Postwar Defence, 1943–45', in A. Deighton (ed.), *Britain and the First Cold War* (London, 1990), pp.91–108.
M. Gowing, *Independence and Deterrence: Britain and Atomic Energy, 1945–52* (Basingstoke, 1974).
M. Grant, 'Clouds of Uncertainty', *The Tablet*, 30.7.2005.
M. Grant, 'Home Defence and the Sandys White Paper, 1957', *Journal of Strategic Studies*, 31:6 (2008), pp.925–49.
M. Grant (ed.), *The British Way in Cold Warfare: Intelligence, Diplomacy and the Bomb, 1945–75* (London, 2009).
M. Grant, 'Civil Defence and British Deterrence, 1958–64: Strategic Imperative and Political Expediency', in his (ed.), *The British Way in Cold Warfare: Intelligence, Diplomacy and the Bomb, 1945–75* (London, 2009), pp.51–66.
O. Greene, *London After the Bomb: What a Nuclear Attack Really Means* (Oxford, 1982).
S. Greenwood, *Britain and the Cold War, 1945–91* (London, 2000).
A.J.R. Groom, *British Thinking About Nuclear Weapons* (London, 1974).
A.D. Grossman, *Neither Dead nor Red: Civilian Defense and American Political Development during the Early Cold War* (London, 2001).
S. Guy, '*High Treason* (1951): Britain's cold war fifth column', *Historical Journal of Film, Radio and Television*, 13:1 (1993), pp.35–47.
S. Guy, '"Someone Presses a Button and its Goodbye Sally", *Seven Days to Noon* and the Threat of the Atomic Bomb', in A. Burton et al (eds), *The Family Way: The Boulting Brothers and Postwar British Film Culture* (Trowbridge, 2001), pp.143–54.
C. Haddon, 'British Intelligence, Soviet Missile Defence, and the British Nuclear Deterrent, 1964–1970', in M. Grant (ed.), *The British Way in Cold Warfare: Intelligence, Diplomacy and the Bomb, 1945–75* (London, 2009), pp.159–75.
A.H. Halsey (ed.), *Trends in British Society since 1900* (London, 1972).
K. Harris, *Attlee* (London, 1995).
P. Hennessy, *Never Again: Britain, 1945–51* (London, 1992).
P. Hennessy, *The Prime Minister: The Office and Its Holders since 1945* (London, 2001).
P. Hennessy, *The Secret State: Whitehall and the Cold War* (London, 2003).
P. Hennessy, *Having it so Good: Britain in the 1950s* (London, 2006).
P. Hennessy (ed.), *Cabinets and the Bomb* (Oxford, 2007).
P. Hennessy and G. Brownfeld, 'Britain's Cold War Security Purge: the Origins of Positive Vetting', *Historical Journal*, 25:4 (1982), pp.965–74.
M.A. Henriksen, *Dr Strangelove's America: Society and Culture in the Atomic Age* (Berkeley, 1997).
J. Hersey, *Hiroshima* (London, 1946).
J.G. Hershberg, 'The Crisis Years, 1958–63', in O.A. Westad (ed.), *Reviewing the Cold War: Approaches, Interpretations, Theory* (London, 2000), pp.303–25.
A.E. Holmans, *Housing Policy in Britain* (London, 1987).

M. Howard, 'Strategy in the Nuclear Age', *Journal of the Royal United Service Institution*, 52 (November 1957), pp.473–82.

J. Hughes, 'The Strath Report: Britain Confronts the H-Bomb, 1954–55', *History and Technology*, 19:3 (2003), pp.257–75.

F.C. Iklé, *The Social Impact of Bomb Destruction* (Norman, 1958).

S. Isaacs, *It's the Job that Counts, 1939–1953: A Selection from the Speeches and Writings of the Dowager Marchioness of Reading* (Privately published, 1954).

A.A. Jackson, *The Institute of Civil Defence 1938–1955: A Short History of its First Seventeen Years* (London, 1988).

K. Jefferys, *Retreat from New Jerusalem: British Politics, 1951–64* (Basingstoke, 1997).

G. Jones, 'The Mushroom-shaped Cloud: British Scientists' Opposition to Nuclear Policy, 1945–57', *Annals of Science*, 43:1 (1986), pp.1–26.

H. Jones, '"This is Magnificent!" 300,000 Homes a Year and the Tory Revival after 1945', *Contemporary British History*, 14:1 (2000), pp.99–121.

H. Jones, 'The Impact of the Cold War', in P. Addison and H. Jones (eds), *A Companion to Contemporary British History, 1939–2000* (Oxford, 2005), pp.23–41.

R.E. Jones, *Nuclear Deterrence: A Short Political Analysis* (London, 1968).

T.L. Jones, 'A Comparative Study of Local Authority Preparations for Nuclear War in North-eastern Wales', *Welsh History Review*, 20:1 (2000), pp.89–115.

R. Jungk, *Brighter than a Thousand Suns* (Harmondsworth, 1960).

H. Kahn, *On Thermonuclear War* (Princeton, 1960).

S. King-Hall, *Defence in the Nuclear Age* (London, 1958).

S. King-Hall, *Power Politics in the Nuclear Age* (London, 1962).

D. Kirby, 'The Church of England and the Cold War Nuclear Debate', *Twentieth Century British History*, 4:3 (1993), pp.250–83.

D. Kirby, 'Divinely Sanctioned: The Anglo-American Cold War Alliance and the Defence of Western Civilization and Christianity, 1945–48', *Journal of Contemporary History*, 35:3 (2000), pp.385–412.

D. Kirby (ed.), *Religion and the Cold War* (Basingstoke, 2003).

E. J. de Kudt, *British Defence Policy and Nuclear War* (London, 1964).

Labour Party, 'Let's go with Labour for the new Britain', in I. Dale (ed.), *Labour Party General Election Manifestos* (London, 2000).

R. Lapp, *The Voyage of the Lucky Dragon* (Harmondsworth, 1958).

R. Lapp, *Kill or Overkill* (London, 1963).

D.C. Latham, *Strategy for Survival* (Tucson, 1963).

P. Laurie, *Beneath the City Streets: A Private Inquiry into the Nuclear Preoccupations of Government* (Harmondsworth, 1972).

J. Leaning and L. Keyes (eds), *The Counterfeit Ark* (Cambridge, Mass., 1984).

B. Liddell-Hart, *The Revolution in Warfare* (London, 1946).

B. Liddell-Hart, *Deterrent or Defence* (London, 1960).

C. Loft, 'Reappraisal and Reshaping: Government and the Railway Problem, 1951–64', *Contemporary British History*, 15:4 (2001), pp.71–92.

K. Lonsdale, *Is Peace Possible?* (Harmondsworth, 1957).

W. Loth, 'Review Essay: General Views on the Cold War', *Cold War History*, 3:2 (2003), pp.157–65.

W. Loth, *Overcoming the Cold War: A History of Détente* (Basingstoke, 2003).

N.J. McCamley, *Cold War Secret Nuclear Bunkers* (London, 2002).

L. McEnaney, *Civil Defense Begins at Home* (Princeton, 2000).

C. Macdonald, *Britain and the Korean War* (Oxford, 1990).

R. Mackay, *Half the Battle: Civilian Morale in Britain during the Second World War* (Manchester, 2002).
H. Macmillan, *At the End of the Day, 1961–1963* (London, 1973).
J. Melissen, 'The Restoration of the Nuclear Alliance: Great Britain and the Atomic Negotiations with the United States, 1957–58', *Contemporary Record*, 6:1 (1992), pp.72–106.
D. Miller, *The Cold War: A Military History* (London, 2001).
L. Minkin, *The Labour Party Conference: A Study in the Politics of Intra-Party Democracy* (London, 1978).
R. Moore, 'A JIGSAW Puzzle for Operational Researchers: British Global War Studies, 1954–1962', *Journal of Strategic Studies*, 20:2 (1997), pp.75–91.
K.O. Morgan, *Labour in Power, 1945–51* (Oxford, 1985).
K.O. Morgan, 'George, Gwilym Lloyd, first Viscount Tenby (1894–1967)', rev., *Oxford Dictionary of National Biography* (Oxford, 2004) [http://www.oxforddnb.com/view/article/34571, accessed 15 July 2005].
F. Mulley, *The Politics of Western Defence* (London, 1962).
M. Navias, *Nuclear Weapons and British Strategic Planning, 1955–58* (Oxford, 1991).
M. Navias, 'Nuclear Weapons and British Alliance Commitments, 1955–56', in A. Deighton (ed.), *Britain and the First Cold War* (London, 1990), pp.273–90.
H. Nehring, 'The British and West German Protests against Nuclear Weapons and the Cultures of the Cold War', *Contemporary British History*, 19:2 (2005), pp.223–41.
R. Neild, *How to Make Up Your Mind About the Bomb* (London, 1981).
T. H. O'Brien, *Civil Defence* (London, 1955).
G. Oakes, *The Imaginary War* (Oxford, 1994).
S. Openshaw, *Doomsday: Britain after Nuclear Attack* (Oxford, 1983).
S. Orwell and I. Angus (eds), *The Collected Essays, Journalism and Letters of George Orwell* (London, 1968).
R. Ovendale (ed.), *The Foreign Policy of the British Labour Government, 1945–51* (Leicester, 1984).
J. Park, 'Wasted Opportunities? The 1950s Rearmament Programme and the Failure of British Economic Policy', *Journal of Contemporary History*, 32:3 (1997), pp.357–79.
H. Pemberton, 'Relative Decline and British Economic Policy in the 1960s', *The Historical Journal*, 47:4 (2004), pp.989–1013.
R.W. Perry, *The Social Psychology of Civil Defence* (Lexington, 1983).
M. Phythian, 'CND's Cold War', *Contemporary British History*, 15:3 (2001), pp.133–56.
A.J. Pierre, *Nuclear Politics: The British Experience with an Independent Strategic Force, 1939–1970* (Oxford, 1972).
N. Pronay, 'British Film Sources for the Cold War: The Disappearance of the Cinema-going public', *Historical Journal of Film, Radio and Television*, 13:1 (1993), pp.7–17.
K. Pyne, 'Art or Article? The Need for and Nature of the British Hydrogen Bomb, 1954–58', *Contemporary British History*, 13:3 (1999), pp.562–85.
G. Rawnsley (ed.), *Cold-War Propaganda in the 1950s* (London, 1999).
D. Reynolds, 'The Origins of the Cold War: The European Dimension', *Historical Journal*, 28:2 (June 1985), pp.497–515.
K.D. Rose, *One Nation Underground: The Fallout Shelter in American Culture* (New York, 2001).

R.N. Rosecrance, *Defense of the Realm: British Strategy in the Nuclear Epoch* (New York, 1968).
D.A. Rosenberg, 'The Origins of Overkill: Nuclear Weapons and American Strategy, 1945–1960', *International Security*, 7:4 (1983), pp.3–71.
V. Rothwell, *Britain and the Cold War, 1941–1947* (London, 1982).
G.M. Routh, *The History of the Institute of Civil Defence* (London, 1956).
K. Ruane and J. Ellison, 'Managing the Americans: Anthony Eden, Harold Macmillan and the Pursuit of "Power-by-Proxy" in the 1950s', *Contemporary British History*, 18:3 (2004), pp.147–67.
B. Russell, *Common Sense and Nuclear Warfare* (London, 1958).
B. Russell, *Has Man a Future?* (Harmondsworth, 1961).
B. Russell, *Unarmed Victory* (Harmondsworth, 1963).
B. Russell, *Autobiography: Volume III* (London, 1969).
R. Ruston, *A Say in the End of the World: Morals and British Nuclear Weapons Policy, 1941–1987* (Oxford, 1990).
S. Schrafstetter, '"Loquacious... and pointless as ever"? Britain, the United States and the United Nations Negotiations on International Control of Nuclear Energy', *Contemporary British History*, 16:4 (2002), pp.87–108.
S. Schwarzkopf, '"They Do it With Mirrors": Advertising and British Cold War Consumer Politics', *Contemporary British History*, 19:2 (2005), 133–51.
L.V. Scott *Conscription and the Attlee Governments: The Politics and Policy of National Service 1945–51* (Oxford, 1993).
L.V. Scott, *Macmillan, Kennedy and the Cuban Missile Crisis* (Basingstoke, 1999).
L.V. Scott, *The Cuban Missile Crisis and the Threat of Nuclear War: Lessons from History* (London, 2007).
D. Seed, 'The Debate over Nuclear Refuge', *Cold War History*, 4:2 (2003), pp.117–42.
M. Shaw, 'From total war to democratic peace: exterminism and historical pacifism', in H.J. Kaye and K. McClelland (eds), *E.P. Thompson: Critical Perspectives* (Cambridge, 1990), pp.233–51.
T. Shaw, 'The British Popular Press and the Early Cold War', *History*, 83 (1998), pp.66–85.
T. Shaw, 'British Feature Films in the Early Cold War' in G.D. Rawnsley (ed.), *Cold War Propaganda in the 1950s* (Basingstoke, 1999), pp.125–44.
T. Shaw, *British Cinema and the Cold War: The State, Propaganda and Consensus* (London, 2000).
T. Shaw, 'Some Writers are More Equal Than Others: George Orwell, the State and Cold War Privilege', *Cold War History*, 4:1 (2003), pp.143–70.
T. Shaw, 'The BBC, the State and Cold War Culture: The Case of Television's *The War Game* (1965)', *English Historical Review*, 121:494 (2006), pp.1351–84.
A. Shlaim, 'Britain, the Berlin blockade and the cold war', *International Affairs*, 60:1 (1984), pp.1–14.
A. Shonfield, *British Economic Policy Since the War* (Harmondsworth, 1958).
J. Slessor, *The Great Deterrent* (London, 1959).
J. Smith, *Clouds of Deceit: The Deadly Legacy of Britain's Atom Bomb* (London, 1985).
M. Smith, '"What to do if it Happens": Planners, Pamphlets and Propaganda in the Age of the H-bomb', *Endeavour*, 33:2 (2009), pp.60–4.
R. Smith and J. Zametica, 'The Cold Warrior: Clement Attlee Reconsidered, 1945–1947', *International Affairs*, 59:2 (1985), pp.237–63.

D.L. Snead, *The Gaither Committee, Eisenhower and the Cold War* (Columbus, 1999).
W.P. Snyder, *The Politics of British Defence Policy, 1945–1962* (Columbus, 1964).
K. Stoddart, 'The Wilson Government and Responses to Anti-Ballistic Missiles, 1964–1970', *Contemporary British History*, 23:1 (2009), pp.1–33.
P. Summerfield and C. Peniston-Bird, *Contesting Home Defence: Men, Women and the Home Guard in the Second World War* (Manchester, 2007).
A.J.P. Taylor, *The Deterrent Myth* (London, 1958).
A.J.P. Taylor, *A Personal History* (London, 1982).
R. Taylor, *Against the Bomb: The British Peace Movement, 1958–1965* (Oxford, 1988).
N. Thomas, 'Challenging Myths of the 1960s: The Case of Student Protest in Britain', *Twentieth Century British History*, 11:3 (1997), pp.277–97.
R.M. Titmuss, *Problems of Social Policy* (London, 1950).
J. Tomlinson, *The Politics of Decline* (London, 1999).
S. Twigge, 'Disarmament and Non-Proliferation', in M. Grant (ed.), *The British Way in Cold Warfare: Intelligence, Diplomacy and the Bomb, 1945–75* (London, 2009), pp.33–50.
S. Twigge and L.V. Scott, *Planning Armageddon: Britain, the United States and the Command of Western Nuclear Forces, 1945–1964* (Amsterdam, 2000).
I. Tyrell, *The Survival Option* (London, 1982).
L.J. Vale, *The Limits of Civil Defence in the USA, Switzerland, Britain and the Soviet Union* (Basingstoke, 1987).
M. Veldman, *Fantasy, the Bomb, and the Greening of Britain: Romantic Protest, 1945–80* (Cambridge, 1994).
W. Walker, 'Nuclear Order and Disorder', *International Affairs*, 76:4 (2000), pp.703–24.
D.C. Watt, 'Britain, the United States and the Opening of the Cold War', in Ritchie Ovendale (ed.), *The Foreign Policy of the British Labour Government, 1945–51* (Leicester UP, 1984), pp.43–60.
M. Wayne, 'Failing the Public: The BBC, *The War Game*, and Revisionist History: A Reply to James Chapman', *Journal of Contemporary History*, 42:4 (2007), 627–37.
C. Webster and N. Frankland, *The Strategic Air Offensive Against Germany* (London, 1961).
H.G. Wells, *The War of the Worlds* (London, 2005).
J. Welshman, 'Evacuation and Social Policy during the Second World War: Myth and Reality', *Twentieth Century British History*, 9 (1998), pp.28–53.
P.S. Williamson, *Hugh Gaitskell: A Political Biography* (London, 1979).
R. Wilmut (ed.), *The Complete Beyond the Fringe* (London, 1987).
L.S. Wittner, *Resisting the Bomb: A History of the World Nuclear Disarmament Movement, 1954–70* (Stanford, 1997).
Women's Voluntary Services, *Report on 25 Years Work WVS Civil Defence, 1938–1963* (London, 1963).
L. Woolf, 'Britain in the Atomic Age', *The Political Quarterly*, 17:1 (1946), pp.12–24.
W. Young, *Strategy for Survival: First Steps in Nuclear Disarmament* (Harmondsworth, 1959).

Unpublished theses and papers

N. Bliss, 'The Role of Sir Norman Brook in the Construction of the Cold War State, 1945–51'. Unpublished MA in Contemporary British History thesis, Department of History, Queen Mary, University of London, 2000.

A. Craig, 'The Joint Intelligence Committee and British Intelligence Assessment, 1945–56'. Unpublished PhD thesis, Faculty of History, University of Cambridge, 1999.

S. Goebel, 'Commemorative Cosmopolis: Transnational Networks of Remembrance in Post-War Coventry'. Unpublished Paper, Writing War Seminar, Department of History, Queen Mary, University of London, 2005.

M. Grant, 'The Impact of CND on Civil and Home Defence Planning, 1958–1966'. Unpublished MA in Contemporary British History thesis, Department of History, Queen Mary, University of London, 2002.

M. Grant, 'Civil Defence Policy in Cold War Britain, 1945–68'. Unpublished PhD Thesis, Department of History, Queen Mary, University of London, 2006.

M. Smith, 'Architects of Armageddon: Scientific Advice and the State in Cold War Britain, 1945–68', British Society for the History of Science Annual Conference, Keble College, Oxford, 4–6 July 2008.

A. Webb, 'The Impact of the Strath Report: The Formation of Home and Civil Defence Policy in the Thermo-Nuclear Age and Its Development, 1954–1965.' Unpublished BA Thesis, Department of History, Queen Mary, University of London, 2001.

Index